THE GREAT
WALKING
ADVENTURE

Hamish Brown

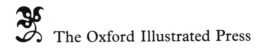 The Oxford Illustrated Press

© Hamish Brown 1986

Printed in Great Britain by J. H. Haynes & Co. Limited

ISBN 0 946609 12 8 (Hardback)
ISBN 0 946609 39 X (Paperback)

The Oxford Illustrated Press, Sparkford, Nr Yeovil,
Somerset, England

Published in North America by Haynes Publications Inc.,
861 Lawrence Drive, Newbury Park, California 91320, USA.

Library of Congress Catalog Card Number
86-80184

CONTENTS

Greetings
to the friends who have shared
the walks described in this book.

Introduction

It is on etched hills and lithoed seas
That the stars appear to spin free
About the sky. Freedom is a glance
At the wheeling stars and we
Find that sight, by choice, not chance.

Walking has given me some of the happiest moments of my life. Few things are more naturally ours, at no cost, than the possibility of placing one foot in front of another — yet what a strange mixture of choice and chance has led my wandering feet. Choice is the master of chance however. Freedom is a glance at the wheeling stars.

I had been working hard, for several weeks, on the manuscript of *Hamish's Groats End Walk*, the story of how my dog Storm and I set off one May morning to walk the British Isles from end to end (the Irish part is told in chapter six) and the result was a thorough dose of itchy feet, a sort of haemorrhoids of the mind. It was doubly hard to keep to the work for I sat in Taroudant, a walled city south of the Atlas Mountains, with a thousand distractions and allurements about me, and I was writing about the longest walk I have ever undertaken. Somehow the book was finished and the sweat-impregnated manuscript posted off to my long-suffering typist at home. That it was to be short-listed for the Smith's Travel Prize and soon appear in paperback were bonuses, not luck, not chance. I had chosen the road to Taroudant and bullied my biro across the pages day after day (a far harder slog than the six months' walking) so when the release came it was naturally to a perambulation that appealed. I'd had enough of sizzling sunshine. I took a bus up into the mountains.

Three days later I was somewhere in the middle of nowhere, having climbed to the Atlas crests and simply turned west to wander till satisfied or till I met the Tizi n' Test road which links Taroudant and Marrakech by an interesting (some would say terrifying) 2,300-metre pass over the mountains. I dropped down off the main crest onto a spur and in the corner between them found a trickle of melted snow from which I filled my water bottle. I then moved out onto the spur and levelled a platform in the gravelly surface. This would be my bivvy site.

The crest of the spur was chosen as it buttressed southwards and I would enjoy daylight for as long as possible and, more important, catch the first yawning warmth of sunrise. A timeless ritual followed: getting armfuls of scrub along the slopes and feeding a small flame, twig by twig, till the blackened dixie simmered cheerily and the tang of smoke hung on the air: lying back, replete with mittened hands cupping the last drink of coffee while the sun burnished the crests copper-red and night swept up velvet darkness from the deeps: waking to some brief noise (the clicking of hooves on stone perhaps) and blinking in wonder at the extravagance of stars overhead. You do not see stars like that above the lurid glare of cities.

It was crackling cold. The stream across the slope had been silenced by frost and my breath had rimed my sleeping bag with white hoar. It was completely quiet. I found myself holding my breath and straining ears for a noise, any noise. Surely the stars should sing!

C. S. Lewis called his autobiography *Surprised by Joy*. As I lay there that sparkling, pristine night this flooding content filled the cat-limbs and bird-soul of me. I had walked into happiness, been ambushed by joy.

It was difficult to sleep and I was content to drift in and out of consciousness. The outside of my sleeping bag was furred with frost and the stars glittered with icy clarity as they wheeled round the sky. My mind was happy to spin off into memories — of other nights, of other places, of other wanderings. That was the genesis of this book.

* * *

As far back as I can recall our family walked. My parents were great walkers so the first debt is to them. So many eastern parents had minimal contact with their children but we went where they went and the sea and the hills are my earliest memories. Very early I began to see — and possess — the beauty and wonder of the world. This overwhelming wonder proved my sheet-anchor as a teenager. Here I knew something unchangeable and true. When I fled to their slopes they sobbed my sorrows dry. When I raced their slopes they laughed my happiness into tears and songs. Here I was supremely at home with things, with peace and freedom not to be found in the 'far below'.

Apart from the earliest days of parents' influence my experience was learnt alone. This is something I rather cherish now — but would not really advocate. I shudder in retrospect at some of the things I did as a boy. However, if they were not wise they were usually calculated. One learns early than an uncalculated risk is highly dangerous. The first commandment for young mountaineers is 'Think'; and the second is like unto it, 'Think again'. This will not make you less bold but it may make you bold, and old. We usually manage to get what we want (and go where we want) if we are determined enough — though in this shrinking world of permitted travel other factors have arisen which are set against adventure.

What walker can be bored, anywhere, with chapters of memories to turn to and read and re-read? Those grim hours connected with air travel, those sick-bed days — such can be made bearable by vicarious memory. Prospect too is always there. I have roughed out many a walk or expedition during a train journey or in the middle of some tedious meeting.

Strangely enough my earliest distinct walking memory is one of disappointment. I would be six or seven at the time, in Japan, just before the war. Our house had a view of Fuji Yama (4,064 metres) the sacred mountain which rose about eighty kilometres, away — so often as a graceful cone above a mist-moist landscape. I knelt at the window feeling forsaken for I just could not see my parents' figures on the far cinder slopes! It took them two days to walk up and for a score of years thereafter they could always cut me down to size by starting a sentence with 'Well, when you've been as high as we have . . .'

The war chased us down the Malayan peninsula and with Singapore falling about us in flames we escaped to South Africa — lucky to have survived, lucky in where we went.

In South Africa I was to live among some of the most beautiful hills in life's most carefree years. How vast they were. I remember Botha's Hill best and how I would wander freely into the 'Valley of the Thousand Hills', an area as beautiful as its name. Its burnt grass slopes sent up clouds of dust under foot, the long flat kloofs horizoned blue skies and in between ran the streams where we sought fool's gold. It was a world of red-hot pokers and arum-lilies, of weaver birds, of chameleons and praying mantis and sometimes snakes. There was a friendly welcome at each *kraal* and strange drinks to quench the thirst.

After two years in South Africa we returned to Scotland and I had, for the first time, more than two birthdays in the same country. It was very much a coming home and though I have wandered all my life Scotland remains home: not any single place in it so much as a symbolic whole. For I came to know it whole.

As soon as my young brother, who had been born in Japan (I was born in Ceylon and mother in Thailand) was old enough, the whole family would cycle off, often for weeks at a time, up to the western wonderland of Glenelg, Kintail, Torridon, Sutherland — names that glitter — and there we walked and explored to our hearts' content. And what of the hills: Suilven? An Teallach? Liathach? The Five Sisters? They rose initially beyond the dreams of a boy: miles high of rock and heather with screes about their sides and guarded by lochans and bogs. The magic of those hills never faded and eventually they were possessed. You could hostel for a shilling a night, live off wartime surplus ration tins and roam the length of the land. To cycle was cheap, to go alone was simple, and soon there were few places I had not been. I came to know the hill passes, and began walking up favourite peaks — a beginning any boy can follow.

The home hills, the Ochils, claimed a great part of my devotion, after all I could lie in bed and gaze along their slopes which rose above Dollar. How ridiculous running round a track seemed to one who knew those heights.

I left school at eighteen and R.A.F. National Service days took me off wandering again: Egypt, Cyprus, Jerusalem, Aden, Jordan, Kenya, Uganda, Tanzania, Malta — a splendid paid holiday on the whole even if some of it was active service or grim policing. (Many places we roamed then are no longer available or are inadvisable.) The hills above Kyrenia, the Ngong Hills outside Nairobi, Kilimanjaro, Mount Kenya (an oil painting I did then still hangs on a bedroom wall) and the Mountains of the Moon — these were abiding influences.

4

I spent a couple of years as an assistant in a Paisley parish and both there and through S.U. camps much of my time was spent with youngsters. I then somehow drifted into teaching and next was appointed (the first such post in a state school) to initiate what has become Outdoor Education. I was actually paid to take gangs off into the wilds! After a decade the school closed and I had an advisory job which I came to loathe for its imprisoning atmosphere. At the age when most people seek security I broke off to freelance anything to do with mountains and writing about mountains. Walking, as can be imagined, was the heart of all these years, and so it remains.

Most years the months of February, March and April are spent in Morocco for it offers a certainty of sunshine wherein to walk, climb, ski, watch birds, explore generally and write free of the distractions of home life. It is cheaper than staying at home. It is perhaps the most accessible of lands which are utterly non-European and having one such place to return to again and again makes It almost a second home, where I can rest, as in an old tweed jacket, with comfort and content. It is very much the place where I can dream dreams and plan ahead. There always seems to be more time there. People still matter. It is a bit like the Highlands used to be in my early wanderings.

Our self-indulgent, greedy, materialistic society I think fails because man was not meant to be a pampered creature. Experiments have shown that rats, given all the comforts, soon go insane but under stress they thrive and multiply. Man seems the only creature to be actively sinning against himself and in our suicidal society there are plenty who seek to escape the insanity by heading into the wilds. Walking and climbing is largely escapism, a fleeing of urban pressures and crazy imposed values. Perhaps it is a vain re-creation but it can give personal adventuring for the taking. *Walking,* recreationally, involves more people in Britain than any other sport or pastime (if you exclude watching T.V.). Thank God for it.

The last fifty years has seen a steady and now accelerating decline in the possibilities of walking adventures. There was an explosion of enthusiasm after World War 1 but even then passports had arrived and the frontiers were being drawn in. Freedom to roam vanished with the Second War, since when country after country has become isolated, dangerous or forbidden. People travel now with all the inspiration and initiative of pre-packed margarine. Sadly, many want it so and homeland values are now jetted off to the corners of the world. The very differences people travel to experience are slipping away into the vast, grey common denominator of our materialistic monoculture. Walking is one of the few basics left to us and even it is threatened by the prissy bureaucrats and the commercial pimps.

> All men are free under the stars
> Yet we bolt our doors and creep to bed,
> All men are kings upon the earth
> But some have sold their thrones,
> despaired, and fled;
> All men, in Adam, walked with God,
> Now God, and walking, both are odd.

Uganda, Zimbabwe, Ethiopia, Iran, Afghanistan, are now no longer possible or advisable. You may now be mugged in the Andes as readily as in London. I would urge you to put legs to your dreams quickly then, before the world is completely rendered in uniform grey and before our freedom to wander is utterly lost. Great walking adventures *are* still possible.

I hesitate over the word 'great' for it is such a relative term. What may be great to one person may be commonplace to another. The greatness is in the aspiring. The actual doing is merely mechanical. Frequently the determining factor is time and for this reason I have restricted the walks described in this book to ventures which could be, and often were, fitted in to a two or three weeks' holiday period.

The walks described ranged in character and style, and in their physical demands. If there seems to be a bias to walking in the British Isles (and Ireland) this is partly to satisfy the nationalistic enthusiasms of the various countries. I could hardly enthuse over the Somerset-Avon walk without Scottish friends being up in arms. I could hardly miss Scotland for there lies the wealth of mountains that makes for challenging trekking to rival any. People tend to think they can only find grand walking at the ends of the earth. I hope this book will encourage more visitors to Britain to bring along their boots (and waterproofs) as well as their London-Edinburgh-Dublin tickets. The South-

6

West walk is one rich in history, a landscape peopled from the dawn of history, and one which could be a good introduction to taking up walking for relaxation — far more rewarding than keep-fit exercises or jogging round the park. The South-West is a set route so to speak. A coast-to-coast walk across Scotland (the Ultimate Challenge game) or across Ireland, is open to infinite variety and the additional fascination of planning and accomplishing one's own creation. A walk across Scotland is a tough assignment as visitors from many parts of the world have discovered. Papa Stour and St Kilda are special cases, unlikely choices. I hesitate to call them British even: Papa Stour is in Shetland, which regards itself as an entity with marginal Scottish connections and St Kilda, as one book about it says lies 'on the edge of the world'. They too offer something quite quite different and would reward both the overseas and home visitor with a unique experience.

A cousin of mine from South Africa considered Britain as barely worth a visit because it 'had no wide open spaces'. He was astonished to find how wild, dramatic and wide, wide open it could be. You can walk for days on end and not see another human being. Golden eagles soar above some of the oldest sculptured peaks in the world and sea eagles are back again among the scattered islands of the golden west. In a book of walking adventures worldwide I make no apology for so much on British (and Irish) interests. These are among the most-visited places on earth and, for me and all who walk, the towering cliffs and St Kilda are finer than the Tower of London. Bring your boots to Britain! Lazy Brits, start exploring your own country, the best way — on your feet!

Scattered through the narratives I hope there is quite a bit of practical advice and hints about actually playing the walking game. There is no mystique about walking. It can be easy or as demanding as one desires and at any level it is one of the most healthy activities available — at minimal expense! The chapters are not written in an increasing order of difficulty but purposely juxtapose very different settings. I hope the result will be one that gives readers itchy feet and if the reaction to one chapter is 'Wow, I'd like to go there, but it's far too hard and needs too much time' then the next may suggest 'Sure, I could do that! Let's give it a try'. Readers, after all, will vary from armchair specialists to those who have done a great deal themselves. Fortunately it is a pastime of unlimited scope.

The emphasis too is on walks lasting days, or even weeks, rather than just a single day. There are scores of guide books on local walks in any country; while they may provide some adventures, such walks must remain rather low-key accomplishments. I believe there are greater rewards waiting for many walkers, if they would just shift up a gear, and press down on the accelerator of imagination. For this reason I have described the Moroccan walks (and Morocco generally) in much greater detail. As I go there most years, the High Atlas being one of the finest walking landscapes in the world, I also know it with a greater depth of understanding than say the Cordillera Blanca in Peru which I've only seen on one, memorable, occasion (and which is perhaps not too safe a place in the present unsure political situation). In the Moroccan chapter I have taken time and space to hint at history, at the cultural or practical background, at artistic or gourmet temptations, in a way not possible for every walk. (Each deserves a book!) In Morocco I have carefully described a possible three-day walk which could be a good one for a first visit to an exotic and different world. It is one that satisfied a group of widely-experienced walkers last spring, so is not to be underrated. It is quite physically demanding — but that too is an ingredient of the rich cake of satisfying accomplishments. Try this walk in the mountains above Marrakech and you'll be a world-wanderer, world-walker for the rest of your days, delighting in new peoples, new cultures, new stimulations, new great walking adventures.

There is nothing like a solitary night under the stars to let the imagination run free. I have had so many nights like that in Morocco (lucky man to put feet to so many dreams) that they are now a special feature of the annual visits which speed the years away. If the genesis of this book was that bivouac, then it is also its exodus.

Eventually the jet-and-glitter sky over my bivvy began to fade, the stars steadily vanished (yet not one could you catch in the act), the edge of the world glowed lemon and pink. Day came shivering out of the east: an explosion of exaggerated brightness heralded by the whir of the doves' wings and a fox silhouetted against the glow. I struggled with the toggle of my sleeping bag and wriggled out like some strange butterfly from its chrysalis. The world was garbed in a white pelt from the frosty night.

Fortunately I'd stored some handfuls of scrubby twigs under my bivvy mat and these were soon crackling below the pan. The smoke rose in a column, straight up but the mere scent of the fire set the mouth watering. As I sipped the first dish of tea the sensuous sun came over the peaks on the horizon. It was like turning on a heater. The frosting fell from the scrub and melted on the rocks in just a few moments. Pebbles, held still all night, began to trickle and tinkle down the screes. On the next spur, much lower down, more blue smoke rose into the air. There would be an *azib* there: a *shieling,* a *saeter,* a *bergerie* — call it what you would — that common development of shepherding the world over, the highest places where man and beast can dwell to live off the fringes of vegetation. Very faintly I could hear an ululating song. Welcome sun! Welcome day! Welcome the walking adventures to come!

* * *

As finding out about new places is both fascinating in itself, and essential if there is a prospect of actually walking or visiting, each section has a brief bibliography and a note about maps. Finding these may not always be easy and the following specialist suppliers may be able to help.

Cordee, 3a De Montfort Street, Leicester, LEI 7HD. 0533-543579.

McCarta, 122 King's Cross Road, London, WC1X 9DS. 01-278-8276.

Edward Stanford, 12-14 Long Acre. London, WC2E 9LP. 01-836-1321.

West Col, Goring, Reading, Berkshire, RG8 9AA. 0491-681-284.

The Travel Bookshop, 13 Blenheim Crescent, London W11 2EE. 01-229-5260.

* * *

I

Scotland

DOLLAR AND THE OCHIL TOPS

Only a hill: earth set a little higher
above the face of earth: a larger view
of little fields and roads; a little nigher
to clouds and silence: what is that to you?
Only a hill; but all of life to me,
up there, between the sunset and the sea.

(Geoffrey Winthrop Young)

The Ochils are not big hills that stun with dramatic grandeur; rather they are bald bumps, tawny and green according to season, which sprawl on the chequered lawn of Lowland Scotland. They are marginal hills, dividing the desert from the sown, the solitary from the urban, the singing heights of the heart from life's troughs. They were my boyhood hills and, as such, are linked by a unique emotional attachment — which only increases with the disillusion (and dissolution) of age. My Ochils are coloured the perpetual greens of youth.

Through all our family's 'Dollar years' my bedroom faced west, looking along the steep scarp of the Ochils. The hills ran east-west, with this abrupt face to the south. Whatever you did, or wherever you were, in Dollar, or the other towns along their edge: Tilly, Alva and Menstrie (collectively known as the ungrammatical 'Hillfoots'), this bulk of hill loomed to the north. Sedbergh has the same situation in the Howgills but there, unlike Dollar Academy, youngsters are encouraged to make use of this natural bonus. Being a 'Hillfits chiel' was no guarantee of inheriting the freedom of the hills; that had to be sought out by restless youth.

The pronunciation of Ochils can prove tricky. They are neither the *Ock-hills* nor the *O-hills*, though this latter *O* is the correct start at least. Add the soft Scottish *ch* sound and you have it: the *Och-ills*. Note the definite article, always a sign of affection, THE Ochils, as much as The Ben can only be Ben Nevis.

To come out of the emotional horrors of war to this pleasant place was quite a shock in itself. Joshua, going in to possess the land, could not have been more excited. Somehow we had all survived to be reunited and to enjoy a few brief years as a complete family: mother, father, the three boys, and granny. I already had the freedom to roam and use it fully, exploring every corner of the boy-on-foot bounds of Dollar. Were our school houses not even called by these mighty loves — Hill, Castle, Glen and Devon?

I relished my junior years at school for a love of the outdoors, and wild nature was encouraged by dear old Ma Wilson. Later years I found discouraging, with a largely out-of-contact staff and peers with few interests in common. Does an innate liking of a subject lead to an enjoyment of its learning or is a subject made an enthusiasm by the contagious presentation of a teacher? Perhaps both but I was extremely fortunate to have mentors who made certain subjects live fully: Art, English, History, Geography, Natural History. These have in odd combinations and all unplanned, now become my livelihood. I must have been a horror, pursuing as I did, all kinds of interests (with the cost of non-conformity) but the library; home and hill-freedom ensured a more liberal education. I was prepared to suffer for my freedom.

Occasionally when frost made the ground too hard for games we were sent to go up King's Seat, one of the 2,000-foot summits of the Ochils — which made the hills a penance, if not a punishment, in the eyes of most rugged fanatics. I once arrived on the summit to find some of the lordly first fifteen lingering there in a thick mist unsure of the way back. 'You, Brown, know these bloody hills. Which way do we go for home?' From the battered ranks of the second fifteen it was with considerable glee I pointed due north! They came out at Blackford I believe and had to borrow fares from the police to bus round the Ochils.

We learnt our way as shepherds do, by trial and error, rather than by map and compass (we possessed neither) and were never seriously mislaid, never mind lost. The basic geography was simple. Unless you went over the watershed to the north, which was not easy to do, any and all water eventually drained southwards to one of those Hillfoots towns. Being lost is quite different from being briefly mislaid; you learn from the latter, in the former you are simply dead wrong, or dead. Experience is the sum of near misses.

The circling River Devon was our boundary to south, east

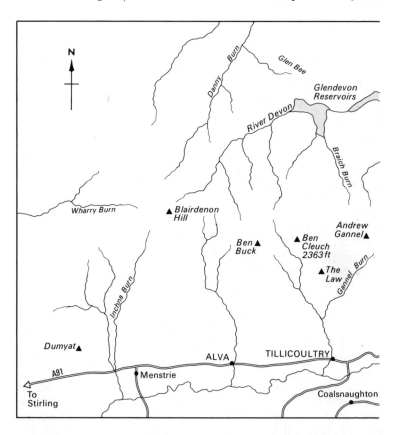

and north. The Ochils continue beyond the Glendevon-to-Gleneagles pass through the hills but to venture thence was more than a day trip. When a youth hostel was built in Glendevon it helped and eventually the possession of a cycle and a tent opened up the whole world so to speak. Economical years in youth were no bad thing. I know my Scotland from foot slogging, from the soil up. There is no substitute for Shank's pony. Skis, canoes, push bikes are extensions not substitutions for they retain the element of self-propulsion and direct contact. The school house called Devon (in recognition of the River Devon), was praised (in rather mediocre verse) by Rabbie Burns after a visit in 1787 and is the anglicised version of its older,

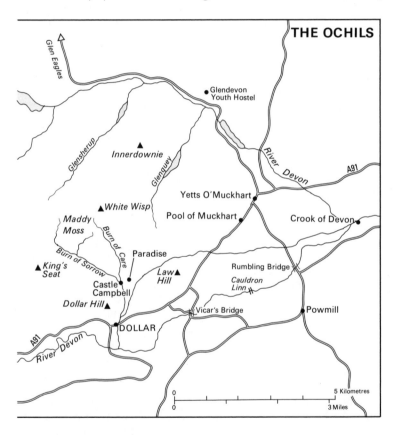

THE OCHILS

Glen Eagles

Glendevon
Youth Hostel

Glensherup

Innerdownie

Glenquey

River Devon

A91

White Wisp

Yetts O'Muckhart

Maddy
Moss

Pool of Muckhart

Crook of Devon

Burn of Care

Burn of Sorrow

Paradise

King's
Seat

Law
Hill

Rumbling Bridge

Cauldron
Linn

Castle
Campbell

Dollar Hill

Vicar's Bridge

Powmill

A91

DOLLAR

River Devon

0   5 Kilometres
0   3 Miles

lovelier, names of Dovan or Dowan. Our house was called 'Devon Lodge' though it was not a lodge and lay a mile from the 'clear winding' water. The river yielded its delights of winter skating and summer swimming and on it I had my first sighting of summer-dazzling kingfishers. The Five-Mile Walk round by Vicar's Bridge and back by Rackmill Bridge was a regular tramp of father's.

The vicar of Vicar's Bridge was Thomas Forrest, an early Reformation martyr who committed such crimes as 'showing the mysteries of the Scriptures to the vulgar people in English' (at his trial his bishop admitted he had knowledge of neither Old nor New Testament!) and outdoing the wandering friars in acts of charity (he would carry bread and cheese up the sleeves of his gown to give to the poor) — for being such a bad example they burnt him on Castle Hill in Edinburgh in February 1539. He was one of my earliest heroes and the second article I ever had published was an account of his life and death. His was perhaps an odd name to find along with Shackleton, Gino Watkins, Eric Shipton or W. K. Holmes. Above Vicar's Bridge a carter was ambushed and murdered and the assassin, one Bell, was reputedly the last man publicly hanged in Scotland. It gave a fear and fascination to the brae up to Blairingone.

Glen school house is named after Dollar Glen, a surprisingly dramatic cleft in the hills. Down into it pour the Burns of Care and Sorrow, which formed a natural moat and bastion for Castle Gloum above. The old laid-out paths had all fallen down during the war so it was out of bounds to school pupils — which made it doubly attractive and fairly private as few adults could, or would, penetrate its fastness. As members of the C.C.F. we sometimes spent Friday afternoons on exercise on the hills. Perhaps typically we went off and the teacher or officer stayed below. On one sweltering day my hill knowledge proved useful. We plunged into the oak-dappled depths to swim away the afternoon in the glen while periodically I would report, on the walkie-talkie, about our (mythical) manoeuvres.

Castle was my school house and Castle Campbell still dominates town and gown from that perch in the hills. It is all one can imagine a castle should be: a square tower, with later outer walls, set high on a precipitous knoll, with a wide view out over the rich lands of Fife, the carselands of the Forth and the Pentlands beyond Auld Reekie. Slowly it was restored from the war's neglect, a solitary mason working there for a decade. We found his work as fascinating as I'm sure he found it satisfying. We had clandestine nights sleeping in the castle and my first real winter climb was Kemp's Score, a narrow rock gash over thirty metres long, up which I hacked steps with an ordinary hand axe borrowed from the woodshed at home.

Romance and adventure link to sobering history. Kemp's Score ensured the castle's water supply. Kemp himself was a freebooter who was once indiscreet enough to carry off the king's dinner from the palace at Dunfermline. Because of this he eventually lost his head (literally) and the body was thrown into the Devon.

Castle Campbell took on that name by act of parliament in 1489, the first Earl of Argyll not liking the title of The Gloum by which it was known. Mary Queen of Scots was there for the wedding of a sister of Argyll's and the castle surrendered to the queen on her march through Fife in 1565. John Knox mentions staying in the castle and both preached and dispensed the sacrament at an open air ceremony. With the ease of youth I was both for kirk *and* king. It was all stirring stuff. The castle was finally destroyed in Cromwell's time.

It still saddens me how little today's youngsters know about the past. The deeper the concrete we lay over the soil of our history, the more we are becoming a rootless people. Walking is a dangerous pastime: it opens up avenues to all kinds of questionings. As a boy, the town of Dollar felt like the solid centre of the universe from which I explored and returned until, as by some planetary centrifugal force, I was thrown out into life's space to be a perpetual wanderer. The security of those days has long gone. Man seems to be within the accelerating drag of some fearsome black hole of his own creation. Incapable of salvation we take to the hills, we seek the wild and beautiful and solitary places of the world, to make the unthinkable bearable. Walking is glorious escapism!

As young lads we found our own way to the Ochils. We only met one adult regularly in our wanderings, the writer W. K. Holmes, and he, quietly, had a huge influence on us. His modest *Tramping Scottish Hills* was the book that took us beyond the Ochils to the hills we could view from their summits: Ben Lomond, Ben Lawers, Ben Nevis itself. He it was who pointed out flowers and birds or historical sites (like the ancient copper mines up the Burn of Sorrow), enthusing us with his own delights and only smiling quietly at our wilder escapades such as pegging routes up the quarry in Gloom Hill with six-inch nails. He also encouraged my own earliest writings and I still treasure postcards in his spidery hand which followed me to Egypt, Kenya and other places during National Service days in the R.A.F. He remained to the end, as he wrote,

> Still a child in a world of wonder,
> Heir of the sky and the earth thereunder . . .

Years later I was to spend twelve years taking youngsters from a Fife school into the wilds and many of them had their first spell of camping at Paradise, a pool east of the castle and now buried in a plantation of regimental pines. The name is still used locally and it was curious recently to see learned suggestions being put forward for William's Stone, another of our names given during those years. This erratic boulder above the castle was simply a regular gathering place of our exploratory clan, and was named from one of our number — nothing whatever to do with William the Lion, King of Scots! As recently as a year ago on a walk across Scotland from Tay to Clyde I camped at Paradise. The magic remains.

> We went out into the dark, sleepy-eyed and vague, into a silent town and a sky all stars. There was a frosted mist and the ring of our boots on the road seemed to be caught by it and swirled away in muffled, unsure sound. Up through the Old Town we went, the dog padding ahead and the pair of us reaching long strides as we found the rhythm to bear us up to the tops . . .

What I wrote about those decades ago has not changed. Let us walk and share the route again.

An early start is advisable for it is a long day and if it is to be savoured, rather than gulped, then time will have to be borrowed from the stars. At the first squint of day we are walking up the burn from the clock tower and, if it is spring, the burn is at its cheeriest and the banks are a blaze of cheery blossom (father's doing during his town council days). The burn had to be banked and controlled after a spate tore the fronts off some of the houses. Across the middle bridge the ruins of the old parish church hold a lantern belfry against the eastern glow of dawn. At the top bridge a notice points out the narrow entrance to glen, castle and hills — the straight and narrow way that leads to Paradise. Unashamedly romantic, I never tire of this approach. Familiarity breeds content.

Once a father and son stood on top of Ben Nevis and gazed at the widest view in these islands. In awe the laddie pointed up Glen More, the Great Glen of Albyn, and whispered, 'Is Paradise there, Daddy?' With unintentional humour and complete lack of imagination came the reply 'No son, just Inverness.'

The path runs tight by the burn and then the constraining eases for the Mill Green. There is no mill or big wheel now and the bleaching green became a grassy wilderness long ago. Now it has been tidied up as part of the outdoors welfare state. Across the burn is the first hole of the golf course, a hole which proves expensive for any golfer with tendencies to slice the ball to the right. A village lad, a bit simple, used to make his pocket money finding lost balls, a source of income respected by the rest of us, however impecunious. We sledged on the golf course, the runs taking on the numbers of the holes. To actually play golf on this scarp of the Ochils it is useful to have one leg shorter than the other. I gave up the game when I lost more balls than I found.

Dollar to this day is different from the rest of the Hillfoots towns. The rest are industrialised but Dollar grew on account of its magnificent school, the result of a bequest from John McNabb, a poor boy born in 1732, who ran away to sea, became rich, and left half his estate to benefit the town. The main academy building is a Doric showpiece designed by Playfair and opened in 1821. It was extended in 1868 and various other additions (like laboratories in 1909) were added without spoiling its park-like setting under the Ochils. While I was staying at Glen Coe Youth Hostel in 1960 Ingrid Feeney, the warden, rushed me through to their television to see the school going up in flames. The interior was gutted but the stone facade escaped and the school was rebuilt inside the shell (with three storeys instead of two) and ceremoniously opened by the Queen.

The wooded glen is a wild place, a mix of oak, ash, sycamore, hazel, birch and rowan. The banks occasionally become sheer precipices through which the Dollar Burn dashes loudly even on the balmiest of days. The odd building by the water's edge as the path rises is the town's water supply intake, the gift of a proprietor last century. In 1950 J. E. Kerr of Harviestoun presented the glen and castle to the National Trust for Scotland and the castle is now in the care of the state.

In 1865 the Dollar Flute Band paraded through the streets and a thousand people gathered for the Glen's opening ceremony. Thanks to long hard labour, plenty of dynamite and some unusual bridging, paths had been created through the gorges. 'Not even Switzerland could have done better' they boasted — and were soon dreaming of a railway up Ben Cleuch. When we tried to force the gorge (as close to the water as possible) there were several places where we had to bang in pitons and pendule across the mossy walls — so to *walk* though such a gorge is still quite dramatic. The heart of the Glen is where the Burns of Care and Sorrow meet. On the prow of rock between the burns the castle sits in its solitary security.

We double back here to traverse 'The Long Bridge'. It goes *up* the stream, a catwalk built on girders lodged into the sheer cliffs, so you look through the slats to the racing waters. What must it have been like in 1877 when the Ochils were battered with waterspouts and walls of water crashed out of the gorges to flood and destroy the Hillfoots towns?

Where the burn curves the Long Bridge deposits one on the cliff again, a path blasted out and known as Windy Edge. It traverses mere feet from the pounding gush of water and is an impressive place. A big boulder is wedged between the narrow walls and we used to scare ourselves as kids by saying that the walls would clash-to if this wedge was ever washed out. Here too is Kemp's Score, the historic gash that leads from castle to burn. Before the Victorian path was blasted out it would be quite unapproachable in normal conditions. You were not regarded as a real Dollar boy till you had scaled it. It is an ascent best left for dry conditions, mud being its main difficulty (hence the winter ascent by brother, dog and myself). The young Walter Scott slimmed up — and later, in *The Talisman,* wrote a description of a castle, La Guarde Douloureuse, which has marked similarities to The Gloume. The dignified first Rector of Dollar, the mighty Dr. Mylne, tried to descend it, lost his footing and suffered the indignity of a thirty-metre tumble into the burn, 'to the detriment of his nether garments and some damage to his person'. Perhaps Kemp's Score should be a prerequisite for teachers rather than the taught.

One escapes the Windy Edge over the Glencairn Bridge and the west bank gives easy walking up to the Shepherd's Fall and Bridge which leads to the neck of land that allows access to the castle. Lady Nairne wrote a song about the castle. Burns kept to the valley.

The castle presents a blank wall to this side with an entrance through a fortified gateway. Before it are two giant sycamores where no doubt unfortunates swung for their sins. The power of pit and gallows was very real. The pit is a tiny cell built into the thickness of the walls and entered by a trapdoor. A tiny slit in the wall would mark time's weary passing for any victim thrown down into this prison. A tiny chapel also exists in the wall's thickness. The original tower is in quite good order with details like this well preserved. The barrel-vaulted roof of the top storey has faces set in it and through the gaping holes of mouths lights were lowered from above. From the battlements there is a huge landscape panorama below — and a backing of bold hills above. It is a castle well worth visiting and if only half a day is available it is worth exploring the paths by the Sochie Falls further up the Burn of Sorrow before returning down the Burn of Care.

We cross at an easy ford east of the neck. This way came a rugged cart track, the only access to the castle, now a tarred road. At Brewlands (currently a scout centre) we double back on the old drove road to Glendevon and Auchterarder, that runs above the Burn of Care for its first mile. What history that path has known, travelled by drovers and packmen, by Cavaliers and Covenanters, by Redcoats and Jacobites. In the 1715 rebellion a Jacobite force came that way just to annoy the Government forces in the castle but on Sheriff Muir, at the west end of the Ochils, that hope of Stuart restoration ended.

The hill on our left is Whitewisp and on its lower slopes (once all cultivated to supply the castle) the bracken now covers the last remnants of what we knew as Library Farm. This was a humble shepherd's house but one particular shepherd John Christie (born in 1721) had a remarkable collection of over 370 books, bound and treasured. Sadly, when he died, they were auctioned off at Dollar Bridge.

The path leaves the new plantings to enter the narrows of the pass. When this begins to open out again, look carefully, on the right hand side, to find a bubbling well of clear cold water. This is the Maiden's Well (on the map it is shown much too far on to the north-east) of which W. K. Holmes told us various tales. The spirit of a beautiful maiden may be summoned from the spring by a visit on a moonless night, but the veracity of this remains 'unproven', for any such adventurers were invariably found lying dead in the pass in the morning.

The smooth hillock on the left as you continue is the Maiden's Castle, a not uncommon name in lore from Dorset to the Lomonds. There is no trace of any earthworks on this particular bump. Legend tells of a piper passing one night and finding a castle ablaze with lights. He was invited to join the revelry and to play for the company. He obliged and had a merry time. When he reached home the next day he found himself a stranger — for a hundred years had passed in that magical night.

Where the fences of the Glenquay Reservoir cross the track turn up the stream banks to 'take to the hills' over the Dun Moss to gain Innerdownie, the most eastern of the 2000 footers — now 611 metres — on the metric maps we are using. On the way you will probably be startled by snipe ricochetting off or have to endure the plaintive complaints of tumbling peewits. The wall on top makes a convenient wind-break for eating 'pieces' (the Scotsman's sandwiches).

A lazier day's walking is to go right through the pass to Glendevon, have a pub lunch at the Tormaukin Inn, and return along Innerdownie and Whitewisp, with castle and glen explorations thrown in as well. From Innerdownie our traverse of the 2000 footers will provide a twenty kilometres of grassy walking but the route never drops below 500 metres so it is not too demanding. The steeper slopes of the Ochils can be very slippery when the grass is dry and polished. (I found studded cricket boots were the perfect footwear.) Given a dusting of snow they become ski-touring hills but the same smooth skin can create dangerous avalanche conditions. The biggest I have ever seen in Scotland was on the north side of Whitewisp.

It is over three kilometres to Whitewisp from Innerdownie and every step of it expands the views. The big hills to the north appear and you can spot two Forth Bridges, one

Kincardine Bridge and two Tay Bridges. The wall from Innerdownie does not go to Whitewisp but bears off along the crest to Tarmangie.

Whitewisp (643 metres) looks a bold shape from across the Devon Valley but is only a spur. Tarmangie Hill, a mile west, is 645 metres and the highest point of these hills that lie north and east of the Sorrow. From Tarmangie Glen Sherup drains down to Glendevon. Its reservoir is over a hundred years old but the massive forestry plantings are new. The Sorrow rises from Maddy Moss, which we cross, to circuit round and up King's Seat (648 metres) on the other side of this mournfully-named river. Maddy Moss has dried out considerably in my lifetime but the Burn of Sorrow is still a favourite route up into the hills. The old pony route through to Blackford from Tilly (Tillicoultry) is joined as it skirts Maddy Moss but the way is now made longer by the reservoir in Upper Glendevon, which I can remember being built. A fifth reservoir has recently been completed to tame the hill-held Devon.

We back-track off King's Seat and pull up a nameless hill on the map. It was nameless on our first-known map so we called it Peewit Hill and we dutifully carried boulders to build the cairn on its grassy summit. It is still a small cairn as there is no stone near at hand for cairnomaniacs. The hill which has the resounding name of Andrew Gannel (sounds like a character out of John Buchan), is 670 metres high and one of four which are circled and drained by the burns that descend to Tilly. As Dollar lads we felt like clansmen entering rival territory when we ventured west of Maddy Moss, which is not so imaginative really. When Montrose's men harried Dollar and Muckhart it was only retaliation for the destruction of 'the Bonnie Hoose o' Airlie' while shortly afterwards the opposition carried fire and sword through Alva and Menstrie in further vengeance.

Ben Cleuch is disfigured with a radio beacon but before following our fence to it we swing south to take in Tilly Law (638 metres), the prow that fills the gap in the scarp above that town. A gentle mile swings us up to the top of the Ochils: Ben Cleuch (721 metres), sometimes Ben Clach on older maps. It may lack impressive altitude but the view is one of the best from any British summit. The peaks of Arran, the Bass Rock, Lochnagar and Ben Nevis can all be seen in a sweep of the horizon's circumference. There is an indicator to pinpoint the distant features. The Ochils are worth a clear day both for the views and because navigation is not easy in cloud as there are few marked features on a landscape of grassy swellings. There are fences in plenty but you have to know where they go before using them as markers.

Ben Buck (675 metres) lies about 800 metres north-west from Ben Cleuch and Ben Ever (622 metres) lies a similar distance to the south-west. It is easiest to add the mere swelling of the Buck first. We lose quite a bit of height to swing down to Ben Ever's high crest which divides Tilly's waters from those of Alva. Alva Glen, while not so dramatic as Dollar Glen, is also attractively pathed, and splits into two with the Alva Burn leading up to our last summits (one possible descent route) and the Glenwinnel Burn coming up to meet Ben Ever. From Alva another old track angles up to the Silver Glen (silver mines 200 years ago), picks up the higher Glenwinnel waters and eventually crosses to Blackford. We contour to cross this path and make for Blairdenon Hill which has three fences meeting on its summit. This part of the Ochils was once famous for its birds of prey, but a few kestrels on high and buzzards lower down are the only common species now.

Perhaps our being on the western Ochils explains the sudden change to peat-ridden country. We look west to Ben Lomond and the Cobbler, to the Trossachs country — from which a great deal of rain is delivered. We seldom explored west from here over Sheriff Muir but usually turned south to return to the Hillfoots proper. Even the names going westward have a novel ring: Loss Hill, Ashentrool, Pendreich, Stonehill, Cauldhame . . . and how about Seamab Hill, Cloon, Ben Trush, Simpleside, Mickle Corum or Whaick?

Draining this changed country to the north are the infant waters of the Devon. This river enters the Forth Estuary about ten kilometres south, as the crows fly, but to reach it makes a tour of the Ochils, about fifty-two kilometres in all. Today's round can be varied by starting in Glendevon and following the tops west to Blairdenon and then tracing the River Devon back, first by little secretive streams, then along two reservoirs. After Blairdenon we were often only too glad to peel off sweaty garments and plunge into the first pool available. The Devon very much bounded our Ochils, both north and south. The burn wends east to Glendevon's road through the hills then breaks out by the Yetts o'Muckhart southwards. In ancient times the Devon drained to Loch Leven but a classic river-capture at Crook of Devon now swings it west to flow right along below the Ochils. The Devil's Mill, Rumbling Bridge and the Cauldron Linn hint at some spectacular features above Vicar's Bridge. After that it is very much the 'crystal Devon, winding Devon' of the last song Burns ever wrote. (He was writing of a lassie at Harvieston rather than about the river.)

Blairdenon (632 metres) has a small top a bit to the west, Greenforest Hill (616 metres) which is a slight sting in the tail of the day's walk. The way off to Alva can be made along the tops or down the Alva Burn. The latter is my favourite: a change from the breezy summits, with the chance of a cooling swim, a return to the world of flowers and scents, of waterfalls and bee-loud trees, and the richer, riper greens of life. Green is the colour of the Ochils as Rennie McOwan sings:

> But the Ochils are green, of every shade,
> moss and emerald, lime and jade,
> lichen and ferns, grasses and rock,
> birch and rowan, hazel and oak.
> They'll all change a little as the seasons move,
> but green, green, above all, is the colour of love.

Alva is eight kilometres from Dollar but there is a bus service, or perhaps you could arrange a second car or a non-walking friend to return you to the start. This is a day walk so you are still tied to such symbols of civilisation as cars. Most of the subsequent chapters will take us well away from cars and into saner civilisations but for all their majesty and strangeness I am still content to return to these gentle hills of home. The Ochils give as good walking as anywhere and there never can be hills to match the first-loved hills of youth. Come, soon, and try the Dollar gateway to Ochil adventuring.

> O some grow old and dream no more
> And some do dream by day, lad.
> And some put feet upon their dream
> And have a song to sing, lad.

BIBLIOGRAPHY
Dollar Chapbook, Dollar Civic Trust.
Seven Dollar Walks (descriptive sheets), Dollar Civic Trust.
BENNETT, D., *The Southern Highlands*, S.M.C.
TRANTER, N., *The Heartland*, Hodder and Stoughton.
HOLMES W.K., *Tramping Scottish Hills*.

MAPS
Ordnance Survey 1:50,000 Sheet 58.

2

Scotland

SEA-WALKING ON PAPA STOUR

Sail forth — steer for the deep waters only ...
O my brave soul!
O farther, farther sail!
... are not all the seas of God?
O farther, farther, farther sail!

Walt Whitman

A certain bias towards mountains and mountain walking is probably obvious in this book. I make no apologies for this. Mountains are plainly enhancing to scenery, to local life and to experiences gained but it would be a bold man who would define what is a mountain or even what is a hill. The Island of Rhum is all mountain from the sea upwards though it fails to gain the magical 3000-foot mark of the Munros. A sea stack may give more genuine rock-climbing than Everest. Seeing importance in height is a very artificial and rather ridiculous convention; scaling summits a rather contrived pleasure.

It is only recently, when walking has largely ceased to be done of necessity, that it has become artificially contrived, enthusiastically promoted and even turned into literature: the hallmark of acceptability. Ironically the real walking adventures go unrecorded. A soldier in Alexander's army who marched from Greece to the Ganga really did know something about walking. So do peasants and porters in the Andes or Atlas or Himalayas — and we are ready to admit their superiority by employing them and paying them to ease the efforts of our walking. We are only playing at walking. We Westerners take playing games so seriously though.

Even to mountaineers walking is the basis of all else. The early Alpine Club volumes entitled *Peaks and Passes* were an

25

indication of this underlying importance. Making first ascents was originally a doubtful pastime. The game was smoke-screened by a clutter of science. The tragedy on the Matterhorn brought the disapproval of the Queen and the howls of the populace. (It still happens every time a climber is lost in our hills.) Peaks were a perversion but passes, well, they were natural, logical and quite proper. We feel this with both head and heart. For as long as men have been on

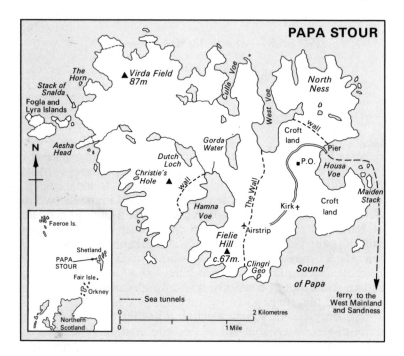

earth, forcing routes from A to B has been important. Migrations, military and commercial reasoning may be behind it, but footing it out is (almost) as old as the hills. It still is in many parts of the world. We, who so easily jump into a car or call a taxi, we who are the lemmings of the air, tend to forget this.

In Britain this fossilised way of life can only be found on the island fringes. To wander round on foot in a society not dominated by mechanical bustle is invigorating and relaxing. People actually matter more than micro chips. Our normal lives are so bounded by time that we burn ourselves up rushing into the future (which hardly bears thinking about anyway) so in this chapter I want to describe a place barely touched by time: the island of Papa Stour, in the Shetlands, off the coast of Scotland. Its highest hill is only 87 metres, it is only a few miles across at its widest, and its nearest neighbour, westwards, is Greenland.

Only St Kilda and Foula can claim a greater remoteness. Foula, another of the Shetland islands, is visible from Papa Stour. A sharp-cut fin rising on the horizon, you almost expect it to dip under the sea like a whale's fin. Sometimes the shimmering haze hides Foula from Papa but this is only one more place that claims the saying 'If you can see Foula it is going to rain; if you can't see Foula it is raining already'.

This is rather unfair, for though it can rain, Papa's situation on the western edge of Shetland ensures that much of the rain-bearing cloud passes overhead to unload on the higher hills of the mainland, a lesson that can be worth remembering in the Scottish hills. If Torridon, for instance, is wet and miserable, slip over to Applecross and you may find sunshine beaming in under the black clouds. The weather in Shetland (or the outer Hebrides) is dominated by wind rather than rain. The wind always seems to be blowing and frequently writing its will across the sky in dramatic cloudscapes. Views in Shetland are dominated by the sky not the land.

It is a good place for summer holidays for the 'three plagues of the Highlands': rain, midges and crowds of people are seldom dominatingly present in the isles. The wind controls the first two and if you've sailed from Aberdeen in the *St. Clair* it probably strongly influences the third. Most people simply fly to Sumburgh, Shetland's airport (which has benefitted from the oil boom). I sailed in order to have my dormobile as a base for touring and exploring the many islands that form the group. My mother was with me and in our first week we ranged from Sumburgh Head and prehistoric Jarlshof to the bird-crowded cliffs of Hermaness and Muckle Flugga (the lighthouse set on the dragon's teeth of skerries that form the most northerly tip of Britain); we climbed Ronas Hill and walked miles of wind-combed moors to see something of the wealth of brochs, chambered cairns and standing stones. The second week we spent on Papa Stour without transport.

I took two rucksacks and mother a wheeled trolley; Storm, the dog, carried nothing. Some day he is going to have panniers made for exploring the wilds.

When Papa folk talk of going to 'the Mainland' this is the Shetland mainland, not that other one with Scotland and England on it. My Scots accent shows enough that all through Shetland I'd be politely asked 'Do you come from Scotland?' in much the same way as they'd ask 'Do you come from Australia?' Shetland is geographically nearer to Norway (Lerwick has a Norwegian church) than to Scotland's mainland. It is actually further north than Leningrad. The islands only became Scottish in 1469 (when they came as a Norse dowry with the wife of James III) and Norse influences linger on, touching a wide range of things and very noticeable in the lively dialect of the people. Papa Stour itself comes from the Norse *Papa ey Stor,* the large priest island. As an ornithologist I found it delightful to deal with such birds as the raingoose (red-throated diver), ala mootie (storm petrel), peerie hawk (merlin), tieves' nacket (lapwing), teetick (pipit), or tystie (black guillemot). The last is the name still used in Norway.

The isolation and independence of Shetland is well-illustrated in a story I heard there. I would not vouch for its veracity but if it did not actually happen, well, it should have. A new economising edict went out from London that exam papers were no longer to be posted by each school but collected by van and sent in by train. The Shetland Council duly considered this and despite its obvious nonsense decided to comply. London was paying after all. So a van toured the islands, a lengthy task with all the ferry crossings, and eventually a ton of paper accumulated in Lerwick to be taken to the nearest railway station. The reaction of London is not recorded when they received the papers (and the bill) for they were despatched from Bergen station, this being 'the nearest station to Lerwick'.

We were lucky to have a gentle crossing, and the motor launch, the *Venture,* was accompanied by a school of porpoises. We sailed past two steep islets, riddled with caves and tunnels. One had a point, Scarf's Head, which was aptly crowded with cormorants hanging themselves out to dry. The ferry made a wide sweep to round into Housa Voe, passing between some towers of rock. The entrance is a maze of stacks, natural arches abound and one of the oldest traditional Papa stories concerns the Frau or Maiden Stack on which a thirteenth-century Jarl imprisoned his daughter to keep her away from men, to no avail, for despite her isolation, she bore a child. Scandinavia and its isles have many Maiden Stacks and similar stories attached to them.

The Shetlanders used to call Papa people 'Scories', the word for a young gull, for killing and salting young birds was an important part of food supplies on places that could so easily be cut off. Handa and St Kilda people did just the same. Gulls' eggs too were a relief in spring.

We landed at the pier from which a single mile of tarred road wiggles across the cultivated end of Papa Stour. The caravan we had hired for the week was at the other end of the road. I carried one rucksack on top of the other and mother wheeled her belongings along. It was one of three caravans beside the Old Manse and the walled enclosure of the school and school house. Our hosts, the Colemans had three children (a third of the school's population) so it must have been convenient having school next door.

One of the sad aspects of living on an isolated island like Papa Stour is that children once past primary school age, are boarded in Lerwick for their education. Unlike most children they cannot even have weekends at home for the Sound of Papa is notoriously dangerous and when you see storm beaches fifteen metres above the sea, composed of boulders which can weigh many hundredweights, you begin to realise why weekends home had a tendency to last weeks at a time.

Papa Stour nearly died as a community a score of years ago. It could have been the St Kilda story over again but an influx of newcomers ('the hippie invasion' some rudely called it) helped stem the tide of depopulation. The isolation and the demands of survival were too much for many of them but even now something like half the population are incomers, a common-enough situation in remote places in the Highlands and Islands. A community of about thirty teeters on the edge of extinction and has a hard time in every way. Piped water is recent and there is no electricity from the grid. There is no nurse or doctor. Beyond the wall west of our caravan lay a rough airstrip and the windsock was stored in the Colemans' barn. Self-sufficiency is no wishy-washy ideal but harsh necessity. Everyone seems to work some land, perhaps running a fishing boat as well, whilst others knit, operate the ferry, are postman or take in summer visitors. It is a deep-rooted way of life very far removed from the normal insecure but self-indulgent city life. A hundred years ago Papa's population was 253; it had been more but many emigrated to New Zealand.

Our particular caravan was the home territory of a goose but Storm and goose came to a quick agreement as to their needs of living space and co-existed quite happily. Storm is willing to be friends with all living creatures and as a result constantly receives pecks from bills and beaks or straight rights from bristling moggies. Before coming to Papa squirrels alone tended to drive him into a frenzy. On Papa it was the great skuas (bonxies) who were to become the bane of his life. These make frightening dives at humans as well as animals and as they try to approach unseen, the last minute rush of wind may be too late for evasive action. I've never been hit but used to walk around with a length of wood slipped down my rucksack so the top end was several feet above head level — and therefore received the dive bombing attacks.

Storm had no such protection and would be harried hither and thither by co-ordinating mobs of bonxies coming in one after the other from different directions. In the end he learnt to walk right at my heels, using me as I used my tall stick. The chicks were football-sized bundles of fluff and ugliness and were much more interesting to Storm who would find them however well hidden. The first few had a thorough sniffing but thereafter it was the finding that gave fun. Failing anything else he would even sniff out pipit nests. Fulmar chicks were a common risk. They have the defensive reaction of spewing out a stinking oily mess and are quite capable of hitting a target several yards away. The recipient will not be welcomed by friends or family. After a few cautionary 'Noes' Storm knew they were to be avoided as carefully as sheep. I had more near-misses than he did.

The bonxies are huge birds, bigger than any gull, but with a juvenile gull's brown speckled plumage, so their attacks can be quite exciting. Even they give way to the lighter but more pugnacious arctic skuas (which go by the fascinating name of 'scutti allens'). These two species could be compared to bombers and fighter bombers. They are both parasitic in that they chase and terrorise gulls until the victims bring up whatever food they have eaten. This is always a dramatic spectacle — unless you are caught immediately below a gull which has just disgorged its supper.

We met bonxies on our first evening stroll and on every subsequent walk. Although Papa Stour is only about five kilometres at its longest it takes a very long hard day's walk to go round it. More often than not we only explored parts of it at a time, being lured off to beachcomb or bird-watch, to botanize or spot whales or to look at the many sites showing man's presence over the centuries — but for convenience I'll describe it as a simple walk.

Our caravan windows looked south across the Sound of Papa to the Mainland and Sandness Hill. The hill was my weather guide. If it was clear I'd be sure of a dry day. Our stay had mostly fresh and windy conditions. I'd work for a couple of hours before breakfast, then make coarse porridge which we ate with fresh yellowy milk which Vicki would bring over in a jug each afternoon. I would only re-appear in time to cook a late dinner. Only on one night when we had visitors in did we light a lamp. In high summer it just does not become dark. The 'simmer dim' they call it.

Life is lived very fully in a place like Papa. It can be difficult, often demanding, sometimes dangerous but it is never dull or monotonous. Everyone helps everyone. Life is rooted in soil and sea. There are families there still with three generations all born on the island and an ancestry going back beyond record. Security like that rather than the numbing security of a nine-to-five life perhaps calls to a gangrel like myself. Everyone is basically self-employed and even set jobs like ferry or post have hours dictated by weather rather than regulations.

Vicki has written about her early years on Papa and a paragraph from her *Living on an Island* may be appropriately quoted.

I have chosen to reject many of the material artifacts that constitute twentieth-century living, but where they do fit into my scheme of things, and can be used without harming the environment, I am not ashamed to use them. There is a school of thought which believes that isolated communities such as this should be retained as living museums. You can still see old-fashioned implements here and you can see people doing things in the old ways. But we cannot escape the twentieth century; we must select from it. Where the old ways are the best we continue to use them, and do not accept all new inventions as being improvements. Weed killers are a case in point, as they kill not only weeds but many quite harmless plants and small creatures, all of which have a part to play in keeping nature in balance. If we unbalance nature too far there is every likelihood that we will destroy our world.

The only practical drawback of life in the caravan was having the toilet fifty metres away in the barn. One day I decided I must find some receptacle and walking on the Kirk Sands found a hospital urine bottle. That's what you call service! The oddest bit of beachcombing was to find a big, perfectly fresh lettuce wrapped in a ten-day-old *Guardian*.

The Hill of Fielie is a good starting point for it is the second highest point on the island and gives a bonxie's eye view of the geography. A coastguard hut is wired down on top and I noticed it was full of artist's materials. The sea lay straight down under red cliffs, sucking and surging on the calmest day. Foula is anchored twenty-eight kilometres off and perhaps only on Hoy or St Kilda do sea cliffs rise more steeply than these. Clingri Geo nearby was a sheer, circular hole like a quarry, and deep in it the sea broke onto the boulders of an inaccessible beach. The sea rushes in through a subterranean tunnel. There are several of these holes on Papa. One is a mere vent and 'breathes' with whale-like vigour, with the compression and decompression of the pounding waves. Another, Christie's Hole, lies a full hundred metres in from the sea yet you look down to sea breaking on a boulder beach. Almost every headland and island seems to have subterranean passages (one is over 400 metres long) and these startling holes are simply the result of a portion of passage collapsing. With an extravagant skyscape overhead and seas crashing and spraying in perpetual motion, this world of geos, *voes*, stacks and passages, sandy bays, farmland and wilderness gives a walking adventure which is quite different from anything I know elsewhere.

Fielie Hill also shows another aspect of man's effect on landscape. It, and the bulk of the island beyond the walled-off croft lands, has no depth of soil. Any turf was removed centuries ago to be burnt as fuel. There was and is no peat on Papa. Once scalped the weather has seen to it that there has been no quick renewal. Coal is now brought in but until fairly recently peat had to be cut, dried and collected from the mainland, or from Papa Little. Several stone groupings left exposed on the hill are prehistoric chambered cairns.

Perhaps a third of the island, all at the south-east end, has been walled-off and is used for cultivation or for sheep and cattle. It is a patch-work of fenced fields and isolated houses with the mile of road wiggling away from below the hill to the pier in Housa Voe. There is a small church and a basic post office and shop. That is all. Two fiord-like lochs, Hamna Voe and West Voe (which faces north!) cut deeply into the island to form a waist. You could walk across in ten minutes yet, round by the coast of the wilderness end, would take all day. We dropped down to follow the shore of Hamna Voe. A fishing boat had come up and anchored in it so the weather must be settled. The voe faces south-west.

Across the loch there is one walled-off croft, now in ruins, and the sheep range freely over the tumbled stones and even descend to nibble seaweed. On our shore are a succession of round walled enclosures about four metres across and about the height of a man. These are *planti crubs* and were used for growing potatoes and other vegetables. Seaweed and manure would be added to build up a rich soil, the walls kept off the constant searing winds and nets were spread over them to counter predation. Very few are now used. Old nets lie in one, nettles fill many and at one the dog and I nearly had heart failure when it erupted sheep.

Shetland has its own distinctive breed of sheep. They are not clipped but the wool is plucked (you *roo* the fleece) and it was once the custom for every woman to knit garments from it.

At the head of Hamna Voe we found the first group of old Norse-type water mills. The last used was abandoned at the end of the war. There are perhaps a score of roofless mill ruins in evidence on the island. The leats for some are still clear and the millstones are usually lying on the ground. Some even have wooden cogs and wheels visible among the interior decay. They tend to be sited in clusters down the few available streams.

It is worth wandering out to the mouth of Hamna Voe for, from now on, the coast faces south-west and that is where the prevailing weather comes from, usually by express delivery. The map indicates just how indented the coast is and in a gale it is a fearsome place. In a big storm you would be unable to stand and the salt spray can be carried right across the island. Children are kept indoors in such weather. T. E. Lawrence (Lawrence of Arabia) was describing the north-east coast when he gave this word picture but his words could equally describe this coast and its thrall '. . . jaws of grey, cold reefs champing white seas outside, all day, all night . . . thrusting out into the maddened sea which heaves and foams over them in deafening surges.'

The coast is backed by Mauns Hill, a fifty-metre dome, scoured of all vegetation except the bobbing heads of thrift. Here live the bonxies. On a bit, near Christie's Hole, there was a nesting ground of terns. The young had flown but still used the site for roosting so the din was considerable. A shiny sprat fell out of the sky to land on Storm's nose and parent birds were wheeling and screaming with beaks full of fish as they sought the right offspring to feed. The bonxies were harrying them which probably explained the fish landing on us.

Further on, green Aesha Head forms a prominent prow with a natural arch which you can actually walk over to gain the point. There is a stack, Sula Stack, in the bay and offshore the larger islands of Fogla and Lyra Skerry. (Lyra is lyrie or shearwater.) These are so riddled with caves and passages that it is possible in places to see right through them. The Aesha stream has several mill ruins. One stone was rough with a surfacing of garnets.

This far end of the island has the highest cliffs and there are several fingers of rock rising straight from the sea. The Stack of Snalda looks and sounds like something out of Tolkien. Sea eagles once nested on top of it. The Horn is a twisted blade sixty metres high. With the boom of the waves and the crying of seals the place had a weird atmosphere.

Storm showed me a sheep in trouble by Akers Geo. The beast, thick-coated from not being shorn, had rolled onto its

34

back and wedged in a runnel. Its wiggling had moved it right to the edge of the cliff. There was nothing to gain any purchase on and I had quite a job to drag it back. Just one wild kick and we could have both gone over the edge. Once righted we both lay for some time and panted at each other. Storm thought it all very interesting. I must say, Shetland sheep smell pretty much the same as any other. (Quite often on Papa we noticed starlings landing on them in search of insects in the fleece.) I had a good wash in a lochan and went up to the breezy top of the island: Virda Field (87 metres), a notable viewpoint.

We could look up the coast over St Magnus Bay to Ronas Hill, at 450 metres, the highest peak in Shetland. (Over it at night came the glow, not of northern lights, but of Sullom Voe oil terminal.) As always it was the sky that impressed; long banners of silky cirrus hung on the lances of day. Six kilometres out to sea the Ve Skerries impressed in a different way. Through my binoculars I could see the spray flying over this notorious reef, the highest point of which is only two metres above high-water mark. Seals alone visit it; a sure sanctuary from man.

It was only given a permanent light in 1979 when the possibility of a supertanker being wrecked finally overcame all engineering difficulties. The work was largely done using helicopters and the latticed structure's strength is gained by super-tensioning rods which pull it into the rock with a strength out of all proportion to size. In any blow it is smothered in water but continues to operate successfully. One of the most horrific wrecks there is still talked about. In 1930 a trawler, the *Ben Dorain*, ran onto the Ve Skerries. It was spotted some days later but the conditions were so dangerous no boat could land or even approach and one by one the figures vanished from the wreckage to which they clung. Those who had tried to help could not bear to watch any longer and sailed away.

Virda Field is the highest point of a whaleback ridge of tweed-tight heather which forms a spine along the island and gives easy access to any point. There are a surprising number of lochs on Papa Stour. Gorda Water, the largest and nearest to the crofting end, is now tapped and water pumped up to a reservoir that can then provide piped water to the houses. Though the Sound of Papa is only two kilometres wide the authorities have still failed to supply the island with electricity. The night sound of Papa Stour is the gentle *chug chug chug* of diesel generators — for those physically able or rich enough. Old women living alone are thrown back on tilley lamps — a dismal state of affairs — but then the votes of Papa Stour don't carry much punch. Dutch Loch owes its name to fishermen from Holland who occasionally came ashore (several hundred years ago) to wash clothes and no doubt themselves after weeks and months away from home.

There is a scattering of smaller lochans in the lee of the spinal ridge and the ground is more broken up. A Viking longhouse has been excavated and there are burial mounds and burnt mounds pointing to its early use. Burnt mounds are an unusual feature being piles of clinker-like stones which had obviously been fired. Apparently water in those prehistoric times was heated by dropping in heated stones so these piles of stones have accumulated at favoured hearth sites.

At Virda Field we are half-way round the island. It is worth following round the coast closely all the way after diverting up Virda Field. The longest passage, the Hole of Bordie, is in the furthest corner and the succession of caves, passages and stacks continues — Papa Stour is over-endowed with these features and you end almost blasé about any more elsewhere. Clunes says Papa is perhaps the most attractive island in Shetland ('to the visitor not afraid of a small boat'), the unique coastal scenery having 'a vividness and life and beauty which gives it a character of its own.' John Tudor, a Victorian enthusiast, writes of its caves: 'none in the British Isles excel those this little isle can show in weird, fantastic outline and rich colouring combined.' The boulder beach by Aesha Head is made of huge tumbled stones which are warm red in colour.

In more prosaic terms these features are due to the ready weathering of various basalts and rhyolitic lavas which are mixed with tuffs of Old Red Sandstone but even the scientific work I consulted on the geology declared Papa Stour produced 'the most impressive series of caves, stacks and arches in Britain'.

From Sholma Wick it is worth cutting inland to see the mounds and so on. Culla Voe is another deeply-cutting fiord and, now cut off at its head, is 'The Loch that Ebbs and Flows'. We found a team from St. Andrew's University marking out one cairn for excavation. A Viking longhouse has already been studied but the whole island is so covered with cairns, mounds, walls and ruins that, unless you are an expert, it is hard to know what is two hundred and what is two thousand years old.

West Voe is even larger than Hamna Voe so takes some walking round. There is a secret sandy cove across which the watery 'pleeps' had left their tracks. A wren (stenkie or Robbie Cuddie) came out to scold us from its territory in a wall. The North Ness is another world of its own, a clenched fist of land thrusting into the north. Unglabreid, Tang Geo, Scopa Wick are names of obvious Viking origin. One geo has The Creed for its name. Concentrations of burnt mounds and homesteads again point to previous settlement. What hardy people they must have been and what adventurers to penetrate to such wild places as Papa Stour or St Kilda. In June 1868 The Creed had an invasion of herring and the people dug holes in the sand in the shallows and scooped them out by the bucket and when a net was eventually set across the mouth it fetched in something like twenty thousand fish, food enough to last till hairst and to relieve the near famine they'd been suffering after a bad winter and spring. West Voe was the centre of the herring fishing industry that once saw Papa's population reach its peak. A thousand boats operated in Shetland waters. In the days before refrigeration the gutting sheds and curing factories had to be built as near the source of the fish as possible. The herring, as elsewhere in the west, suddenly vanished from their regular grounds (about 1907) and the industry collapsed. Saithe seems to be the commonest fish now. The real self-sufficiency of a hundred years ago has largely gone. Sheep are now the dominant money-earner yet they depress the quality of the land even further. When the Nature Conservancy Board took over Rhum the first thing they did was to remove all sheep and in half a dozen years the scalped slopes were lush in vegetation again. Islanders from Papa or Foula when out fishing in a fog used to home-in on their islands by smelling the scent of its flowers and grasses. A mono-culture is a dangerous thing and Papa perhaps escapes, just, by the sheep being insufficient in themselves. Think too of the marketing side: a dangerous crossing to the mainland and long transporting beyond; there is not much profit left.

The round of North Ness brings one back to Housa Voe and the small pier. The southern sweep of the bay is sandy and leads out to the scattering of stacks through which the ferry chugs to reach Papa. The sands are likely to have the odd boat on them and others anchored off. One or two are not likely to sail again. If you get chatting to the locals about life on Papa you will hear some hair-raising tales of storm and wreck and salvage. Housa Voe is not entirely safe and more than one boat has gone down in it. Since our visit we have heard that the ferryman has been drowned and the *Venture* lost. This is the price of living on an island.

Though one mourns such a loss, for it affects everyone in a closely-knit community, it is really part of nature. At least, here, life is close to nature, however beautiful or cruel. The people of Papa are not shooting each other or throwing bombs. A child growing up here has a special security. The suffering they see (an injured bird, a lamb with eyes pecked out by crows) is natural while so much outside the isles is artificial and crazy in its cruelty.

Brei Holm beside the Maiden Stack is indicated on the map as the site of a leper settlement. Leprosy in Shetland only died out last century. Sufferers were removed from the community and had to eke out a miserable existence in lonely huts with whatever food the populace left for them. Papa Stour was long known as such a place and Brei Holm could well have been their prison.

An equally unhappy prisoner was the Hon. Edwin Lindsay who was confined on Papa for twenty-six years early in the nineteenth century. He had refused to fight a duel and his family sent him to Papa in disgrace, the factor being instructed to hold him there under the pretence of insanity. He stayed until a quaker lady, Catherine Watson, making a preaching tour of the islands met him and took up his case. After much legal dodging he was declared sane and restored to his rights. There is still a Lindsay's Well on Papa.

We return to the caravan by the school along the bay of Kirk Sand. A flight of silent gannets wings up the sound. We return ready for a cuppa and with an appetite made huge by windy miles. Afterwards there will be a dram and the little sounds of silence to wrap up the day: a distant voice calling hens to roost, the goodnight murmurings from our goose which sleeps by the starboard wheel, the sad '*pwee-wee-wee*' of a redshank or the eerie call of a loon as they fly overhead, the '*put put*' of the generator, the fluffering of wind. Always the wind, the alpha and omega of these islands, the cradle-rocker and the life-shaker.

RONAS HILL

Sullen Sullom Voe
is visible,
seen from the chambered cairn
on Ronas Hill.
There is always wind,
always wind,
blowing in the mind
on Ronas Hill.
Are all summits hollow,
man-empty,
marking our beginning,
marking our end?

BIBLIOGRAPHY
BALNEAVE, E., *The Windswept Isles*, John Gifford.
BERRY, R. J. & JOHNSTON, J. L., *The Natural History of Shetland*, Collins New Naturalist.
COLEMAN, V. & WHEELER, R., *Living on an Island*, Thule Press.
FOJUT, N., *A Guide to Prehistoric Shetland*, Shetland Times.
LINKLATER, E., *Orkney and Shetland*, Hale
NICOLSON, J. R., *Traditional Life in Shetland*, Hale.
SHEPHERD, S., *Like a Mantle the Sea*, G. Bell & Sons.
TULLOCH & HUNTER, *A Guide to Shetland Birds*, Shetland Times.

MAPS
Shetland is covered by the 1:50.000 sheets 1, 2, 3 and 4. Papa Stour is on sheet 3 but it is worth having the 1:25.000 sheet HU 16 if visiting the island while Bartholomew's 1:100:000 sheet 62 gives a useful map to the whole of Shetland.

3

Morocco

AFOOT IN THE HIGH ATLAS

We are the music-makers,
And we are the dreamers of dreams,
Wandering by lone sea-breakers,
And sitting by desolate streams;
World-losers and world-forsakers,
On whom the pale moon gleams:
Yet we are the movers and shakers
Of the world for ever, it seems.

(A.O'Shaughnessy)

You may have gathered from the Introduction that I have a special affection for the High Atlas Mountains. Most winters I have managed to enjoy some weeks or months in the mountainous region south of Morocco, so selecting a single 'walk' is not easy. The one chosen is straightforward and accessible — a good 'Open Sesame' to the attractions of the Atlas.

Marrakech, with its magic mountains rimming the southern horizon in improbable snowy silver, is pure romance. It is little further away than some parts of Europe but is so utterly different in colour, culture and everything else. A hundred years ago it was still a despotic, mediaeval kingdom, today it is one of the most vibrant and prosperous countries in Africa. The very name 'Atlas' has a ring to it. Here, beyond the Pillars of Hercules, in ancient mythology, the earth and sky were held apart. In early spring the Atlas mountains are one of the most beautiful places on earth.

This is a place *not* to explore in a large group, organised by some tourist enterprise. The tourist route is a busy one and is harassed by touts which the tourists with their unwitting extravagance have brought on themselves. One of our party was told there was 'nothing to do in Marrakech', another that it was 'a country of beggars, dirt, flies and upset tummies', another was told about the constant badgering of people trying to sell everything from kebab sticks to amethyst *geods* or leather belts to Spanish fly! Such comments are more a reflection on the speaker than the country itself.

After over twenty years of Moroccan visits I find there is always more and more I still want to do. Beggars there may

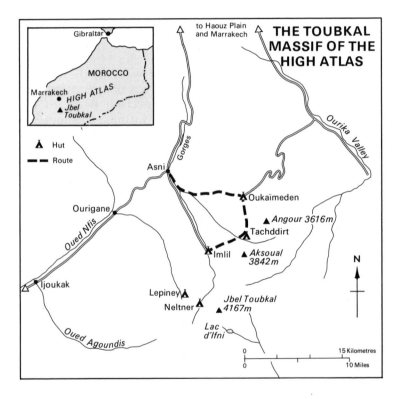

be, but the alms given to them fulfills a Muslim obligation and replaces our cumbersome health service (which tends to shut the handicapped away out of view), so it is, as so often, the visitors' sight that is defective. There are far worse places for dirt and flies. Dust is the inheritance of any hot country. In Marrakech and the Atlas in spring there are far fewer flies than in Britain in summer and I have had no more upset tummies here than wandering in Europe.

Morocco is used to this criticism but it ill becomes Europe or America, with their riches, their strikes, their bureaucracy, their frustrations, to criticise any other country, especially one so hard-working and comparatively poor. The single most common criticism I object to is that Moroccans are lazy; 'they seem to do nothing all the time'. No doubt some do, especially those attracted to the touristy areas (which aren't typical of the rest of the country) but let the descriptions of the trekking dispel all these and other glib comments.

It is the element of romantic mystery which perhaps makes people hesitate to go to a place like Morocco under their own organisation. When I first went to the Atlas I treated it as an expedition and went about it with all the seriousness of a sponsored mountaineering party to the Himalayas. (Trying to hurry gear through customs at Tangier on the eve of Ramadan returned us very quickly to sanity.) The fine Berber people inhabit even the remotest of mountains. They eat. So why carry food there except as a gift to be shared? It is the same in the Himalayas, or anywhere. People are basically the same. All eat, all have individual customs and cultures, all make music, all trade and travel, all laugh and cry, all marry and reproduce because their world is one worth living in. We are all made of the same dust and the same dreams. This realisation is probably the most important thing to grasp before going abroad.

I am actually writing this (and much else of this book) in March at Imlil, a hamlet in the hills above Marrakech, which is a superbly colourful spot but also a staging post on the way to the magnet of Jbel Toubkal (4167 metres), the highest summit in Morocco and all North Africa. A party of sixteen Swiss have just come down from the mountain hut (built with 40 beds but sleeping 60). They made several ski ascents and tours for it is a magnificent mountain range for all forms of alpine sports but Toubkal, as ever, was the grand climax. They did it yesterday. Now they have come down to the road end at Imlil and are waiting impatiently for the hired bus to bear them down to their Marrakech hotel. They have one day for Marrakech, then home. For all the differences they might as well have had a week at Zermatt; they have come and gone without having had any contact with local people or their culture.

Mohammed comes and joins me for a drink. He is delighted, having just bought a pair of skis off one of the Swiss, knowing he will sell them tomorrow for three times the buying price. He called the seller stupid. What would the banker from Basle think of that opinion I wonder? They are both astute capitalists in fact, with so much in common, if only they knew it. The bus bears the Swiss away; sun-red faces peering out at the sunburnt village. The dust settles. The call to prayer rings out, long-drawn notes, trembling like sun-shimmer on the crisp air. Mohammed excuses himself and hurries off to join the others crowding into the small room that serves as Imlil's mosque. (The people of Imlil built it themselves, just as they built their own school.) They kick their shoes off and vanish. The sound of their chanting travels gently up the street. It is actually very hard to sit and write in Imlil; there is always something happening — and, besides, the sun shines so deliciously through the blossom-bright trees that half hide the walls of rock and snow and the distant tip of Jbel Toubkal. Where to begin? — Morocco is so much part of me now.

★　★　★

My plans to lead a party on the Imlil/Asni based circular walk had been made late and the only cheap way I could fly was to go to Agadir on the wrong side of the High Atlas. Agadir, flattened by a disastrous earthquake in 1960, has been rebuilt as a modern seaside resort, splendid of its kind no doubt but offering few of the attractions a walker wants — other than cheap charter flights. Gatwick was left on a miserable, freezing day; southern England stippled with snow, and most of the journey was made above a sea of cloud. We descended through this to the semi desert of the south side of the Atlas. The warm earthy smell of Africa greeted us as we walked from the Boeing 747.

Two lads with ice axes and crampons on rucksacks could only be going to Imlil so I introduced myself to David and Russell, suggesting we team up to share the expenses of taxi, etc. They were glad enough to find someone who knew the ropes — it all takes longer when you have to find where buses go from, where tickets are bought, what happens with baggage, and all these things. We went out and grabbed a taxi which sped us in to the back side of Agadir and we thought we had just missed a bus till we realised Morocco had advanced its time by an hour. We bought our tickets at the office, registered our baggage and nipped round the corner with forty minutes of eating time available. We had been given an arrival time in Marrakech of 1.30 am.

The menu was full of strange-sounding names like *harira* and *tagine*, which was what we had to eat. *Harira* is a thick soup with which the day's fast is broken during Ramadan. It comes in big bowls and is almost a meal in itself (there was delicious fresh bread with it); *tagine* is a way of cooking meats and vegetables rather than a single dish. Local restaurants will have rows of dishes cooking slowly on charcoal braziers; the conical lids (holding in the steam and the flavours) look like 'coolie' hats. I've seldom had a poor *tagine;* the variety of ingredients and spices ensures they are delicious. Mint tea, the national beverage, ended the meal. The bill was about £4 for the three of us.

The bus puzzled me by setting off up the coast instead of taking the direct route to Marrakech. Perhaps the bad weather had blocked the hill route? There was plenty of brown water in normally dry river-beds and an hour out we had a diversion for an exciting river-crossing because a bridge had been washed away. It would certainly have snowed on Toubkal. The route was the normal one however, as subsequent arrivals found out. The bonus was watching the sun setting into the sea, which it did with some splendour, while we swept along above jagged cliffs or sweeps of empty sand. We then climbed higher, inland, among the *argan* trees (goats were browsing among the top branches) while slowly the glow faded and night tried and failed to light the stars. It rained. (It was the only rain for the next five weeks.) We dozed until a longer break was made at some lonely village so we could all pile into the transport cafe.

The next stop was Essaouira (try saying Essa-wee-ra) which is perhaps the most charming coastal town in Morocco. Those of us staying longest returned to it a month later for a few days of blissful ease; David and Russell ended their first Moroccan fling there. I'd recommend room 301 in the Hotel des Ramparts for it is a suite rather than a room (4 or 5 beds) and one panoramic window opens right onto the sea wall. The surf roars into one's dreams. The old Portuguese harbour is a busy fishing port and the sea food here is justly famous. It is a white town, decorated in blue (surf and sky colours) and its narrow alleys and *souks* (markets) are quite charming. Woodwork is its craft speciality and boxes and bowls, often inlaid, are attractive souvenirs. There is no arguing over prices and the frantic badgering of Marrekech's Medina is entirely absent. It has everything one could desire as a contrasting end to a walking, climbing or skiing holiday in the mountains.

There is a huge sweep of sand, with Mogador Island offshore protecting it from the storms, and in the busy harbour fishing boats are still being built in traditional style, their graceful lines seen clearly from the flowery promenade. Flower beds have been laid out with blooms of almost unreal brilliance. In the cool, hazy morning light, their petals fold up, giving a mere hint of colour but by noon the hot sun makes them explode into a riot of colour. There will be a score of football games being played on the sands — it is a popular game in Morocco. You can easily tell when they are showing a last year's First Division game on television — the streets empty and the tele-cafés fill solidly. Yet through this modernity veiled women walk shrouded in white or brown robes as they must have done a thousand years before. That too is Morocco, 'the *Maghreb*', 'Land of the Furthest West', whose setting sun travels on to wake America.

Essaouira is three or four hours west from Marrakech and I've actually been skiing in the morning and swimming in the breakers at tea time. The bus climbs inland through mimosa forest and much of the countryside is cultivated — always a surprise: Morocco is *not* all desert. The fields can be as lush and flowery as alpine meadows, red-stained with poppies, or orange with a million marigolds. We slept most of the way, sprawled out on several seats each, and duly arrived at 1.30 am. There were no taxis at the bus station but a dilapidated pick-up hijacked us (or was it the other way round) and for a fee took us to my regular base, the Hotel de Foucauld. I've known the night manager for twenty years so we were soon installed in a room. Even direct flights to Marrakech arrive at midnight so they are used to late arrivals and the welcome is always friendly. The Foucauld is much used by hill-bound parties, of all nationalities.

It stands at the edge of the Medina (the old town); the bus

to the Gueliz (new town) leaves from across the road; it serves excellent Moroccan food in its decorative dining room; the management is helpful; the prices reasonable and it has some atmosphere unlike the identikit monsters erected in the last few years. The name is also indicative of Moroccan liberality in general. One of the finest boulevards in Marrakech is the Avenue de France. (You won't find that next door, in Algeria!) Morocco still has Jewish communities and is refreshingly free of racial or colour bigotry. About 60 per cent of Moroccans are of Arab descent; about 40 per cent are Berber. Islam is the state religion but it is not extremist in character. Morocco has always been herself, at odds not only with Europe but with Turkish-dominated Islamic states over the centuries. European incursions were usually short-lived and even the French 'Protectorate' lasted less than one man's lifetime. Those ten years of conflict leading to independence are now history too. The good is more often recalled than the bad: good communications (the AA says Morocco has some of the best roads in Europe), a consolidated unity and a modern administration. Today Morocco has enjoyed its longest period of peace, since 1956. Its history is fascinating and worth reading, before a visit, for so often questions in Morocco begin 'Why?' rather than 'What?'. Gavin Maxwell's *Lords of the Atlas* is compulsive reading and Neville Barbour's *Morocco* is the best general history of recent years.

David, Russell and I came down to breakfast rather late and were spoilt, as ever, with as much good coffee and crisp French bread as we cared to eat. We then followed a pattern which I've followed for years: a Number 1 bus to the Gueliz to change money and do all the shopping in the market there — which means a taxi back (cheaper than any bus in Britain) and the afternoon free to explore the Medina. A Foucauld dinner and next morning it was bus to Asni and taxi to Imlil, where the boys and I parted company — they to begin their expedition, I to complete preparations for mine.

Back at the Foucauld again my team members began to arrive. We were an odd assortment: Hamish (doctor) and John (dentist) were fit young New Zealanders; Jack was enjoying his new status as fit OAP; Luigi was an Italian working in Bonn (on the equivalent of the British Council) whom I'd got to know well in St. Kilda; Howard was a town planner from Glasgow and we were later joined by Stan

Bradshaw, a mere 73-year-old who had only stopped running marathons a couple of years before.

I took them to the Gueliz market which had their cameras clicking. It is a covered market with everything you need in the way of food, all conveniently placed under one roof. The stalls of vegetables and fruit made colourful patterns and in the shadows the brilliant flowers put paid to any preconceived notions of a desert country. We filled a kitbag with oranges, grapefruit, two varieties of potatoes, carrots, onions, parsnips, aubergines, green peppers, cauliflower and so on. Strawberries and tomatoes were regretfully left — their survival rate on mule back is low — but various cheeses and sardines went for day snacks. You don't just buy sardines in Morocco (with Portugal and Peru, the world's largest producer), you have *sardines piquantes* or *sardines aux citron* and several other varieties. Nor did we forget Grim, an unhappy name in English for prepacked packets of toast. While not up to Scottish oatcakes, Grim was an excellent hill substitute for the days after bread had turned to stone.

After shopping we plunged into the alleyways of Marrakech: the *souks*, rightly renowned the world over as a unique spectacle. Alas, all too much of Marrakech is now tainted with the tourist contact but behind its glare this world of trade has hardly altered in hundreds of years. It is *not* there primarily for the tourist. A row of stalls selling anything from wedding *babouch* (slippers), to pots and pans, to mention extremes, is not there for the visitor. Part of the fascination lies in the crowds of locals, though they are not so local some of them, for Marrakech is a trading centre of national influence as well as for the people of the plains and mountains to the south. When business is done they crowd the *souks* and the Jmaa el Fnaa just like anyone else. It is one of the greatest shows on earth.

Areas still operate like mediaeval trade guilds: there will be, in turn, ones for woodworkers, silversmiths, leather workers, potters, dyers, weavers, spice merchants, carpet makers and dozens of other skilful trades. We actually stood for half an hour watching the scene in the carpet market. It was fascinating, if somewhat sad too. Dozens of men, who had come in from all over the south, would bring up a carpet, the family's output of a month, and unfurl it before a suave merchant. He as like as not would dismiss it and the asking price with a brief '*La!*' (No!) and it would be carried off to the next shop. Little men frantically bore their carpets round and round. It was a colourful display to us but a matter of importance to many a poor family in the hills.

Goods in the *souks* of Marrakech are not sold at a fixed price but a price reached by negotiation. For a carpet worth many hundreds of pounds this can be a serious business. You may sit all day over mint tea while a badminton-court-sized area is covered with carpets for your inspection, discussion, and, hopefully, a sale. Just where and how things sell only experience will tell. Most visitors don't have time to find out. Touts will meet every tourist bus in hope of a quick sale. As long as everyone enjoys it and is happy, the system works. I must confess to there being several carpets on the floors at home, my tea is poured regularly out of a pot-bellied pewter teapot, the walls are covered with patterned plates and bowls, my dressing gown is a *djellaba*, my porridge bowl is Berber, my favourite chess set one I first drew and then had turned, piece by piece, by an eight-year-old craftsman, thus introducing chess sets as an item to sell to visitors. The white pieces are in orange wood, the black pieces are cedar wood. It is kept in an airtight box and when I open it the scent brings back all the memories of magical Marrakech.

The shops are simply stalls or cubicles with every inch of their space covered in merchandise. There is hardly room for the owner. He as like as not sits outside on a cheap orange-wood stool (I've one of those at home too) and eyes up the throng that passes for likely customers. '*Shuft*' he will urge. 'Just look!' I'm equally happy to sit and look at the people passing as well as the goods on sale. The world ebbs and flows along the alleys of Marrakech:

> The Genouah from Timbuctoo, with their head-dress of shells and string, and their clanking cymbals; the dark Susi in blue linen dress; the hardy mountaineers, tall, and of commanding appearance; the men from the fertile plains enveloped in the folds of their coarse blankets; while through all this strange throng, pass, and repass, the rich merchants and townsmen in their flowing white robes, walking or riding, and shouting, '*Balak! balak!*', (get out of the way).

48

'There are strings of laden camels with their drivers; the stalls with the fruit of the season; nuts from the Atlas; almonds, dates, and figs from the plains; other stalls piled high with gaily coloured carpets and all kinds of native dress; the gun maker with his old flint-lock guns, some most beautifully inlaid with ivory and silver, the brass-mounted and silver daggers. Then to pass the idle minutes, there are the snake charmer, the conjurer, and the story-teller, each with an eager listening audience squatted on the ground around him. Groups of Moorish women, enveloped up to the eyes in the native *hyke* (veil) selling their bread, small cakes and biscuits. These, with the throng of idlers in picturesque Eastern costumes, all go to make up a picture as un-European and novel as fancy can paint.

Those words were written in 1906. I found them in an old leather-bound volume of *The Dollar Magazine,* my old school's publication, but the description fits today as much as it did then. When the newcomers had satiated themselves with the experience we retreated to the Marjorelle Gardens, a botanical garden echoing with the chatter of bulbuls and garlanded in vivid bougainvillaea colours. Fat goldfish, frogs and terrapins filled the pools. It is an oasis of shade and quiet in the busy city. Marrakech is a garden city. Its ancient walls are surrounded by thousands of palm trees and there are huge olive groves with royal pavilions reflected in pools of water. Water was the symbol of power, prestige and wealth. Marrakech was nothing till water was piped to it from the mountains sixty kilometres away. The first tunnels were made in the eleventh century. The system still works.

Churchill often came to Marrakech where he found the brilliant colours matched his bold style of painting. He could easily have earned a good living as an artist; I wish he had — Morocco deserves a fine artist to record it before too much of the old crumbles and vanishes. Actually it has had its artist but Graham Munro's work of the twenties and thirties has only just surfaced in the mid eighties; hundreds of superb pastels that are as fresh as the day they were done. A dealer was looking at something quite different of his

when he saw one Morocco scene on a wall of the Munros'
Edinburgh house. 'Do you have more of those?' he asked.
'Oh there are drawers and drawers full' came the astonishing reply. 'Nobody would be interested in them.' A
display was arranged for the Edinburgh Festival. An advert
for it caught my eye as I waited for a flight from Orkney to
Edinburgh. The paper was several days old. The exhibition
closed that day. I made it and wandered round in a daze of
delight. It was my Morocco too. I could actually recognise
street scenes and views in the many-hued countryside. Yet
these had been done fifty years earlier. I was lucky enough
to meet Graham Munro (in his eighties) and his wife Ruth,
and hear something of their impecunious years living and
working in Morocco under French encouragement. There
have been further exhibitions and the pastels have sold well,
ironically in the artist's old age. Pastels are actually the
perfect medium, for watercolour is difficult (it dries
instantly in the heat) and oils are awkward (they don't dry
quickly enough!). The only sad thing is that his pictures are
now scattered all round the world so their vivid massed
effect will never be seen again.

It was a leg-weary gang who assembled for dinner that
night but the Foucauld does excellent Moroccan food and
we were soon making the most of it. We took our coffee onto
the rooftop to sit looking at the floodlit Koutobia, the tower
of a mosque but dating from the time of bad King John. It is
the symbol of Marrakech ('the City of Morocco' in old
books) and is actually big and dominating but so perfect are
its proportions that this is not noticed — unless you live
opposite it as we did in the Foucauld. From the rooftop we
could also see the big moon illuminating the whole spread of
the mountains where we were bound on the morrow.

We were told there was a bus going to Asni from the Bab
er Rob gate at 8 am and were there then. A bus eventually
turned up at 9.30 and by the time we'd heaved our baggage
up onto the roof rack (among live chickens, a bike and boxes
and bundles of every description) the seats had gone. I had a
seat on the engine (which eventually grew uncomfortably
hot) while I half-nursed a poor goldfinch in a cage for the
owner who had a baby to look after as well. Howard was
standing in the crowded passage and when we came to the
policeman, always stationed at the exit to Asni, everyone in

the passage was made to squat down out of sight (standing is not permitted). Howard couldn't get up again to everyone's amusement. When the bus swerved a *djellaba* fell off the rack onto a rather dignified man which caused even more laughter. The driver kept a series of tapes blaring out local pop music which we all felt to be an improvement on European pop. It set my foot tapping and a neighbour leant over to ask 'You like Moroccan music?' He looked pleased when I said yes, that I had several tapes at home and recognised what they were playing.

There are many miles of Haouz plain which year by year is being won back from the desert to join the sown. We had one diversion where a huge new irrigation canal had to be bridged and a roadside notice saying 'Pedigree Holstein Herd' looked incongruous as for miles there was only a purple waste of stone. When the angle steepened slightly roadside water channels *(seguias)* could be seen flowing at speed and every now and then they were diverted into mills. As we neared the foothills the vegetation grew richer and through the heat haze the snowy peaks began to take shape. The bus swung its way through some really beautiful countryside, the valley bottoms so vividly green in contrast to the arid country higher up. The forestry folk have done an immense work of stabilising the landscape by planting pines (Aleppo pine I think, a species that can stand drought anyway) which now are beginning to look like real trees. Here and there the web-like nests of pine-processionary caterpillars could be seen, a Mediterranean pest I had not seen here before. Jean Fabre's book, *The Life of the Caterpillar* is worth reading to learn about their extraordinary habits of nest-building and going for long walks in a line, all nose to tail. They are highly poisonous, a fact made use of by the Borgias, while the hairs are used for itching powder, a fact made use of by generations of nasty schoolboys. After a few wilder bends, which made one poor girl sick, the road crossed the river and did a long out and back round a hairpin bend to gain height, for it now ran through the Moulay Brahim Gorge. As we charged into its third bend, horn blaring, the driver suddenly jammed on his brakes and we stopped a few feet off the precipice. The steering linkage had gone it was discovered. A hammer was found from somewhere and used underneath after which everything seemed all right again, but it was a quieter

51

busload that twisted in and out the cliffs high above the river.

The gorge relented and the chatter began as we drove up the Asni basin, a hollow in the hills which is intensely planted with almond, apple, pear, cherry and other blossom-bright fruit trees. It was at its showiest for our arrival and all its delicate tints were set off by the green pines and the brick-red soil of the hills. With a backcloth of snowy peaks adding their share of tinting against the bluest of skies it was breathtakingly lovely. When the bus arrived and 'Shotgun' yelled, 'Asni! Asni!' our gang just sat, shocked by the beauty. ('Shotgun' is our nickname for the rear door, luggage-minder, ticket-collector bloke who does everything except drive the bus; one of his tricks is to nip up onto the roof to store the new baggage, then climb down the ladder and round in through the back door while the bus is doing 50 mph.) We had quite a pile of baggage eventually sitting on the roadside and my tip was greeted with scorn. The altercation soon drew the touts. Some tried to explain that handling luggage merited a tip and being foreigners a bigger one than locals paid, but other touts leapt to my defence. We were not just foreign tourists. This was a Monsieur Hamish gang! While the argument raged we shouldered our rucksacks and the kitbags and staggered up the road to the Grand Hotel du Toubkal where we were spending one night of luxury.

The hotel does not look anything special from the road (Howard suggested a Foreign Legion outpost) but as soon as the doors open its opulence greets one with cool dignity. The walls are fabric lined in red and the pillars and roof are richly ornate with Moorish plasterwork. All the furniture is hand-painted in a welter of colourful motifs; there are coloured lanterns hanging down from the high ceilings; a huge fireplace and many paintings on the walls. The whole south side of this magnificent room (all the tables set for luncheon) is just glass for nothing man-made could improve on the view nature provided: the highest peaks in North Africa rising only a few miles away in a wall of white beyond the fields of blossom. Just being there was magic. 'I don't care what it costs' someone gasped.

In reality it did not cost much but one big meal at night was all we needed so we went through the *souk* to have a picnic lunch by the river. The sun shone, as it did nearly all that spring, from a cloudless sky. Everyone was enjoying everything and I knew then it would be a good gang, however odd its composition.

In comparison with some expeditions I've led, this group were keen to savour every aspect of their walking adventure, so accepted everything as enriching, and in turn were welcomed as real people. The Moroccans are astute in the extreme and if the mountain Berbers are hospitable and friendly they are no fools.

The old man in charge of the hotel thoroughly spoilt us at dinner, leaving a vast bowl of soup for second helpings, grilling a scrumptious fish dish while the main course *tagines* or steaks left us hardly able to cope with Moroccan sponge cake as the sweet. Coffee was on the house and we'd had a good wine or three with the meal. One of the waiters was the old man's son. I've known them twenty years, and care for them very much. As I lay in bed I could hear the rattle of beaks from the storks nesting on the roof, the odd barking of a distant dog and elusive, all-pervading night whizzle of the cicadas. I could also hear Jack's stentorian snoring. I wrapped the familiar content about me and was no doubt soon snoring myself. It was like coming home.

In the earliest light of Saturday we could hear the clip-clop of donkeys and mules passing. While breakfasting on the terrace, with that view renewed overnight in pastel shades, we were aware of the buzz, such as comes from a concourse of excited people. It was the sound of people gathering for the local *souk*, which in Asni is held just once a week and attracts people from a wide area: all the villages up to Imlil (itself a dozen villages) or up to Tachddirt or up to the plateau on the other side of Asni. Men bring in what they want to sell and take home what they have bought from other traders; there are few women at the *souk* for trading is man's work. Hundreds and hundreds of donkeys and mules come and are tethered or let loose in two paddocks, each a couple of acres in extent. They make a considerable din as they bray and bicker and mate. Donkeys have members out of all proportion for their size so this is quite a spectacle in itself.

A certain permanence was given to the *souk* a few years ago by walling off enclosures and having a colonnaded front of shops (a few are open every day to supply Asni's needs as a route junction) and a double line of butchers' shops was also constructed leading to the abattoir. The rest is all very temporary with flimsy reed-covered shelters and mud-built foundations marking out Saturday stances. Even the permanent shops are just cubby-holes with a slab of counter. It is amazing what you can find in them. I asked one grocer for '*des bougies*' (some candles) which I thought he might have. He at once produced a packet of sparking-plugs and asked were they the size I wanted. *Bougie* was also sparking plug I knew (from Corsican capers) but I hardly expected them to be stocked by the village grocer. As there was a twinkle in the grocer's eye I was probably the butt of an inter-language leg-pull — which would be quite typical. The mountain people have a tremendous sense of fun.

Hamish and John headed straight for the abattoir, as did Stan, he having been a tripe manufacturer all his life. They were all very impressed with the efficient, ritualised slaughter of sheep, goats, cows and poultry. The butchers' shops were soon hung with fine-looking meat. As at home it is relatively expensive, and not practical for trekking or climbing. Tinned meat is almost unknown in Morocco, but tinned fish is plentiful: sardines of every variety, mackerel, tuna and so on. Oddly enough cheese is not made in the hills (the cows produce little milk) and only processed cheese is manufactured in the cities. Other cheeses are imported so are expensive. Disappointingly, nuts, which are grown in Morocco, are expensive but salted almonds or fresh walnuts are hard to beat when taken along with the national beverage of mint tea.

When I am alone at Asni hostel (or anywhere else) for any length of time, usually writing rather than walking, I find I am living on about 60p a day. Breakfast is porridge *(tagoula* — a Quaker tin covered in Arabic script), an egg, bread, marmalade and tea. (I'll have coffees all through the day.) At lunch I'll have a cheese portion and jam pieces. In the evening, soup, a tin of spiced sardines or something with a vast plate of vegetables, coffee and biscuits, maybe an orange, maybe apple flakes from home. (Dried fruit is worth taking out.) When I think about it, this is the sort of eating we do while trekking too. The odd question I'm always asked is 'How can you afford months in Morocco at a time?' It is really the other way round. I can't afford Britain!

Near the donkey park there are a score of men who spend all day shoeing the animals, a fast, skillful task which even the locals will stand and watch. Asni *souk* has nothing to do with foreigners and only the odd tourist bus stops briefly from its tour to give the occupants ten minutes to wander round. Near the entrance archway jewellery and ornaments are on display to catch this occasional traffic but even these shops are basically selling to locals. Luigi spent half an hour buying a satchel bag (as carried by the men) as a present for his wife: a handbag that is different.

There are rows of clothes, rows of household goods, rows of foods and fodders. You can have you hair cut or visit a chiropodist, have your fortune told or purchase a good-luck token, you can buy your bread hot from the oven or doughnuts straight out of the vat and when, after a couple of hours, you are exhausted there are rows of cafés and restaurants. We went to one for lunch.

The roof was a flimsy frame of reeds over which sheets of polythene had been hung for the day. The walls were matting or just cardboard (a donkey was steadily eating away the latter beside our corner) and matting was spread on the ground, leaving the centre bare. Shoes were kicked off and everyone sprawled on the matting. A big kettle was kept boiling in the middle of the room and the various pairs, or groups, would boil up their own mint tea from it — the café providing the teapots and glasses. (Imagine a café at home if we all took in the particular tea we wanted and insisted on brewing it personally!) We ordered a *tagine* and it was placed in our midst. A couple of loaves were provided, both to mop up the delicious gravy and to act as a cutlery-substitute. All hands (right hands) dip into the one dish. We made short work of the *tagine,* then relaxed over several glasses of mint tea. Wandering minstrels came in to serenade the company. One asked us our nationality and the reply, "British, Italian and New Zealand" only slightly took him aback. He gave us an impromptu, personalised, serenade in English, Italian, and what he claimed was Maori, with a last verse, no doubt very personal and rude, in Berber, that had everyone else in stitches. He earned his *dirham.* A desperately poor old cripple was given our left-over bread. A child with no legs was towed in by another child as he sat on a home-made trolley. He sang and piped and his companion went round with a hat. It was not begging. It was a performance and a good one. He too earned his *dirham.*

By about two o'clock we were groggy from having seen and eaten too much so went up to the Toubkal hotel to collect our piles of baggage, ready to move on to Imlil. We lugged it down to the gateway where all the transport to Imlil congregates on Saturdays: trucks, taxis, pick-ups, anything and everything is pressed into service. A big red lorry was being loaded, so we threw up our rucksacks and kitbags and climbed aboard. Howard, partly disabled, was yanked up by helping hands and everyone on board greeted me by name and shook hands all round. This really was coming home. There must have been twenty of us plus boxes, sacks, livestock and all our gear in the back of the lorry before it condescended to go. A rangy character, a wilder look-alike to Omar Sharif, green cloth wound round his face, was riding shotgun and collected fares by climbing round outside the lorry or over the top of us. There was endless banter and people seemed to jump on and off at every track end of the eleven-kilometre road up to Imlil.

Imlil has grown steadily. Michael Peyron in his guide compares it to Le Bérade or Fort William! People in other valleys tend to mock Imlil ('They sit and play cards all day') but this is not quite fair. Imlil's fields are no more neglected than theirs. It is the surplus male population that can be seen sitting around but in fact they are waiting to provide tourists with guides, mules and supplies. (Carrying several pairs of skis up Toubkal is not exactly earning easy money.) Playing cards at Imlil, with a good income, is preferable to playing cards in the city of Casablanca, with no work at all. Imlil now has a row of shops selling to the surrounding villages, various cafés, some basic accommodation, and a sports shop and is highly geared to the business of mountain trekking or climbing Toubkal. Everyone has to go through Imlil to go anywhere else so naturally there is a competitive commercialism in the dust of the air.

I consider Imlil to be even more beautiful than Asni, for whereas Asni is basically just a view up to mountains, at Imlil you are in them, surrounded by them; here you can lift your eyes up, up, up, to towering snow walls. Imlil (1760 metres) is a cross-roads for side valleys going up to *tizis* (cols) which lead to parallel valleys east and west, while straight on leads to Jbel Toubkal, lord of all, the sun-catcher, the cloud-maker. All round the hollow of Imlil there are villages (like piles of boxes) on the dry slopes.

Water channels run round them; spread below is the shocking-green blanket of terraced fields and glistening trees, lit here and there by puffs of almond or cherry blossom and sparkling with the glint of sun on water.

We stayed at the Imlil hut but it was uncomfortably crowded. The hut has a pleasant garden however, and being beside the square something of interest is always happening: perhaps just a five-year-old driving thirty goats down the road; or a mule breaking from its lines and careering about; or a truck full of girls in gorgeous kaftans returning from a wedding, singing and clapping in hypnotic rhythm; or Mohammed in full flight from a swarm of bees that have invaded his shop; or a game in the gloaming with a frisby or the memorable night I laid on a fireworks display (one of the first questions I'm asked on returning year by year is 'Have you any fireworks?'). That is Imlil, about which everyone is so rude. Most visitors hurry through it, racing up to the even more crowded Neltner Hut, or hurrying back down to grab a night in Marrakech before flying home. I'm fortunate to be able to spend months at a time in this country so that I can do things more slowly. I use Imlil as a base (my gear stays there from year to year) and in this way can go off for several days at a time on round trips.

Haj Brahim, the guardian of the hut at Imlil is now an old friend, a charming character who with the help of his family sees the hut is kept spotlessly clean. Mohammed his son is now officially his assistant but brother-in-law Llacem also helps for he can greet groups in fluent English, French and Spanish and enough German and Italian to fix anything for them 'pas problem'. He has the souvenir shop, ski-hire business, and the 'Shopping Center' and a prime site for a future hotel when the promised tarring and widening of the road comes. (*That* really will be the end of Imlil.) He is all go, is our Llacem, and I remember us all laughing when 'my Mohammed' (as Llacem calls my friend and guardian Aït Idir Mohammed) pointed at Llacem and said to me, 'He is a capitalist'.

'Mohammed's young brother Hassan has grown up into a fine young man, an accomplished skier, guide and linguist. How I would love to take him to the UK for a few months' work at Glenmore Lodge. Imlil only absorbs half his talents and energy.

We were not long in when 'my Mohammed' came to greet

us. He does all my 'fixing' (not always *pas problem*) and I needed two mules; they were promised for crack of dawn. He brought my gear out of storage (smelling of hens and with a hole chewed through my karrimat) and we all set to, to organise the round tramp — to Tachddirt, Oukaïmeden and back to Asni — I'll describe in hope that it will be copied. It is one I've done several times but I'm quite prepared to go again tomorrow; it is walking of the finest quality.

★ ★ ★

We were off just before first light. We had to climb out of a hut window as the door was still locked — nobody stirs much till the sun hits their village and Imlil is a 9.30 sun-touch-and-come-alive place. Mohammed, having collected our gear, went home for some breakfast. The mules would catch us up easily enough. We had $2^1/2$ hours of walk up the eastern *tizi*, the Tizi n'Tamatert, just time to do most of it in the coolness of mountain shadows. It is a great time to be walking and careful planning and an early start can provide a surprising amount of shade. Eventually the ragged shadows wilt away as the sun powers up into the sky. From noon to five it can be very hot though the very heat itself may set up welcome breezes. If not, you can always lie up in some shady nook and walk the last few hours of the day. Our early start would land us at the Tachddirt Hut for midday.

There are silver and pyrite mines above Imlil and a road has been carved out of the valley to service them — but fortunately it takes a different line from the original mule track, which is the walkers' way. The new road is followed for a bit but it is left when you twist up through the village of Tamatert. In such a small village it is surprising how easily you can lose the way. Houses can extend right over the 'street' and the route can seemingly go round in circles. It can be confusing, but the eye takes in little details: the pokerwork pattern on some shutters, the pedal Singer sewing machine standing in a yard, a single red stone set in a house wall of crocus purple, a blind child tracing the pattern of a window grille . . . Among the walnut trees beyond Tamatert there always seem to be green woodpeckers calling and swooping about. How appropriate the Scottish name of

'Yaffle'. Up onto the road again, then off it by a dammed pool and some beds of cress, the landscape harsher but rejuvenated with forestry plantings. The Barbary partridges go squealing off as we near them. The path steepens to the col. We reach it just as the sun spills over its lip and floods down to Imlil. The mules catch up. 'Bonjour Mustapha' I greet Mohammed's son, and he grins at being recognised. He is eight but he rides the mule like an emperor; the second muleteer I don't know, but he grins too.

There was a pile of white stone by the roadside and a track from it rounding the hillside so we went to investigate. It was a new mine: a fifty-foot slice into the hillside. The men were already at work in the narrow adit: real pick and shovel work with the ore being taken by wheelbarrow to the road side for the lorry to collect eventually. Half an hour later there was an 'wumph' sound and we saw a plume of smoke rise by the col. It was not all just pick and shovel work after all.

From the Tizi n' Tamatert, (2279 metres), a path drops to the valley below in 27 tight zig-zags, then claws its way up to a *tizi* at 2928 metres, to reach Oukaïmeden the ski resort. This is far too grim a route so we were breaking the journey by staying overnight at Tachddirt, up the valley, and at 2314 metres one of the highest permanently inhabited villages in the country. It is an easy traverse on the road, then one drops down to cross the river, and joins the main track to the village which, like all the others, lies on the northern flanks where it catches the early sun. We had a cross-valley view of their coming to life: the goats pouring out, young girls setting off, singing, for the upper slopes to collect firewood or fodder, women going down to the stream to do the clothes washing, an odd mule bearing a man off on business, others off with mattocks on shoulders and long, hillmen strides. No wonder they have kept their freedom through history, What fighters they must have been. Even today the mountain Berbers receive minimal state aid or control. They exist as a semi-autonomous state within a state, electing their own village councils and looking after their own affairs.

The mules had already been unladen and soon set off back to Imlil. At Tachddirt the guardian was Mohammed. Yes, another Mohammed and his old father was Mohammed and so is the first of his seven children. Mohammed welcomed us grandly with cans of Fanta cooling under the tap. He has changed over the years. I first knew him as one of the Tachddirt kids, later he would swoop down on skis to my dormobile at Oukaïmeden for a coffee (he crossed a 3000-metre col, a five-mile ski trip each day); then he became family and businessman, and today too portly for much skiing he is the fixer for Tachddirt walkers and skiers.

We had left Hamish and John to climb and ski the slopes of Aksoual opposite and could now see them as tiny dots on its huge bowl of snow. Tachddirt looks south to a wild and huge bank of mountains, which, being north-facing are deeply snow covered till late in the season. The northern side of the valley however comprises south-facing rock ridges (on which we made some new routes in our fitter young days). It is an extraordinary effect to have the two opposite seasons simultaneously, one on the right hand, the other on the left.

Luigi, after lunch went zooming off to try and reach the valley head, the Tizi n'Tachddirt (3172 metres), which is several hours' walk while Jack and Howard wandered up the village in an orgy of photography. Someone was extending a house, hammering in a clay-gravel mix behind shuttering just as if it had been concrete. Even at Tachddirt holiday homes are being built: incongruously lavish compared to anything else. I wonder what the locals think of them? I wandered up to recce the route for the morrow and spent an hour on a knoll enjoying the sun. A brilliant Morocco redstart (Moussier's redstart) nearly landed on my bent knees and lesser kestrels were calling up above on the crags. A party of choughs swanked down the valley.

Cloud slowly began to form in the valley and eventually clamped down as a raw mist. It brought Jack and Howard home from the hill. We began supper: soup, corned beef and heaps of fresh vegetables, apples and raisins, coffee, cheese and Grim. It was just ready when the weary skiers appeared. John was so tired he could hardly eat. 'It's a big country'. Hamish gasped. We had almost finished when Luigi appeared in the dusk. He had lost the path in the mist and had to be rescued by a young goatherd — though not before he had fixed his price! We paid Mohammed and were early abed for an early start. The mists cleared in the cool of night and a half moon rode at anchor among the stars.

We set off at seven o'clock by torchlight with the moon

60

dodging in and out of view round the bluffs but it was soon light enough to see. I regretted not having my binoculars as there were birds in plenty: partridges, black wheatears, rock buntings, choughs, and others which were voices only. There are two paths to the Tizi n'Ouadi (2928 metres), the upper being a pedestrian shortcut over a rocky spur, while the mules traverse the lower to join the long path up from the valley to the col. By the upper route we were on the col by nine reaching it by an icy traverse from the crag. The mules had been scheduled to leave at eight o'clock and would also take two hours we assumed, so we traversed into the sun and sat for an hour to wait for them . . . and another hour . . . and another hour. There was a sneaky wind which chilled us thoroughly. Our duvets were with the mules. We cursed and were about to go and investigate when we spotted the beasts. Even the lower route had some big patches of snow on it and we wondered how they would cope. Badly it proved. One mule baulked completely and while both muleteers were dragging it over the icy track the other started rolling down the slope. There was much rushing about and we learnt a few naughty words of the Berber dialect. Mohammed had seemingly sent the oldest and youngest inhabitants of the village. We never did discover why they were so late. We quickly unloaded and trudged off round into blessed sun, *sans* wind, where we sat to watch Hamish and John ski from the col down the valley we were traversing. We met up again at the ski resort an hour later. The path angled down gently to the level valley bottom. Horned larks and wagtails were about as usual and the first jonquils were in flower. There were only about six cars in the car park yet the chairlift was working, as were most of the tows. The price of tickets is now a discouragement for you to pay per run rather than per day and with no queues you can do a great deal of skiing. We sat with cool drinks for a while then settled into our dormitory at 'Chez Ju Ju' where we had decided to stay.

We took the chairlift up to the summit of Jbel Oukaïmeden (3273 metres). When built before the war it was the highest chairlift in the world. Few can yield such an extensive or such an impressive view. We looked over to the massive Aksoual snows with Jbel Toubkal behind and the Tazharhart Plateau to the right. All the western peaks were clear and, eastwards, hill succeeded hill to the horizon. It took an hour to absorb. The clinging clarity of the air made every detail sharp. Howard and Jack went down by the chairlift but Luigi and I went along the crest down to the Tizi n' Oukaïmeden. Avoiding the snow where possible we had the odd scramble and also reconnoitred a planned new way back to Imlil that Howard and I might do with a bivvy en route. It was too snow covered to be practical so after some discussion in the dormitory we decided we'd walk down to Asni over two days, so as to still have the fun of a bivouac. The skiers decided to ski and Jack and Luigi planned to climb a nearby summit (which took them seven hours: 'It's a big country'). We were all glad of the meal when it came. French cooking, good, and plenty of it: two bowls of soup each, *escalope panée* with mashed potatoes, cheeses and crêpes, coffee. Dinner, bed and breakfast was £8. We slept hardly lighter in pocket and decidedly heavier in tummy.

A full moon filled the Ouka plateau when I looked out first thing. I roused Howard. Our trip was on. The journey ahead from Oukaïmeden was very much the best part of the round trip. We had motored up from Asni to Imlil after all and the way to Tachddirt and Ouka had been made relatively straightforward by the mountain geography. The descent to Asni however is different, I was looking forward to it.

It is a good thing to set off early on the long tramp down to Asni for the way is long, the sun can be hard and the possibilites of going astray are legion. Paths fork and fork with a chess-board liberality of alternatives. If unlucky enough to encounter a day of thick cloud either postpone the journey a day or hire a guide. Sometimes the cloud forms a vast sea spreading over the Haouz Plain, with its edges lapping over the Tizarag scarp onto the Oukaïmeden basin. In these conditions a journey up to the top of Jbel Oukaïmeden can be even more spectacular than usual, comparable to and a deal cheaper than a private air flight which is the only way of seeing a similar scene.

Good intentions of an early departure may not always prove effective in reality. We were assured of breakfast at 7.30 am. At 7.30 we were ready but the ordered rhythm of Chez Ju Ju obviously was not. The floor was swept and mopped round our oasis of discomfiture as we sat at the table and only then was the gas lit and the water brought to a boil. We left at 8.30 with the sun flooding the basin and the air so delicious it deserved bottling.

It is worth pausing on that rim for it divides worlds of scenery, culture and much else. Behind lie the snows of Jbel Oukaïmeden and the rocky bastion of Angour (a world of mountains); nearer are the half-buried *azibs* (summer dwellings) of the shepherds, some of whom already have their flocks grazing the jonquil-bright meadows (a world of Biblical agelessness) while superimposed on this is the angular, brash, creation of a ski resort and summer retreat for the wealthy (the world of Chez Ju Ju!) — all this then battles, behind, in a shocking juxtapositioning but take a few steps forward and down off the plateau and it vanishes on the instant. The world superglues itself into a unified whole: ageless, fresh and utterly charming.

As Howard and I took those first few steps I was conscious of a sudden cessation of noise (part mechanical, part the wind) and also of stepping into cool shadows from bright sunshine. It was a change of sensation such as one has on plunging into a swimming pool in mid winter. Breathlessness was not just from altitude.

It is a deep-end view. The Tizi n' Oukaïmeden is 2668 metres high, Asni is 1165 metres and the Haouz Plain 450 metres. From the Tizi you see clearly down to the latter — 2218 metres — of which most will be walked; a giddy prospect. At Asni there is an old road sign that says, in faded paint, 'Oukaïmeden 3 heures'. In our innocence, the first time, we took this as a pedestrian estimate and set off from Ouka confident of beating any such 'book time'. Eight hours of 'hit and mist' later we realised this was the time of motoring, not walking, and it was several more hours before we bowled into the hostel, hurried by a dust storm, weary and famished. (Morocco constantly cuts one down to size — be warned!) Howard and I were determined on no such escapades and in fact planned to bivouac out at the foot of the brutal descent and walk down the valley to Asni in the cool of the morning. This would be easier for him too, being somewhat handicapped and I would take the chance of writing down a description of the elusive route.

This can confuse from the start. I wrote 'At the bend in the road on the *tizi* (pass) a path drops westwards. Take this', but there are actually several paths as humans and goats have worn short cuts and variants. The true path

63

zig-zags down a hollow, right of a spur, and this dominant spur is what matters. The path eventually uses it to wend down on its *left* side. We just wandered down to it direct as we could see everything. The spur acts almost like a rifle barrel along which the eye aims for the depths below. Such down-ness! It has to be experienced rather than described. In the morning play of sun and shadow the many slopes, spurs, ridges, cliffs and gorges were seemingly multiplied endlessly. The vivid hues of purple, red, buff and yellow soils, of docile tree-greens and the wild greens of irrigation gave colours as dramatic as the shapes. There was a scattering of *thuya* trees, none very tall but many gnarled and thick with generations of growth on the upper limits of survival. Crushing the leaves between our fingers brought out the rich juniper aroma.

We wandered down the flank of the spur on the stony path and at the first obvious junction, above the village of Gliz, right towards Agadir, a prominent village on another red spur of hill ahead. Agadir is a common enough name everywhere for it means a fortified granary and a site like this no doubt originated in the need for security rather than its dramatic outlook. We crossed a new motorable road or rather it swooped down the hillside to cross our centuries-old path. There are new mines near Gliz and the road to them cannot penetrate up the gorges so comes over the crests in dramatic fashion. A bright yellow lorry down at Gliz struck the most incongrous note in the day's pastoral symphony. Shortly after crossing the road there was a less obvious junction and the route bore sharply back, down, leftwards. We went on a bit to look closer at Agadir and a possible line beyond but the spur was almost precipitous beyond. A magpie chackered at us. They look and behave like the British species but have a bright skyblue patch above the eye. Women were out washing by the *seguia* and laughed and waved at us in a mixture of curiosity, shyness and friendliness. They were not veiled, wore bright garments and their infants romped about with a physical daring and confidence that would have horrified a European mother. Toddlers just don't fall off the flat roofs I'm assured.

Our turn-off was onto a much poorer path which made a tortuous descent down to a scattering of houses nearer the river. It was eventually a matter of choosing the most likely of many variants. One hopeful track led us straight into someone's house, to the consternation of the resident who waved us off down another way. It was hopeless to ask directions. One shouldn't approach women on their own and they would only speak the local Berber dialect anyway. There were only women and children because the men were all away working in the fields or off on business elsewhere. Every corner where water could be led had been terraced and was carefully tended. The high slopes of Grindelwald were not better tended. Fortunately there was one feature which can simplify navigation and which I recognised at once from years previously: a prominent rock block perched on a pedestal of gravelly soil which in turn topped a sloping boulder set in the hillside. (Howard suggested the earth pillar was not a good landmark as it looked most impermanent!) It can be seen from well up the hillside and a route chosen to reach the sunken lane leading down from it.

This we followed down to bypass the lowest house just above river level. The view back up the valley was one of the day's best. The purple irises that edge the fields (they hold the soil and retain precious water) were just coming out and trees like our poplars were shimmering their new green clothes by the rush of water. The tweedier tones of dry hillside above were flecked with the *thuyas* and above a cirque of cliff the snows of the mountain veiled the heights. I was so busy looking at the view that I slipped on loose gravel and only just kept upright. There were shrieks of laughter from the dark interior of a window overhead.

The track wended along northwards on an easy traverse with the perched houses of Agadir now a thousand feet above us. We stopped for a bit to eat as we were coming to the edge of the shadows which had kept us cool as we walked. In the quarter of an hour we were there the sun shoved the shadow hundreds of yards along and left us in the delicious first hour of sunshine. After that it becomes hot. We looked across another green crook of the river valley to the three villages of Tidili opposite. They had had the sun for an hour or two so all was bustle with the goats streaming out under the charge of boys who would be with them all day as the nimble beasts foraged for food above the cultivated levels. Six and seven year olds would climb thousands of feet and romp about (in plastic sandals probably) on rocky hillsides as casually as their charges.

Stray beasts were brought back to the herd by accurately thrown stones. Many years ago I saw an angry tourist make the mistake of throwing a stone at a child. He missed but the child and his instant reinforcements were deadly accurate in their retaliation. From years of throwing stones (or snowballs) at objects in competition with British kids in the wilds I am fairly good as a mere adult goes. At Imlil I could score about 40 per cent hits, which earned dignified praise from the infants whose accuracy was 90 per cent. I'd never make a goatherd obviously.

Tidili was no distance away as the chough puffs but each of the villages stood by a descending stream and before reaching them at all we had to cross a side valley which flowed out from a deep set valley of its own. The path did a deal of wiggling and at the third village, instead of going into it, went down to the river and followed down the bouldery bank where there was really no sign of its existence. This is quite a common trick of paths in the Atlas. I'd recognised it but at the same time a man waved from a rooftop, then sped down to show us the way. We crossed to the left bank at the first bend in the river and in order to diplomatically lose our 'guide' we had a pause, nibbled some biscuits (sharing with the local) and conveyed that we did know the trail. His concern was quite altruistic and typical of the friendly helpfulness of the people. When we had shaken hands he wandered up to inspect some young walnut trees — and, I suspect, to see we did keep to the route. Had we asked for tea, or hospitality, it would have been freely given I'm sure and in such cases it is hard to recompense the host. In such a situation an offer of money could be highly offensive — quite a change from the Morocco seen by the tourist! It is a bit like the Scottish Highlands I knew as a boy, before the invention of B & B signs.

We were soon lost to view as the path did some tight turns up onto a spur ('They must have articulated mules'), and then swept along to another jutting crag from which we peered down a huge flight of zig-zags. With just a little traversing of the path the river was suddenly far below. Howard took a tumble on the twisting descent but his lack of balance had long made that part of his normal experience (it did not stop his scaling Toubkal a few days later). We had a good view to a village ahead and the river bank was well cultivated. A man was hoeing a vegetable patch and a girl

66

was cutting grass to take back to the cow at home. A boulder in the *seguia* diverted water into her lush field and it was so divided and shared that the whole surface was saturated. Portions of the field were cut and by the time the far end was reached the start would be ready to cut again. That was a one-cow field. The sale of the cow's calf would be that family's main cash income. When the snows fail the rivers dry up and it is a desperate crisis for everyone. Most local squabbles are about water rights.

The river ran tight against a bluff so we had to traverse along the rock face but the next bend produced a bridge: two logs with many slats nailed across. As they are often washed away there is no point in anything more elaborate. Tinoughâr was a small village but one house had gaily coloured windows and at the end of the village there was a very smart house indeed. Inserting a wrought-iron window grille and painting the window surrounds white is the first visible expression of prosperity in a village. Interiors can be cool, clean and even luxurious in some wild and lonely places.

We paused for a bite of chocolate and a swig at our water bottles on the outskirts of the village, for a wall gave a small patch of shade and we could see the path heading determinedly uphill ahead. It was now very hot. Someone was being seen off so there were constant *'Bon jour'* and *'Là bas'* interchanges as they set him on his way. A donkey in the field retained by our wall began to bray. We fled, in bottom gear up the brae, then on a grand highway of a path set far above the gorge which has cut deeply down through a wild craggy landscape to join the main river which comes down from Tachddirt. (The walk down from Tachddirt to Asni is another long-day trek of character.) It is a landscape on a big scale and one of the best parts of the day. An isolated 'peaklet' stands in the main valley while the more wooded slopes beyond are that vivid red colouring that is such an African speciality.

This hill is purple and tawny in colour and moated by the river while the Tachddirt-Asni path crosses the neck behind — and thereafter becomes a motorable road as the valley relents from this last show of geological petulance. As we tramped on past this 'island' our track began another of those 300-metre series of zig-zags as it made its way down to the river. There were ilex trees mixed with juniper. The path was taken over by a real road which we could see curling down to ford the main river and join the Asni road. Imsker, a big village, could be seen a mile on. This last sweaty descent in the noon sun was really the last of the slog. It was a gentler valley walk thereafter. A good place for the main pause of the day.

We were hot enough when we reached the river to be glad of its cooling waters, paddling across to a nook under a jungly bank, where there was welcome shade. A wren perched above us and trilled with noisy wren gusto and periodically a kestrel would beat its way up the valley or perch on one of the walnut trees opposite. A surprising number of people observed us, and we must have been stranger than any migrant bird.

A middle-aged woman, watching over her one cow on a field no bigger than a living room at home, waved to us as we reached the ford, indicating stepping stones. When we went on past these she yelled '*Lá! Lá!*' (There!), and doubtless thought we were crazy when we took boots off and paddled over instead. For some hours she sat in the sun, occasionally retrieving her brown cow when it strayed onto someone else's tiny field. Like all Berber women she was unveiled and dressed in a colourful array of clothing. Two younger girls came down on our side of the stream and she waved at them to cross before coming on us but they were not having anything of this and came down to our spit before crossing. They had a good look and shrieked with amusement. They splashed across and soon had the older woman in hysterics as well. They had brought baskets and spent some time washing watercress — when they weren't stealing looks at us and giggling helplessly as a result. They were in kingfisher garb too. They vanished without our noticing it and the woman led her cow off by a rope halter. It grew cool enough that we crossed to sit in the sun to read or write, shifting from boulder to boulder as the sun dodged among the red tiers of hillside above us. An invisible hand wrote patterns of cirrus cloud on the sky which was a bit worrying. They usually predict a bad spell of weather. A bright green tree, possibly an aspen, in vivid new leaf glittered with back-lighting over our picnic spot. (The greens of a desert landscape are the greenest greens in the world.) Across on the south-facing hillsides there was a remarkable variety of soil colours: purple, red and yellow spurs in turn, spotted with the ilex and thuya trees. Some fine terraces were being carved out of the red soil just upstream. The people only use a simple mattock yet, even today, they are fighting out new prosperity from this arid landscape. In the four years since I'd last walked this way, six or seven new fields had been created in this one crook of the river. Three of them were patterned with an array of new fruit trees, each tree set in an individual square which was surrounded by a soil wall six inches high and fed by the *seguia*. Each tree was being shaped by pruning and sticks inserted to push branches apart. A woman spends all day looking after one cow; two men have created seven fields in four years; their dedication is astonishing. It is a shame that the Moroccans who hang around the tourist centres give visitors the wrong impression of the Moroccan people.

The growing cirrus decided us to move on down to Asni then rather than bivouacking overnight. We were equipped for cold (it *feels* cold in contrast to the heat of the day) but not for rain. The hard ground does not absorb water as at home so an assault by heavy rain would be unpleasant in the darkness. We had no torches either. Even when the walk down to Asni is planned for one day a long lie-up at the ford here is recommended. It was five when we decided to move on and we made some tea and had a snack first — and still reached Asni at dusk. With our slower pace we still completed the journey in average time because we did not go astray as so often happens. This is why a separate route description is given for this day (see appendix): the map by itself is quite inadequate and hours can be wasted extricating oneself from the wrong choices of the innumerable alternatives. I say this from considerable experience of being mislaid in the Atlas. You would be hard put to become lost as against mislaid for as soon as you step over the rim of the Tizi n'Oukaïmeden all water eventually flows to Asni so you only have to follow a stream and you get there. It is the geographical and human deviations that complicate navigation — that give it an unforgettable flavour in fact.

Our sheltered nook was hemmed in downstream by a crag so rather than have more paddling we went upstream a bit and scrambled up the steep slope. Two *seguia* channels ran along the near-cliff face, the upper even went under the road to end high above us, spilling down in a curtain of vivid green grass, studded with young walnut trees. The main road had destroyed the original mule track but on its stony and largely unused width the mules had beaten out a narrow path of their own, which gave the best surface for biped travellers too.

Imsker is a bigger village. Being so near the picnic spot I've never explored it for a shop or the chance of a drink and the road keeps round outside it. There are some kilns outside the first house and the half mile before it is a blaze of cherry blossom in March. Above track level there is an unusual area of Spanish oaks. It is a very lush spot compared to the barren slopes above. There was a great deal of field work being done and in the village walling was in progress and stacks of planks lay beside the road. We walked through in a chorus of greetings as usual. The *piste* (track) could be seen slicing along the slope of the valley ahead but we broke off to take a path down into the valley.

This leaves the road to pass the village well where there is always a gathering of young girls or women. The children are shy but friendly: smiles reveal fine teeth, and dark eyes twinkle. There is a great deal of laughter in the villages. Life may be harsh but it has its rewards in a freedom and independence, a self-dependence, all too rare in Africa today. Running water in the home is unknown so the village well or river water source has an importance familiar from Biblical references. Villages are built up on spurs or such places not just for strategic reasons but as an economic factor. All land below *seguia*-level is wanted for cultivation, not building. After all there are women and girls enough to fetch water — from however far away. (A new tribe has settled in Asni and its black-garbed women walk almost half a mile to the river to fill their huge earthenware water pots.)

There is another of those startling views from the edge of the Imsker. The valley floor is packed with shimmering green trees, which may be our aspens. The green has a brazen brightness which, in clothes, would be bad taste. In the fiery sunshine the effect is a brilliant perfection. The trees sweep round to a narrowing of the valley and on a spur opposite another village is built, box on box, up the slope, with the bluest of blue skies beyond. The path zig-zags down. A woman indicated the main road to us but we said we preferred the scenic route. It is amazing what you can manage by dumb-show.

There was a bridge in place this time so we did not have to

paddle or play boulder-hopping games. By bridge we mean two logs with plenty of branches nailed across. They are surprisingly sturdy but obviously at risk of being washed away by any spate. Several years ago we made it to here from Tachddirt for our lunchtime picnic and paddle. The gang then was from the ship the *Eye of the Wind* which was heading for Australia and the Pacific. She had been the base for 'Operation Drake' and while re-rigging at Gibraltar I had taken the crew of youngsters off to Marrakech and the High Atlas. They had raved about it enough that when the ship was setting off on further adventures the following spring, Morocco was the first port of call.

Below the village there is a mill powered by water from a *seguia* which is diverted down a pipe no more than ten yards long. The force produced can turn a big stone; all the gears and working parts are made of wood. Grinding is women's work. The men are agriculturists, traders and artisans in case you think all work is done by women. Until not so long ago they were also fighters, for the land was usually in a state of feud or war. Since Independence Morocco has enjoyed her longest period of peace — and it shows.

The path went on through fields. In one a family was planting grass, plant by plant, adding manure and building the usual irrigation hollows. They were all at it from grandfather to a toddler who could hardly lift the ubiquitous mattock. With varying widths of blade and lengths of shaft this is the single tool with which the Berbers have carved out their world in the mountains. 'Patience is the badge of all our tribe,' Shakespeare's Shylock said, but it is true of these people too.

The path came to a ford under a big cliff which was riddled with caves but there was no bridge and the day's melt-water had covered the stepping stones. It did not really matter as there was a path keeping to the right bank. There was a great deal of karst-like limestone in the valley hereabouts and the flora was the richer for it. The scent of lavender was strong and there was a pretty blue flower which neither of us could name, besides a wealth of different shrubs. Oleanders grew by the river. A nightingale sang. It was very pleasant for the sun only caught us briefly when it shone through the lowest col of the ridge opposite. The ridge steadily descended in altitude and eventually ended in an old flood plain which was chequered white with almond

71

blossom. This was the junction of the two big rivers from Tachddirt and Imlil, the start of the rich Asni basin, which grows apples, plums, cherry, almond and every possible blossom-bearing fruit tree, in a riot of spring colour.

The road down from Imsker crosses to the right bank by a ford (there is a bridge for mules and pedestrians if you have crossed at the caves) and climbs up to join the old *piste* from Asni to Oukaïmeden, now seldom used and fit only for lorries or jeeps. The surface of the road is hard-beaten stone, it is exposed to the full glare of the sun, and it takes an unnecessarily devious line along and down to Asni. Having walked it once I now carefully avoid it, much preferring the original mule track which wends between the floral agricultural plain and the arid limestone hillsides. There is a wealth of birdlife. The sun finally dipped for good as Howard and I ambled along so it was suddenly deliciously cool. Dawn and dusk are the hours of glory in these hills. The villages across the valley were smoking as fires were lit for evening meals, cows were being led homewards and from a mosque tower a raucous, pre-recorded call to prayer sounded over the vale. If Gray's Elegy describes certain similarities there were a deal more of contrasts.

Several times we hopped across a water channel which had decided to share the path line, then turned up a sunken lane behind a mule and its rider, onto the barren flanks. The power line to Oukaïmeden passes overhead here — a useful navigational check. The biggest village of the day sprawled ahead: Tansghart, with its prominent white mosque, new since my last visit three years ago. Mosques have sprung up in most of the mountain villages of any size in just the last few years. I'm not sure whether this is due to increased prosperity or increased zeal.

We managed not to lose ourselves in the sprawl of Tansghart. A dog barred the path at one stage but when we came up it wagged its tail — all animals are treated more kindly in the hills. After all a mule is as big an investment to a villager as a car would be to a European. One sees some ill-used donkeys in the city however: cities are the same everywhere and I'd like to bet those who make disparaging remarks about Morocco have only stayed in the cities. There has been a mighty surge in the package holiday industry of late and the results ebb out with ill effect, which is why a walk like this is so useful in seeing something of the reality behind the hassle and artificiality. Eyes are best worn in one's boots!

Howard and I chatted on these and many topics for the remaining miles home. The light faded fast. A lorry was being washed in the last ford as we crossed to Asni. There was a bridge. Behind the whole horizon was a jagged pink array of mountain summits. If, after three hours, we seemed to have come no distance at all, now it was the other way. Could we really have started the day away up at that snowy skyline? The scale impresses still, even after years of familiarity. A solitary star hung in the west as we turned in to the hostel grounds, the walk accomplished.

We had a small meal and turned in early. It did not rain in the night and when we pushed open the shutters the sunlight flooded in as usual. I nipped down to buy bread and we had a lazy breakfast, thinking of the others as they began their descent off the Oukaïmeden plateau. How would they do on their own? What might they not give for the route description I'd made on our descent? We went to the Hotel du Toubkal for *café au lait* and on the way back collected a bag of vegetables for lunch. Several potatoes, carrots, onions and parsnips cost all of 20 pence and over these we broke a tin of spiced sardines. We sat under the trees of the old olive grove. The family cows were turned out on it, grazing the lawn as efficiently as any lawn mower. White iris were bursting into bloom, a fringe to match the view up the river to the shimmering mountains. As usual the serins were jangling in the trees overhead.

As hostels go Asni's is primitive. The interior walls are spotlessly white and there are the usual bunks but there is no running water and just a couple of tables and benches in the common room. Water comes from a well, cold and clear. The toilet is at the far side of the garden, mercifully, for it was a French-style, footprint-squatter over a hole, *sans l'eau*. (There are more reasons than one for a coffee at the hotel.) Since then running water has been restored at the hostel, after a twelve-year lapse. You used to turn a big wheel to pump water from the well into a rooftop tank which then served showers and kitchen. When it broke down you used rope and bucket instead. Now it has all been re-assembled, in half a day's work — just twelve years behind schedule. There is nothing so desperately urgent as *mañana* in the Atlas.

What a difference there is in Asni over the score of years I've known it. The bare, overgrazed slopes leading up to the 'Stanage Edge' scarp of the Kik Plateau has been afforested, the old market site has been walled-in with a colonnaded façade of shops and ornate gateway, there has been a vast increase in agricultural acreage (mostly fruit trees, so attractive in the pinks and whites of blossom time) and a line of rich holiday homes now lines the old road by the river. The Hotel du Toubkal is bright and sumptuous as ever and the view from it, to the improbably snowy peaks of the High Atlas is simply as splendid as any in the world. It is the Imlil hills rather than the Oukaïmeden ones we see from Asni, for there is another, nearer scarp blocking off these latter peaks. The Grand Hotel du Toubkal would be the classic place for a honeymoon I once suggested to a visitor on the terrace. He replied 'I'm here celebrating my divorce!' By staying in the pound-a-night hostel we felt justified in dining again in the hotel.

Everyone was in before dusk. Howard had wandered back up to take photographs and met Jack and Luigi. It was after that meeting they managed to go astray in the cultivated fields and only extricated themselves by wading the main stream. Hamish and John were in last, as usual crowding in experiences, this time of having mint tea (and walnuts) in a village and discovering this was a ceremony, taking a couple of hours, rather than the 'quick cuppa' they were craving.

All declared it one of the most interesting, colourful and spectacular walks they had ever enjoyed — and between them they had tramped in New Zealand, the Andes, Alps and Himalayas.

A week later they were saying it over again when we tramped off westwards with a bivouac under frosted stars and an amazing seven-thousand-foot descent to Ouriganeg another ten miles up the Tizi n'Test road from Asni. That walk ended at an equally rewarding inn with the name *Au Sanglier Qui Fume* ('The Boar that Smokes') where the best French-style cooking in the south is to be found. It is not to be mistaken for the larger, new hotel across the river, which is expensive, and gastronomically ordinary. The hotel is set in a wild garden (our hillside room was smothered in scented wistaria) and every table will hold a vase of flowers. On one wall there is a boar's head with a large pipe in its mouth, hence the name of the *auberge*. It was only after years of wandering those hills I read that wild boar can still be found, but they are now rare, rather than the object of hunting. Man has wiped out most of the animal life of the mountains, though Morocco remains a rewarding country for the ornithologist.

This seems to be ending as a gastronomic description of the area but as Luigi had taken his belt in two holes and Jack's trousers would hardly stay up there was both excuse and desire to indulge a bit. Morocco is a country with a considerable and underestimated cuisine of her own to which has been added the legacy of the French years, including some palatable wines. You can dine very well, at a reasonable cost. We did, both at the Hotel du Toubkal in Asni, and at the Sanglier, enjoying a touch of startlingly different luxury to round off the hard days' walking. Their visit ended with two days in Marrakech, staying in the Foucauld, eating there the first night and on the last night going out to the 'Ksar el Hamra' which is described later. By the time they flew home Jack's trousers fitted and Luigi had expanded his belt by one hole.

Hamish and John had gone off on a round trip to Zagora and the desert south while we did some more trekking and climbing and Stan joined us after the usual arrival at the Foucauld at 1.30 am, and bus, then taxi to Imlil. We still had a week left and that time we all spent variously on different excursions and expeditions. For our last night we went up to one of the villages above Imlil to dine with Aït Idir Mohammed: we began with mint tea on the rooftop and enjoyed watching the activity of the locals at dusk as goats were herded home and the yellow glow turned to starry darkness. The pointers of the Plough indicated the Pole Star above the cleft of the valley: down to Asni, Marrakech, home. We went indoors for *cous cous*, a modest repast, and more mint tea. We chatted of this and that.

Cous cous is the national dish but is one open to countless variations. The best will have plenty of meat, a great variety of vegetables, sauces to add, and a mix of many spices. Mohammed's was basic: a few bits of meat and ordinary vegetables over the cornflour base. This is a rice-like base of ground sweet corn (maize) and not cornflour in the British sense. It is steamed in a dish which sits over the pot in which the meat and vegetables are cooked so none of the flavours are lost. Originally it was eaten by hand, only the right hand,

75

which would be washed before and after by the host going round with the fancy ewer and basin. Mohammed would neatly knead a ball of *cous cous* and pop it into his mouth while we would end up to the elbows in the sticky grains and a trail of bits on carpet, trousers and beards. Times change. Everyone now just uses spoons. Our third glass of mint tea served, we drank up and took our departure. That is a custom the west could well imitate: the third cup or glassful indicating the end of a social visit. Mohammed shakes us by the hand and hopes to see us next year, *Insh' Allah*. We edge down the track, past his grey mule, over a *seguia*, and through the bramble-edged fields to the road home by the school.

The next morning we were in the square early hoping to travel ahead of the rush but discovered that all transport had been commandeered to take the locals, for free, down to Marrakech to welcome King Hassan II who was driving through. There was nothing for it but to sit and wait.

The world seemed deserted. Only a couple of tourist cars came up but even they soon departed again. It was three o'clock before the familiar drone of a taxi was heard, and out stepped 'Le Grand Noir' who as can be guessed, was a hefty, dark-skinned Berber. The nickname had nothing derogatory in it. He was quite a character as well as being physically powerful, and how he managed to squeeze himself never mind the usual eight others and half a ton of baggage into the ageing Opel was a mystery. His head rested hard against the roof which must have been well battered on the dirt track of a road.

It was a silent ride down to Imlil. The blossom had advanced up the valley by many miles and feet. The broom was out now and the fig trees were in leaf. Only the walnuts remained bare, always the last trees to burst into new life. Time seems to have stood still in some ways, yet subtle changes go on all the time: a new field carved out here, trees planted there; telegraph poles by the roadside (for Imlil by next year should have the telephone) and work should start on the tarring of the *piste*. Asni was as empty as Imlil. A couple of the regular touts were the only others there and few tourists came up the road as Marrakech was cordoned off by the crowds along the king's route. The touts had seen all of us often enough and came to chat rather than sell. More hours slipped by. At home it would have been infuriating but we were old enough hands to accept the situation. Eventually a bus arrived.

The king's route was lined seven deep, with people squatting on the ground and as many standing. I caught the eye of a policeman who opened a passageway for us and we were hurried over and pushed through the crowd on the other side. It would have been frustrating to have been stuck so near yet so far from the Foucauld. An old man with a handcart passed by and we off-loaded our gear thankfully onto him. He wheeled it to the hotel. They were glad to see us for rooms were suddenly in great demand and they were wondering when they could allocate ours! Hamish and John came in from Essaouira the road from which, for the last two hours, coincided with the King's route from Agadir. They wondered what was happening.

The king duly came, bravely standing up in an open car (no Popemobile or bullet-proof glass) while the crowds yelled and the women ululated, a sound quite impossible to describe but it always makes the hairs tingle on the nape of my neck with its weird, wild sound. As soon as the cavalcade had passed everyone poured into the city. The Jmaa el Fnaa was packed solid and, for once, the entertainment went on long after dark. We could hear the pulsing beat of it from the dining room in the Foucauld.

Those about to leave spent the morning visiting the Saadian Tombs. The Saadians were a sixteenth to seventeenth century dynasty and their tombs survived simply because they were so built around that they vanished from sight and memory. In 1917 someone knocked a hole in a wall — and there they were! Theirs is a miraculous survival for each ruler, never mind each dynasty, usually pillaged and destroyed the palaces and buildings of his predecessor. They are now Marrakech's architectural showpiece, surpassed only by the tower of the Koutoubia (twelfth century!) and the miles of walls and defensive gateways.

For our last night we forsook the pleasant atmosphere of the Foucauld to go to the Ksar el Hamra, for what could be called a Moroccan banquet with a floor show added. That of course conveys all sorts of wrong images. The Ksar has no sign out and is hidden away in a corner of an alley in the depths of the Medina. The alley reeked and a blind beggar chanted for alms as we walked down the dark lane yet, turning two corners and dodging into an ordinary doorway, we were suddenly transported into a world as fanciful as the Arabian Nights. A tiled courtyard, pillared and colourful, had orange trees (laden with fruit) growing round a fountain while rows of conical straw baskets covered *tagine* and other dishes, keeping them hot until carried into the dining room. We were ushered in by a uniformed attendant and I enjoyed watching my companions' faces. None had ever been in such sumptuous surroundings before.

It was basically a restored and altered palace so it was both spacious and ornate. The purist would complain that the vital 'space' had been spoiled by a colonnaded platform in the middle, the stage for what was to come, but our gang just goggled like anyone else. We sprawled on velvet divans round a corner table and I had my usual task of translating the seven menus available. We chose several different ones and swopped and tried each others' choices till we were all replete. Howard started with a *pstilla*, which is a pigeon pastry dish. A quarter of it left him full and there were still three courses to go! We gladly helped him out. Traditionally the pastry took twenty-four hours to prepare, being rolled and folded all that time, so it became unbelievably thin and flaky in texture. The pastry is good still but mechanical aids I'm sure now do the work rather than slave girls. Honey and almonds and spices are mixed in with the pigeon. It is a dish unlike any other and is both delicious and satisfying. Several *tagines* had come so we all tried them too: chicken cooked in oranges and spicy oils, lamb with a rich sweet prune sauce, vegetables with flavours we never knew existed. Someone else had ordered *mechoui*, traditionally a whole sheep roasted on a spit, basted and dusted with cumin, the outside crisped like crackling. They kindly allowed an intermission before bringing on the equally varied *cous cous* dishes. Luigi had a soft spot for them since his introduction *chez* Mohammed ('They remind me of pasta'), but even he could only manage a few mouthfuls of each gargantuan plateful.

The Ksar beat us easily and while we were lying back to recover, the Andalusian musicians who had played all night suddenly stopped and were replaced by other musicians. The waiters brought in a huge bowl of oranges just to keep us going. We each ate several over the next hour and pocketed some and there were still several kilos left over. Four girls in folk costume entered and performed what looked like a work dance, but the significance of most of it was rather lost on us. They had no sooner left than a party of lean 'Blue Men' from the desert entered and stomped and banged hypnotically through the simple steps of a dance. They were swathed in blue gowns, faces wound round with black cloths, and they flourished long daggers. The contrast between them and we fat, overdressed European spectators was comical. Had one of them stepped off the dais I'm sure the spectators would have fled. They conveyed all the fierce freedom and blasting sun of the far south.

There was a rotund snake charmer next, almost as ridiculous a contrast to the Blue Men. but he was vastly entertaining with an endless flow of patter as he played with his boxes full of snakes. His cheeks blew out into perfect spheres when he piped. One French female was persuaded to go out and have a huge snake wrapped round her neck. Everyone tried to look small thereafter. He might choose another victim! He went off to thunderous applause from the relieved audience who had not had snakes draped round their necks.

The most interesting act of the evening was a team of tumblers who performed a variety of feats on and off stage and built more and more impressive towers, culminating in one man having another on his shoulders, and another on that man's and on top of his a young lad stood on his hands, upside down! This is straight circus stuff and the troupe does actually work in Europe in summer, using Marrakech as a winter training ground, but their final performer would probably be banned in Europe. I watched Hamish, our doctor, and his expression was a mixture of both horror and professional curiosity.

The last lad was a contortionist and in defiance of human anatomy he bent and twisted into 'impossible' positions. I've seen spectators actually become sick watching. His climax was to bend over backwards so his head came through between his legs and he then crossed his arms to grasp the ankles opposite — and then he 'walked' round the stage, for all the world like a figure playing football with a detached head, only it wasn't. Hamish shook his head in disbelief.

A belly dancer finished the evening off. I noticed the two septuagenarians Jack and Stan quickly changed seats to have a better view. For once the girl was not all belly and she performed her seductive measures so satisfyingly that an annoying German who had photographed everything, but everything, sat still through her whole performance. As she left to maximum applause the waiters came in with mint tea and Moroccan cakes to round off the evening. The cakes are sweetmeats, usually full of honey, nuts and spices. Some look unusual but all are delicious, though so rich that we actually left some behind.

When we went out into the dark alley the blind beggar had pulled his ragged *djellaba* about him and was lying asleep. A black cat sat beside his protruding bare feet. The Jemaa el Fnaa was empty. The stars glittered with their intense indifference, the Plough mocked us: 'North! North! Tomorrow,' but I defied him, whispering back, 'Next year! Next year!' then, as all Moroccans would do, I hastily added, *'Insh' Allah'*.

BARBOUR, NEVILL, *Morocco,* Thames and Hudson.
CLARKE, B., *Berber Village,* Travel Book Club.
COLLOMB, R., *Atlas Mountains, Morocco. West Col.*
HUGHES, RICHARD, *In the Lap of Atlas,* Chatto & Windus.
KININMONTH, *Morocco,* Cape.
MAXWELL, GAVIN, *Lords of the Atlas,* Longmans.
PEYRON, MICHAEL, *La Grande Traversee de l'Atlas Marocain.*
Morocco, Guide Bleu, Hachette.
ELLINGHAM & McVEIGH, *The Royal Guide to Morocco,* Routledge & Kegan Paul.

MAPS
The 1:100,000 Oikaïmeden-Toubkal, Sheet NH-29-XXIII-I of the IGN series covers the area described. There is also a 1:50,000 Jbel Toubkal sheet which some prefer. It shows more paths but is older and less clear generally. Either map can be obtained from Mountain Holidays, 21 Carlin Craig, Kinghorn, Fife KY3 9RX at £6.50 plus postage. The Collomb guide £6.75 is also available, and the Peyron may be obtainable.

4

Scotland

THE ULTIMATE CHALLENGE GAME

'Tis not too late to seek a newer world

(Tennyson)

1979 was the Jubilee Year of the Scottish Youth Hostels Association and I had written suitable pieces for the SYHA newsletter and for *The Scottish Field*. Writing about my early Scottish wanderings for these articles brought home to me again just how big through-treks had been my normal approach to fun in the hills. As a lad it was bike and hike of necessity — and that freedom to roam, day after day, on foot (or at least self-propelled) is one of the finest aspects of living near mountains. Rock-climbing, ski-ing, winter-climbing, these are extensions merely. The core of mountain adventuring is foot-travelling.

Scotland offers a wonderful freedom to roam. It has a landscape second to none for long treks and (happily) none of the frantic competition of pedestrian motorways like the Pennine Way. Competition does have a place of course and many climbers and walkers have enjoyed taking part in orienteering, fell-running and other mountain events. Fun is the vital reason, the *only* reason, for any or all of our hill ploys. Could we not have something similar — challenging, sociable, formal yet free — on a coast-to-coast basis perhaps? The outline of what was to become *The Ultimate Challenge* was committed to paper.

The Ultimate Challenge is not a competition or a race but a highly individualistic and demanding backpacking trek across the widest girth of Scotland. There are a dozen starting places, scattered on or between the scenic western railway terminals, and the finish is anywhere from Arbroath to Peterhead, with a subsequent calling-in at Montrose. It is

81

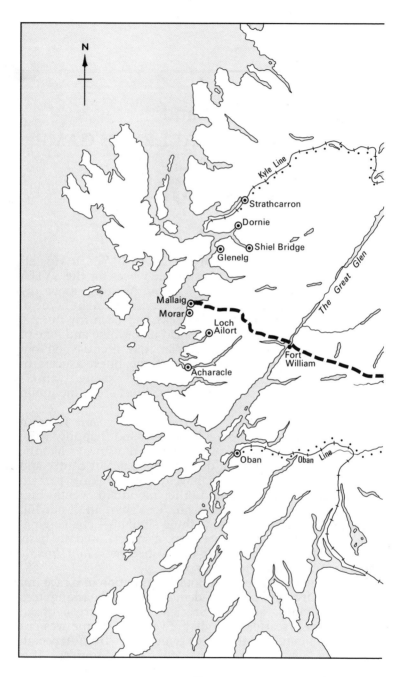

N

Kyle Line

Strathcarron

Dornie

Shiel Bridge

Glenelg

The Great Glen

Mallaig

Morar

Loch Ailort

Fort William

Acharacle

Oban

Oban Line

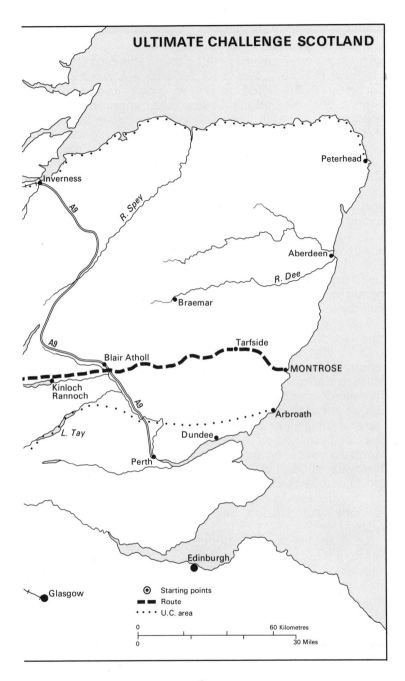

ULTIMATE CHALLENGE SCOTLAND

Peterhead

Inverness

R. Spey

A9

Aberdeen

R. Dee

Braemar

Tarfside

A9

Blair Atholl

MONTROSE

Kinloch
Rannoch

A9

Arbroath

L. Tay

Dundee

Perth

Edinburgh

Glasgow

⊙ Starting points
━ ━ Route
• • • • U.C. area

0   60 Kilometres
0   30 Miles

completely planned and carried out by the individual participants who may carry out either a standard crossing or a high-level route. (The latter includes a dozen Munros or Corbetts, those listed peaks of 3,000 and 2,500 feet respectively.) An optional badge (dated appropriately and a different colour each year) and a certificate are available at Montrose. To date nobody has said they don't want these mementos of what may well be the trip of a lifetime.

The finish is the comfortable and friendly Park Hotel in Montrose where a room is set aside with welcoming armchairs and refreshment facilities. The event covers two weeks including their weekends and Montrose is manned during the second week when the majority come in. It is an odd sight to see tweedy country types, oil-industry executives and hikers in shorts mingling for bar lunches. There have been some memorable dinners at night too when the flatness of finishing gives way to the bedlam of battering memories. I'm a bit of a loner but have found this growing friendship of the hills a real pleasure.

A few people have crossed every year and many make repeats so tradition — and folklore — are rapidly accruing to this vigorous young event. The first 250 applications are accepted (from several times that who apply) and this is whittled down to about the required 200 starters, a number that avoids economic or ecological pressure but still gives a unique atmosphere. Seldom have more than 30 given up *en route,* although one fanatic ornithologist became so carried away he branched off down the Spey instead of crossing to Montrose. Some army lads dashed across to make it before they were whisked off to fight in the Falklands. John Moore and David McArthur, in 1983, covered Oban to Montrose in just 2 days and 4 hours while others take it more leisurely. It is not a competition, but you still walk every inch of its miles.

Rules are kept to a minimum and are mostly a matter of common sense. Sadly, for someone whose most constant companion is a dog, dogs are banned. May is still lambing time in the wilds and it would only take one or two untrained dogs to change the good relationship the event has with local people. Part of the idea behind the Challenge was to put back something into the local economy and this it is doing. May was chosen to avoid the summer plagues of rain, midges and crowds. Inadvertently it cut out students and teachers but, with hind-sight this has given the gain of a higher average age for participants — 43 — who are therefore more experienced and sensible. Routes now are bent to take in favourite B & Bs or revisit keepers and others met en route. In 1983 one party did take a dog but the reception at Montrose, from Roger Smith (Springer spaniel owner), Bob Dawes (Alsatian) and myself (owned by a Sheltie), who had all dutifully left dogs at home, was not the best one to have chosen. No certificate, mate. Our three dogs bore the names Cloud, Misty and Storm, which is probably significant!

The first three years of the Challenge gave about one day apiece to rain, the fourth gave one dry day and how number five went you can read below. May was chosen, above all, to increase the chances of good conditions — and the weather gods have viewed our goings-on with benevolence it seems, giving the lie to the saying about there being statistics, statistics and damned weather statistics.

People may travel alone or in groups to a maximum of four people. If alone some safety system of phoning-in is advised and often the Park Hotel base acts in this capacity — and becomes the main source of trail gossip. It is possible to go for days at a time without seeing another person, which seems incredible in these overcrowded islands but, due to long lochs like Loch Ness or Loch Ericht, there are odd places where there are bottlenecks (Fort Augustus, Dalwhinnie and Braemar spring to mind) and in these other U.C. participants will be encountered — which usually means a good night in the local. There is nothing like a return from the wilds to set tongues wagging, or to set feet merrily to the steep braes again. At Fort Augustus newcomers can be a bit subdued. The west is so very tough, so different from the imaginings.

'I saw the west as a land of dreams
But high were the rocks and deep its streams.'

Ahead may lie the Corrieyairack or Ben Nevis or the empty Monadh Liaths, challenges indeed, but behind, already, are memories cut sharp as the Cuillin. The Great Glen is a good place to meet others, to regroup and prepare the advance. For a few days this exotic band straggles through and then they hirple on to the east. The line of the

A9 is the next great milestone. From the friendly Monadh Liath Hotel at Laggan to the gourmets' delight of the Ossian Hotel at Kincraig the strays drift in again, relax, rejoice, and go away singing into the comfortable Cairngorms. If you reach the A9 only something serious will stop you east of its line. Feet have recovered, bodies have hardened, spirits soar. In Braemar the evenings have an element of frenzy. Just the bends and glens of Angus to go. From Tarfside and Bridgend they exit onto the eastern plains — heading for Arbroath, Montrose, Stonehaven or even for Peterhead if Dee and Don have called. There is a sting in the tail of course and the road miles can be sole-and-soul destroying. The Park Hotel is very understanding and welcomes both the punch-drunk and the emotionally high with practised skill.

There is a comments book in the reception room and it bulges with heart-felt rejoicings. It *is* an achievement. 'Moleskin is marvellous . . . Goretex and Mrs Guthrie saved our lives . . . a journey of Mammals, Munros, Muck-ups, Munchies and Malts . . . now practising the Ultimate limp . . .' Even the agony has an irresistible tone of triumph. I liked two other entries: 'might bring my husband next year' and 'a great honeymoon. Pity the wife had to retire half way through though'.

Though the event itself is not competitive (it is almost unique in that respect) there is the chance to submit a write-up of this trip and *The Great Outdoors* publishes the best Mountain Route and Standard Route accounts in its November issue — which also carries the details of the next year's event. This, along with regional reunions, rounds off the U.C. year and naturally sets the mental adrenalin flowing as the next year suddenly grins provocatively ahead. Some people seem to be hooked on walking across Scotland.

The reunions were a spontaneous happening and are now part of the tradition. We are not likely to forget the years Bob Dawes organised Lakeland weekends with dinners in the Glenridding Hotel, nor the Scottish evening held in Edinburgh Castle, nor John Bourke's party at his home outside Dublin. And what characters have turned up: Ivan Waller, Iain Mathieson, Jack Griffiths, Jim Cosgrove and George Fyvie to just mention a few of the over-seventies who keep on coming. The last pair were 72 and 78 and I'm never sure whether such oldies are an encouragement or a

86

despair to the merely middle-aged. It was interesting to see that age rather than youth coped best with the deep snow of 1982 and the monsoon of 1983. In the first three years of heatwave it was the younger members who suffered heat-exhaustion — an aspect of walking in Scotland that is seldom foreseen but is quite a common hazard.

Some people have made all the crossings. Glancing at a list (pre-U.C. 1985) I can see Dave McArthur from Mold, Ron Reynolds from Studley, Bob McClurg from Inverness, Bill Robertson from Perth, John Donohoe from Blanefield and Bob Dawes from Glenridding. Characters all. Others may be one down but are equally part of the scene: Chris Townsend (an early Munro-maniac), Eric Pow, Cliff Hunt, Keith Pickup, John Needham (a river-crossing expert), Chris Munford, Tony Wilson, Ray Swinburn (the maxi-comfort man), John Brown from north of Inverness, the team of Downer and Bean (who are neither down nor has-beens), the irrepressible trio of Minnie Robertson and Frank and Jean Maud, Ron and Joan Smith, John and Jean Brown or the ever-changing, ever-fresh teams of Doncaster Wayfarers, or Bernie Hynes who, quite unintentionally, was given number 57 and now claims it as a traditional right.

Of my own crossings, the solitary crossing was the longest as it linked Ardnamurchan Point, the further west mainland point of Britain (48 kilometres west of Land's End), with Buchan Ness, the most easterly corner of Scotland. Acharacle, actually a day's walk from Ardnamurchan, had been added as a starting point to open up the splendid wild country west of Loch Linnhe and the coast north of Aberdeen had been added as a finish to open up the historic Buchan and Donside regions for those not so set on big hills. What a romantic litany there is in just reeling off the names of the starting places: Oban, Acharacle, Lochailort, Arisaig, Morar, Mallaig, Glenelg, Shielbridge, Dornie, Strathcarron. Perhaps 'reeling off' is not quite the best term. Acharacle requires some practice. And try pronouncing Glenelg backwards.

The hardest decision is choosing a starting point. For the 1984 crossing that I am to describe, there was the option of making an initial boat journey, after clocking-in at Mallaig, to reach Tarbet, a lonelier, starting point on the western seaboard. I couldn't resist the idea especially as I had originally met my three female companions at sea. Sandy

Stokes, from Ireland, was even more seasick than I was on that voyage and as my bunk was above hers we had this bond of misery. Sandy and two others there were all student nurses in London and had teamed up for various interesting holidays. Now in 1984 they were to accompany me on the Coast to Coast challenge. They had never been to Scotland and were not walkers, but they leapt at the idea of a new challenge — while I revelled in the anticipation of their good company. Hamish going with three girls would give the trail gossip its best gas in years!

We sorted out equipment. Boots were bought before Christmas to ensure they were well broken in. 'We wear them always' Sandy wrote, conjuring up a picture of night wards echoing to the tramp of vibrams. There is something fascinating in imagining all the different entrants working away at their preparations. Old friends would ring up and discuss routes and as the year changed I began to receive batches of Route Plans for vetting. This is a useful system whereby an eagle eye can be cast over plans by those who know the Highlands well. John Hinde, of Outward Bound Lochiel had borne the brunt of this for years and had even prepared duplicated information sheets to help. Dangerous rivers, over-ambitious ridges, missing bridges, shops or telephones no longer existing — information like this could be passed on without in any way inhibiting routes.

Over 600 people applied for U.C.84. Our team changed a bit as one nurse returned to Germany and the other had to choose between a honeymoon or the Challenge. The Challenge lost, but Claudia, another friend brave or innocent (both it proved), came instead to join Sandy and myself.

For four days before the official start, I carried out the final preparations. I enjoyed wandering the hills and glens of Knoydart and left a great stack of food, a stove, dixies and other things hidden near Glen Pean bothy which would be our first overnight stop. Then, when everything was at last done, I met up with Sandy and Claudia and together we took the train to Mallaig where we were to check in at the West Highland Hotel. There were plenty of other challengers on the train to Mallaig. After Fort William we shared a compartment (and cups of tea) with Frank and Doritta Crooks, who were starting at Lochailort. Our original route through Knoydart was altered because so many seemed to be going that way and after checking in we set sail (with other challengers) for Inverie. Several challengers had decided to start there but we went on, alone, to Tarbet on the other side of Loch Nevis. The three of us, the ferryman, several boxes of groceries and a bag of mail was quite load enough for the wee boat that splashed its way in to a rough jetty. There can be few more isolated post offices anywhere.

After a brief chat with Mr Macdonald, the bay's sole permanent resident, we tramped over the shingle to join the rough track up to a pass which was the gateway to our adventure. This was it. We were committed with supper, safety, everything now at the working of our legs.

The crags bore a shiver of trees and as soon as we started uphill a pair of cuckoos came swooping overhead from one green gully. Another flew up opposite, yelling 'Cuckoo, cuckoo' — the annual refrain of the Event — and the girls were excited at actually *seeing* the noisy birds; not one but three of these normally elusive birds.

I kept quiet about my thoughts which were dwelling on three other, pedestrian, cuckoos. There was a wealth of secret emotion in our last backward look down to shadowy Loch Nevis. *The Western Isles* ferry had already put-putted out of sight and its wake had wobbled and died on the shore. A soft eider voice came over in the pulsing heat, its sound simply deepening the silence. It is very difficult today to find the true sounds of silence, free from mechanical and man-made batterings. We turned our backs on the sea.

Half a mile and a few hundred feet of ascent on and we had grabbed the view beyond: another loch and lonely hills but glittering in the sun. This was Loch Morar. We sat and finished a big container of apple juice and ate the last of our extra picnic goodies. (That was all weight to be carried in belly rather than on back!) The cuckoos never stopped for a minute. Loch Morar is a fjord-like length of fresh water which is only just above sea-level and is linked to the sea by one of the shortest rivers in the country. It is the deepest natural hole in Europe however (300 metres) and you have to go away out past St Kilda or Rockall to find the sea reaching that depth. It is probably a fault which has been further gouded out by glaciation's JCBs but no one seems to know much about it. Like Loch Ness (almost as deep and closely-linked to the sea) this loch has a history of sightings of an unknown water creature. With that British flippancy which so often hides the incomprehensible or frightening, the beast has been given the cheery name of Morag. We did not see her.

The girls had probably never been in so remote or empty a place but the sun gave it warmth and the glen down the other side overflowed with a vivid birch wood. It was a misleading kindliness as they found out over the next few hours but, if we suffered the smiting of the sun, it was preferable to the more familiar Morar thrashings of wind and rain. I felt it keenly for the responsibility of such a dramatic start was all mine. The nagging doubts had to be firmly battered down. Complete ignorance has its own strength born of innocence. By the time they knew what they were doing we would be half way across Scotland!

A solitary figure suddenly appeared above the trees and zig-zagged up the rough spur of hillside beyond. It might have been a challenger who had started at Morar station but we never saw him again to ask. It was surprising to see anyone but his passing indicated a path and we set off to find it rather than fight down through the trees to follow the shoreline. It was a lucky choice for a strong, experienced party, was at that moment doing a shore-level traverse and were to describe it to us later in one word — which cannot be repeated in print. We hit the path at once and in the wood's sun and shadow stucco, with a frieze of primroses, violets and anemones, it was briefly cool and delightful. As soon as we left the shade we exploded into sweat. I did anyway. Maybe the ladies gently perspired. 'Time for shorts' I gasped — and found shorts were the first thing I had forgotten to pack.

We ended many hundreds of feet above Loch Morar and basically used the height gained by that initial toil to traverse along and down to the other end of the loch, a mere eight kilometres but kilometres that were to take us nearly five hours. It is hard to describe the difficulties. It was steep, it was rough, it was complex and though never excessively so, gave wearying, unrelenting, unrestful hours of hot labour. How we dripped!

A small group of figures appeared below on the shoreline and were obviously making as slow an advance as we were. When they stopped (to brew presumably) we passed ahead, but later they caught up steadily as weariness began to slow our own progress on ever rougher, steeper terrain. We lost height more quickly and the leading figure below came on a converging course. It was a man in a kilt, bearded, thumb-stick in hand; it could only be one person: the Cumbrian hill enthusiast Bob Dawes.

'Lost one already I see' he cracked. 'You girls want to watch these old men. Here's us all changed our route to find you — and we can't keep up.' Five minutes with Bob was just the restorative Sandy and Claudia needed. We straggled on to the end of the loch and made tea on the shore. 'Brought my own chef this year,' Bob joked, but he had, for Max Fuchs (also in a Bob-made kilt) is a professional chef. 'Ray and Smiler are a bit behind. They stopped for a brew.' These two pairs deserved each other. Both Bob and Ray Swinburn had done three Challenges already and Ray and I had done other crossings before the first event. Smiler proved to be Chris Trumpess, on his third crossing. Some of us seem to have caught the Challenge bug rather badly.

It cooled down as the shadows lengthened but when Ray and Chris had not turned up after an hour we had to push on. The others only had to round the head of the loch to reach their bothy but we had many miles and a pass to cross to reach ours. We took our different routes after scrambling over the crag that plunges into Loch Morar at its head.

We seem to have found a second wind for the pull up to the deep gash of pass, one of the finest in Britain, which is held tight between steep, rocky mountain slopes and in its heart holds a tiny lochan, as hidden as a raindrop in a lady's mantle leaf. The track did one of its several vanishing tricks and a big moon rose to push the last red lines of day into the west. The watershed was passed but the miles seemed endless. We passed through tiredness to walk as automatons. Fortunately I knew the path shown passing north of a loch is a figment of the O.S. imagination. We crept past on the south and the improved path promised an end to our tramp. I recognised the last crag's silhouette against the stars and at 11.30 pm the gable end of Glen Pean bothy appeared. Stopping was an ache!

There was a rucksack by the wall and this proved to belong to Rob Aitken, also on the Challenge. He must have thought a herd of elephants had invaded. Although it was late we were not so tired that we did not relish a big meal. So

I went off to uncover the food and cooking equipment I had hidden nearby. It was a bitter cold night of great clarity. 'You don't see stars like that in London,' one of the girls remarked.

Although tired, we rose early to be away in the cool of day. (The sun has been the undoing of several Challengers in the past.) We ate in the six o'clock sunshine. We followed the river bank down for three kilometres and crossed to follow a glen and then up onto a ridge to complex country which led to Gulvain. By the time we had gained the ridge the heat was belting at us and legs were like jelly. We dropped down and brewed tea by a stream, paddled, and set off more cheerfully for Drimsallie Bothy just through and down an easy pass. The hill slopes were crowded with red deer, too hot to do more than canter off a few hundred yards. Two hours of gentle descent brought us to the bothy and there we stayed, making a lazy day of paddling and brews and catching up on needed sleep whilst the frost dropped off the stars to whiten the landscape.

Refreshed, we were up at five and away an hour later for, after dropping down through the forests to the Mallaig–Fort William road, we were faced with many miles of road to reach the latter town and Glen Nevis. The early start was rewarded and the walking proved easy rather than punishing. A picnic by Loch Eil had a view of Ben Nevis looming ahead. There was some satisfaction in hauling it in, mile by mile. At Corpach a shop was open and cool drinks and ice cream were welcome. A local purchased some booze which was carefully put into a brown paper bag. It was the Sabbath after all.

We crossed the sea lock of the Caledonian Canal, that greatest of Telford's engineering feats, and went by Caol to Inverlochy and Fort William. Inverlochy was the original centre here. The fort came later. The original castle ruin still had solid corner towers and a high wall. We had more drinks below it. It was here that the Great Marquis Montrose swept down out of the hills to defeat the Earl of Argyll in 1645, one of the most extraordinary military escapades in Scottish history. Montrose was a liberal genius in a time of bigoted religious wars and if his king was to lose his head so did he in serving that selfish monarch.

Paths have been created along the banks of the River Nevis so the walking was easy. The clegs (the Gestapo of the insect world) were bad. Just before reaching the hostel we ran into the warden, Dave Gunn, enjoying the sun so stopped for a chat. Later, Challengers Barry Sykes and Mike Rea, arrived and did the girls' spirits a good turn by admitting that the walk along from Glenfinnan had proved hard. They had seen our tracks along the verges. It is always satisfying to reach the Great Glen, a psychological third of the trip, with the next milestone, the crossing of the A9 road, some days ahead. Those western days are perhaps the most rugged too. Easting from the Great Glen one gains and holds something like 300 metres right across till one suddenly descends to the coastal plains below the Braes of Angus. *That* seemed a long way off but 'ane by ane makes ane an aw' as they say.

Glen Nevis, dry underfoot, in golden early sunshine, was a delectable dander. We kept to the north side, flanking along under the Ben, to Polldubh, where the falls were reduced to nothing, and really only had tarred road for the last mile. Beyond the road end lies a fantastic gorge, carved down by millennia of water-action so old pot-holes are left visible hundreds of feet up on the cliffs and the waters still work through a long 'sculpture park'. We took the lowest of the three paths to look at the water-carved rocks. The gorge suddenly ends at a green meadow which is backed by the Steall Waterfall, a classic tumble of water, even in the drought. A mile beyond I had buried our supplies for the next few days so we stopped to brew. Barry and Mike caught up and for the rest of the day we seemed to leapfrog them. They were amazed when I wandered off and returned with three carrier bags full of groceries.

We staggered off with the heaviest rucksacks of the trip, heading steadily east on the old drovers' route, 'The Road to the Isles' of song and fancy. The watershed is a bit confusing and we had time to brew while the other two wandered back and forth trying to cross the river. Two miles on an abandoned house, 'Luibeilt', might have been a possible overnight stopping place but in the two years since I had seen it vandals had completely wrecked the place. An arch of intertwined rowans stood as a forlorn memorial to a once-loved home. We paddled over to the bothy but rather than having a mere hour's walk the next (rest) day we pushed on there and then to Staoineag Bothy. 'A huge meal and bed at 8.30' was my last log entry.

We had twelve hours in bed and a breakfast that 'sort of ran on into lunch'. Challenger Dave Sleath shared that and while he headed off east we went for a stroll along the silver links of river to collect wood for an evening fire. We hauled a sheep out of a bog but it was unlikely to survive. A supper of chili-con-carne warmed us inside and Sandy, with one match, soon had a grand fire to warm the outside. We sat round it and blethered. 'Late to bed — 9 pm,' I recorded. It is amazing how fast a day of doing nothing can go!

Loch Treig was our first loch next day. It is fed through a 22-kilometre tunnel to the aluminium works at Fort William and in turn is fed by a string of lochs almost to Speyside. It was one of the largest and earliest hydro schemes. It was downhill to start, then uphill to Loch Ossian. We crossed the Fort William railway line, up which we had travelled in what now felt like some other incarnation, and watched 'our' train caterpillaring across Rannoch Moor. We took the south shore of Loch Ossian and for the first time rain found us. We walked the rest of the day in waterproofs: up the Uisge Labhair and through the Bealach Cumhann to Loch Ericht. We lunched with two more Challengers, Greg and Paul Hodgson. They carried on up the Uisge Labhair for the Bealach Dubh *(the black pass)* to round Loch Ericht's north end; our route would round its south end. Loch Ericht drains to Loch Rannoch and the River Tay and the North Sea. We were over the great divide that night in Ben Alder Bothy.

The map shows a Prince Charlie's Cave on the hillside. This is probably inaccurately sited but is historically true. After Culloden, when he wandered as a fugitive, he spent several days here with Cluny Macpherson, the local chief. Stevenson describes the setting in that grand yarn *Kidnapped*. The bothy is supposedly haunted but we slept sound enough. An older walker arrived down the loch and a couple came in from the other end. Such crowds!

They were all asleep when we set off. A black sky looked ominous but the hours slowly brightened. On opening the door a herd of deer clattered off from just outside. Blackcock were making the weird sounds of their display in the woods. The daily cuckoo chimed in. A loon cackled out on the grey waters of the loch. These were the sounds of silence and wilderness. The moorland miles we walked east, and then south east, to reach Loch Rannoch, were the loneliest of the whole crossing, a marvellous Empty Quarter, with the beacon of Schiehallion clear ahead. The descent through green fields and spring-bright birch wood was like discovering another world.

Mrs Macdonald made us welcome at Kinloch Rannoch. A B&B night was relished as a contrast to the more austere nights we'd had: 'the rewards of virtue' I suggested. We met Sue and Douglas Barnett in the bar and swopped yarns over a dram. Claudia and Sandy seemed to have things drying all over the house. Mrs Macdonald, being of farming stock, happily provided breakfast at seven o'clock. The rather dismal forecast proved wrong and the day grew sunnier and sunnier all the way. I think it was the day I most enjoyed. We were fitter, our loads were lighter (we left sleeping bags and a few other things: the girls had learnt how inessential much of our daily bits and pieces are — when you have to carry them all the time!).

The green lushness of the Rannoch strath was a vivid contrast to the dark moors and empty heights we'd tramped through since Glen Nevis. We wandered through quivering birch woods where shy roe deer danced off at our passing. The tang of myrtle was strong on the breeze. Schiehallion would be glimpsed across the valley, a keel-up, stranded boat shape now instead of the symmetrical cone that had beaconed our route the day before. We crossed the old military road (from Aberfeldy to Speyside) and by Easter Bohespic farm were back to windy heights for a tramp of some miles through the forestry plantations of Tummel Forest.

These required careful navigation for there were changes not yet on the map. Over a rise we suddenly saw the familiar shape of the Beinn a'Ghlo hills. They lay *beyond* the A9! Loch Bhac was a delectable lunch spot. When we were able to fill the dixie with water (without any tadpoles in it) we made tea. We paddled. We lay in the sun. We brewed again an hour later. 'This is the way to walk across Scotland.'

Heathery moors led us down steadily towards the valley. An increasing surge-of-sea sound turned out to be the rush of traffic on the A9, which had recently given up afflicting Blair Atholl. The Duke's castle was gleaming white in the parkland. We could hear the shriek of peacocks above the juggernauts' din. A couple of days after the event we came back by car and explored it, for it is a bit better than most castles open to the public. The Duke of Atholl bears more titles than the Queen and is the only person allowed to maintain a private army. During the 1745 Jacobite Rising the castle suffered the last siege of any in Great Britain, with one brother defending it for King George and another brother bombarding it for the Pretender. That's an 'auld sang' now but the place oozes with history. It is reached by a mile-long avenue of lime trees which, during a stroll that night, buzzed with a million bees.

Our first stop in Blair Atholl was the old Mill. This still works and can be seen by visitors who are encouraged to have tea and eat something made on the spot. As we entered two tanned walkers were leaving: Peter Evans (of *The Great Outdoors*, whose wife is now U.C. Organiser) and Clive Tully. Later, in the hotel, we found the Barnetts again and it shows the variety in Scotland that they had come from Kinloch Rannoch by a completely different route. Another Challenger there was Dorothy Wilson. Claudia and Sandy were quite glad to see another female on the event, though the energy of Dorothy was rather daunting.

We enjoyed the luxury of Laggan House overnight and the Stephens (also ex-farmers) produced an early breakfast — which makes all the difference on long, hard, hot walking days. The miles before noon are always the easy ones. We were to be glad of them.

There is a hard ascent out of the A9's valley and by the time we were back to the heather slopes, on Beinn a' Ghlo, it was blazing hot. We followed a path through to the south of this group of isolated peaks and found a pleasant spot beside the burn to brew-up but had to move on as we were sitting almost on top of a sandpiper's nest and the mother bird was none too happy. To me the sandpiper's is the voice that heralds the cheerful new season. You can keep the monotonous cuckoo and its anti-social offspring.

A pass took us through to Glen Loch (which comes from the oddly named Loch Loch) and the five kilometres down it were memorable for the sad tally of dead and very smelly red deer corpses. We counted over twenty. Having lost height we had a prolonged stop before facing a climb over a hill range which would allow us to reach another glen running down to the Spittal of Glen Shee. It took us up to the lingering snow patches of winter. Deer were lying on the snow for coolness. A herd of sixty streamed up the slopes ahead of us. Our 300-metre ascent was made much more slowly.

Glen Lochsie used to have its own little estate railway but the Victorian Lodge is now a hotel. We walked down the long drive to the Spittal, collected the key from the hotel there, and so entered Dundee Ski Club's luxurious Gulabain Lodge: hot showers, comfy beds, a modern kitchen.

I'd left food there so we dined on game soup, a curry, fruit and cheese, with a bottle of French wine and Moroccan-bought coffee. While dining we saw another trim figure walk along to the hotel and shortly afterwards *run* round to join us. It had to be Dorothy! After thirty-five kilometres I don't think we three could have run. We had a chat and parted. This is one of the joys of the Challenge: meeting and enjoying the brief company of like-minded folk. Sometimes you actually met two days in a row, seldom more. Scotland is large after all so the permutations are endless. We had a pancake supper to round off the day.

Tomb was the first map name we passed; at 6 am not very encouraging! Nor was the weather. We had two ranges to cross and in the gut of pass under Monamenach the cloud and rain swept down on us. Grouse had been giving us heart-failure as they rose at our feet. There was a surprising amount of snow about and the melt water had swollen the streams. We had a picnic sitting beside the River Isla, which helped to reduce the angle of ascent afterwards. 'If in doubt, eat,' is a good rule.

A good stalking path took us steadily upwards. A herd of about 200 deer careered across the ridge, the biggest herd we saw. The clouds just cleared the corries of the Caenlochan Forest but at the price of a bitter wind. It was quite strange to pile on clothes because of cold. The huge plateau country we reached was Arctic in feel as well as in flora. The damp turned to sleet and then snow while we sat in the decaying stable on Finalty Hill. Fortunately it came from the north so was behind us for the indeterminate miles to Mayar which, at 928 metres, is above the magical Munro altitude of ye ancient 3000 feet. (Remember when hills were measured in feet?) The girls had climbed their first Munro.

As we would reach the youth hostel too early we compounded this felony by going on to snatch Driesh (947 metres) as well. Being the weekend there were dozens of men, women, children and dogs commuting between them. It was the only day of the walk on which we met 'others' on the hill. We descended by the Shank of Inchgrundle into the massed forests of Glendoll, slithering down a path which would have done well in Darien. It was a brutal descent which left the girls weary and Claudia hirping the last rise to the Glendoll hostel: a white lodge buried in the trees.

One owner, many years ago, tried to close Jock's Road (the track from Braemar), saying it was his and private. As one of the most historic rights-of-way in the land he, not surprisingly, lost his case, the appeal and the House of Lords appeal. So costly was this litigation that he had to sell his house in Glendoll. It is now the hostel and Jock's Road sees up to two score of Challengers crossing it each year: a change from warring armies, drovers, caterans and packmen. There was quite a gang sitting outside waiting for opening time: a quarter of an hour that passed in an atmosphere of pleasant banter and a display of plastered feet. The three kilted police lads from Fife went by the nickname of 'The Grousebeaters', a name given by Bob Dawes. Bob and Max, we heard, were just over Jock's Road at Braemar. There would be quite a *ceilidh* that night.

It was a steep ascent to gain the slopes overlooking Glendoll but even our 'rests' produced magic touches — like the diamond-bright jewels of water held in the leaves of lady's mantle or the vixen that appeared out of the cloud and took her time sniffing across the slope a mere twenty yards off.

The cloud was down to top-of-forest level so we zig-zagged blind to the plateau country but just where was impossible to say. I explained to the girls the difference between being lost and merely mislaid. Claudia at once suggested the difference was they were the first and I was the second. I was not going to be let out of sight, not round a single peat hag. Loch Brandy was a target easy enough to hit and when we found ourselves on its corrie rim within four minutes of a time estimate given an hour before, they thought this was magic. I always think so too when tricky navigation works out. Thanks be to St Silva!

We cringed by a cairn on Green Hill to have a snack. Procrastination failed to move clouds. We never did see Loch Brandy. (The crags were edged with creeping azalea, a bonny alpine.) We tramped off on timed bearings along the well-named Long Shank as an alternative to the ominous-sounding Burn of Slidderies. A great deal can be read into the names hereabouts: Watery Knowe, Black Hill of Mark, Wolf Hill, Hunt Hill, Benty Roads and the like.

There was an extraordinary crevasse-like hole in one snow bank but the Long Shank gave springy walking of blissful ease before turning into a fine example of the local peaty chaos. As always there seemed to be endless bits of dead hare lying about. On Mount Keen one year two shot off at our approach and 'hared' round a peat hag just ahead, one to each side. There was a second's pause and then a great thud and two hares spun into view over the hag. Walt Disney could not have bettered it. We all just about died when a grouse rose at our feet and went flapping off in a distraction display. There were nine eggs. Later we saw dipper and pipit nests and at night a thrush chick landed with a clatter on a car roof beside us.

We came down to the Water of Unich and with all the visible snow rims pouring melt water into it there was no chance of boulder hopping. It ensured we had a chilly paddle. I crossed and then came back for the girls' rucksacks before scampering to a ruin to put on a brew. Ignorance has some advantages — but they will not forget their first river crossing.

The descent by the Falls of Damff and the Falls of Unich is one of the most memorable places in Scotland. Very few gorges can surpass it. The blaeberry patches were artificially vivid in colour and the spraying waters would soon be hanging gardens. We tramped down an old path, a gem of its kind compared to today's indecent scourings by bulldozers.

The O.S. do not bother showing the bridge across the Lee and if there is one thing worse than bridges shown not being there it is the opposite. (We even have the odd Wade bridge that has never made it onto the map!) We boulder-hopped across — and then I saw the bridge up the gash in the pearly-grey sculptured rocks. Being a coward I did not point it out.

Loch Lee never seems a very cheery water. Perhaps it is too haunted by sad memories of all the departed people of a century ago. The lodge's kennels were built of solid granite, far better building than the dispossessed had ever known. We stopped to look at the ruined churchyard and had a last brew while Claudia replastered her blistered heel. Several eighteenth-century stones here are still in good legible condition. A local teacher, Alexander Ross, was a poet once admired by Burns, but now forgotten.

Invermark Castle is a pepper-pot of a tower, with nasty loopholes at ground level and the entrance with its iron *yett* fifteen feet up the wall. Not much you could do to it if armed only with an ice axe! It stands at glen junctions and must have been a thorn in the flesh to cattle thieves, mercenaries, gangrels and smugglers — of which the area had its share. The castle was built by Sir David Lindsay of Edzell who lived a cultured life in the brief years before the bloody seventeenth century came in, and who made Edzell Castle such a unique creation. Claudia was interested to hear he had introduced German miners to work the glen. (The old workings could still be made out.) Sandy noticed the door above ground level and compared it to Irish round towers, without knowing we would see one of Scotland's two Irish towers (at Brechin) next day.

The original route cut over Hill of Rowan and we took this rather than the hard-surfaced road down to Tarfside, our destination. It has a narrow gap of a pass cut in the heathery slopes. On top of the hill is an odd conical cairn which is the dominant feature of Glen Esk. Our weary legs rejected a visit but I could tell them it was built by an Earl of Dalhousie in 1866 'in memory of seven members of his family already dead, and of himself and two others when it shall please God to call them hence.'

As we straggled off the hill Claudia asked if we knew what her name meant. With a sigh she said 'the lame'. Never mind, we were at the old cross stone (one of the earliest Christian carvings in the country) and The Parsonage was at the foot of the brae. There is no name or B&B sign but the old Parsonage is a home much-loved by walkers. Routes are regularly bent to take in a night at The Parsonage. The roadside episcopal church has been restored very pleasantly. Historically this was a Jacobite and episcopal region — and it suffered accordingly after the Forty Five.

It is amazing what tea and pancakes, followed by a bath can do to those who have tramped for nine hours. The supper table beat us as usual though. What contrasts that day had given: the plover-crying moors in the mist, the wonders of the Unich, bleak Loch Lee in the rain, the Hill of Rowan in rainbowed evening, the silver of waters which we had traced from threads on the brown tweedy heights to the wide satins of Glen Esk, the glitter of the trees, the birch trees that form a tapestry all down to Edzell. This is called the Glen of the Rowans but it is really the Glen of Birches. Tarfside too is haunted by history. The Fungle and Firmounth come over from Deeside and many a pony stepped out for the Clash of Wirren and the south with the local distillation on its back.

The Parsonage that night was given over to Challengers. I wondered what on earth anyone not involved would have made of the company. When we arrived at six it was to be greeted with 'We hoped you weren't coming'. Beds were at a premium — and we had booked many months before. Mary (Ray's wife) went in with Sandy and Claudia, I had the wee room, and David and Shirley Emerson the other bedroom. Shirley's brother Brian slept on the floor as did Eilir Jones, a young lad with 'a voice of silver and a heart of gold', and the Slawskis. There were two sittings for supper and late night tea and hot pancakes. The Parsonage is quite an institution; Gladys Guthrie spoils us all.

We had planned a rest-day anyway and it passed very easily, and usefully. Mary was up to cheer Ray over the last couple of days so we went with her down to Edzell where she shopped for Gladys and we visited the chemists to buy something effective for Claudia's big heel blister. We visited Edzell Castle, a red keep, with a surprising walled garden laid out by Sir David Lindsay. We were having a picnic by the river at the head of Glen Esk when Bob, Max, Ray and Chris arrived. Challengers seemed to be passing all day. The Guthries that night had fourteen tents on their lawn and there were three sittings for supper. Such a crush is not normal but came about because Terry Smith, the original organiser of the event, was 'retiring' and a dinner/presentation was planned for her two nights hence — so all the old hands had trimmed schedules to be there for that night. There were old hands enough at The Parsonage: John Needham, Ron and Joan Smith, the Barnetts again (Blair Atholl), Eric Grice, Chris, Ray, Max and Bob.

Bob, demonstrating Cumberland wrestling on the lawn, was my reveille, at 6 am. Ray and Chris, Bob and Max, Claudia, Sandy and I set off together for a hilarious morning's walk down the green glen of the North Esk. A stone had somehow found its way into my rucksack but was instantly noticed. I played along till the culprit betrayed himself. After a lunchtime brew Ray went steaming off but the rest of us could not resist a pause by a black pool on the Muckle Burn of Kiltrie. A treecreeper worked up the trees beside us. The main gorge further on had the odd name of The Rocks of Solitude. From the brae above we had our last look back to the hills before crossing rich fields into Edzell. The Panmure Arms was proving a popular meeting place. Mary had found Sandy and Claudia a B&B but I decided to push on that evening to Montrose so the next day could be spent at the finish rather than having to go home for the car in the midst of everyone arriving.

Ray and Chris walked with me for several kilometres of the twenty-two to go, then Mary collected them and they returned to Edzell. The Montrose steeple can be seen from twelve kilometres away and it just never seems to grow bigger. (If the event is ever short of a symbol or a logo I reckon that spire would do!) It was a blazing hot end to the day but we were 'sun-proof' by now so I enjoyed the tramp. Short of the finish I tidied up a bit and strolled in. The end is actually a very anti-climatic moment. The fun is participating, not finishing. After a brief chat with Malcolm Cullen who was in charge of Finish Control, I romped off for the train, collecting a Chinese carry-out to eat on the way. It was strange to be in my own bed at home again.

I drove north and reached Edzell at 8 am in time to join Claudia and Sandy at breakfast. Poor Claudia had been hit by some bug which was sweeping Angus at the time; several Challengers caught it. It takes something much worse to stop you when only twenty-two kilometres off the finish (with 265 kilometres behind) and Claudia staggered on with Sandy, Bob and Max. I drove past them several times and had brews or snacks ready when they passed — or when any other Challengers appeared. The Park Hotel buzzed all day with people finishing their crossings. We sat down 58 to dinner that night. I don't know when the ceilidh finished. Bob was just getting into his stride when we retreated to our tents by the eastern sea — which really was the appropriate place to finish.

BIBLIOGRAPHY

The Great Outdoors monthly magazine (each November issue) carries the best two accounts of high and low level crossings made the previous May (1979 onwards). *The Scottish Mountaineering Club Journal* has a coast-to-coast account 'The Jubilee Jaunt' in its 1979 issue, while the 1972 issue has Sandy Cousins's 'Hill Walking from Cape Wrath to Glasgow', a similar sort of expedition.

GENERAL BOOKS

MACINNES, D & K., *Walking Through Scotland,* David & Charles.
McNEISH, C., *Backpacker's Scotland,* Hale.
MACINNES, H., *West Highland Walks.* (3 vols), Hodder & Stoughton.
BROWN. H., *Hamish's Mountain Walk,* Gollanz/Granada.
BROWN. H., *Hamish's Groats End Walk,* Gollanz/Granade.
Scottish Mountaineering Club General Guides Series.

MAPS

The following 1:50,000 maps cover the UC 'bounds' but only a few would be needed in practice and planning is best done on a larger scale map. 25 – 30, 33 – 38, 40 – 45, 47, 49 – 54.

BENNET D., *The Munroes,* Scottish Mountaineering Club.
Information on the Ultimate Challenge can be obtained from the U.C. Organiser, 16, Glenbo Drive, Denny, Stirlingshire. (Please enclose sae.)

5

Corsica

CORSICAN CAPERS

I wrap my heart
on the starlight stair
and rest my feet by the silver stream.
I lay my head
by the overhang
I watch the hills
and I dream:

Dave Gingell

Corsica is one mountain place I keep returning to every few
years. It has the attraction of being an island, it has a
dramatic mountain world to explore, the weather is better
than in the Alps and it still retains a friendly, antique
atmosphere. Nothing seems to change suddenly or dramatically, despite politicians' promises, the odd Home Rule
gesture or even a French League Cup Final (this last is the
nearest to a revolution I think I've seen!). There are many
similarities between the Scottish Highlands and inland
Corsica, which only vaguely considers itself part of France.
(Sailing to Marseilles people say they are 'off to France'
which is like Shetlanders 'going to Scotland'.) Corsica has
had the same bloody history for the same reason —
neighbourly interference — only they have more neighbours. It was in a skirmish at Calvi that Nelson lost his eye.
Economically the island is depressed and relies on its coastal
tourist resorts to balance the books. The hills, like the
Highlands, have largely emptied of people. Corsica remains
one of the most attractive of all playgrounds for climbers
and walkers.

One regrettable change is the loss of the *bergeries*, the
bothies or huts used by shepherds, the equivalent of the
Highland *sheiling* or Moroccan *azibs*. These would be sited

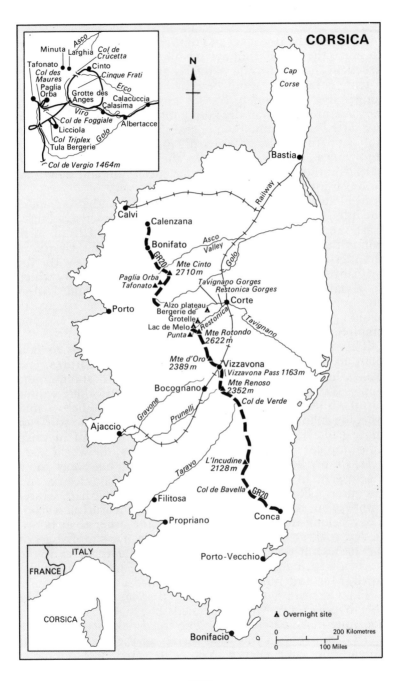

CORSICA

Minuta
Larghia
Asco
Col de Crucetta
Tafonato
Cinto
Col des Maures
Cinque Frati
Paglia Orba
Erco
Grotte des Anges
Calacuccia
Calasima
Viro
Albertacce
Col de Foggiale
Licciola
Col Triplex
Tula Bergerie
Golo
Col de Vergio 1464m

N

Cap Corse

Bastia

Calvi
Calenzana
Bonifato
Asco Valley
Railway
GR20
Mte Cinto 2710m
Golo
Paglia Orba
Tafonato
Tavignano Gorges
Restonica Gorges
Porto
Alzo plateau
Bergerie de Grotelle
Corte
Restonica
Lac de Melo
Punta
Tavignano
Mte Rotondo 2622m
Mte d'Oro 2389m
Vizzavona
Vizzavona Pass 1163m
Bocognano
Mte Renoso 2352m
Col de Verde
Gravone
Prunelli
Ajaccio
Taravo
L'Incudine 2128m
Col de Bavella
GR20
Filitosa
Conca
Propriano
Porto-Vecchio

ITALY
FRANCE
CORSICA

▲ Overnight site

0   200 Kilometres
0   100 Miles

Bonifacio

105

on or above the tree level and to them would come the flocks to graze the upper summer pastures. In spring they made excellent shelters for the wanderer and saved having to carry a tent. Now they cannot be relied on as the shepherds no longer live their lonely life for months at a time and the *bergeries* are either rapidly falling into ruin, or in a few cases, are tarted-up as holiday huts and therefore kept locked. In July and August their loss hardly matters. Rain is less likely and you can just sleep out under the stars, a joy in itself, but earlier in the year, May and June, it can rain and they used to be an interesting alternative.

May and June I reckon are the finest months to wander the hills, even if the weather is not at its summer steadiness. Last time we ran the meteorological keyboard from shrill winds through hail, sleet and snow to the bass chords of thunderstorms but scenically were rewarded with the brilliance of spring colours and the beauty of snow, which soon vanishes under the summer smiting of the sun. Unless you really revel in great heat, high summer is worth avoiding. Some practical experience of using ice axe and crampons is advisable for spring visits.

This is a skill every walker should have anyway as it is both an 'open sesame' to greater walking adventures, and makes life so much easier on lesser ones. In summer the upper slopes can yield vile screes and heart-breaking willow scrub while the *maquis* has been known to turn heroes into weeping maniacs. How much easier it is with the worst of those evils buried under snow, to be setting off in crisp dawn, up corries and peaks, or over passes, the world at its best, simply because of a few spikes under big boots and a magic wand in hand. There is no mystique about ice axe and crampons. They may be the tools of the hardiest winter climbers but they are also the weapons of the wariest walker. They belong no more to the one or the other than boots, stoves, rucksacks or anything else. They are simply part of the basic hill-wanderers' equipment. Use them and, the world of spring discovered, you will wish the months of April, May and June came several times a year.

The Corsican landscape is rugged so any aid, like being able to move on snow, is welcomed. The highest summits do not quite make 2800 metres. The 'yardstick' becomes 2000 metres, rather than the 3000 metres of the Alps. You will expend the same energy. You will gain a less populous solitude and have to be largely self-supporting. The rockier Alps are quite good training for coarser Corsica.

The peaks are, practically, somewhere between the Cuillin and the Alps. Perhaps the Julian Alps or the Pyrenees are the nearest to them in character. Quite a few of the major summits, including Monte Cinto (at 2706 metres, the highest), are quite easy ascents but in a wild and barren setting. You may well start from deep valleys with foaming rivers and grand forests of pine and beech but it is possible to wander, above the tree line, for day after day. Paths are fewer than in many countries and of vital importance. To go astray in the scented garden-tangle called *maquis* is no joke. *Maquis* is a scrub covering with all the friendliness of barbed wire. It is a stage worse than purgatory. Purgatory might describe the willow scrub higher up the peaks. Forcing your way up it is comparable to a caterpillar trying to traverse a hedgehog — from tail to nose! Add to this great gorges and precipitous ridges, acres of boulders and scree and you will realise Corsica is quite challenging. The GR 20 guidebook warns that it is not a place for the 'débutant'. It is best to have cut teeth on tenderer joints.

The GR 20 — Grande Randonée 20 — is one of the many long-distance trails established all over France. It is one of the toughest (there are 10,500 metres to ascend).and right into July snow may still lie on some of the cols and high places it crosses. Three weeks at least are required for its 240-kilometre length as it wanders from Calenzana (near Calvi) in the north, to Conca (near Porto-Vecchio) in the south. There is a guidebook, in French, to it and it is one of the few waymarked routes I'd actually recommend, for it is immensely varied in character and choice of route. This is Corsica's main problem in fact — there is far too much to do. If you like tough back packing with a feel of exploration to it, Corsica is the place. Even the GR 20 touches few villages or roads and its services are not those of other pedestrian motorways. The first guidebook had some comical riders to certain stages '. . . reaches a chalet hotel (the hut is not yet built)', 'this shelter was burnt down ten years ago, not yet replaced'. It is slowly being more organised but the landscape is beyond taming. It is not beyond spoiling however: bad roads, the lack of facilities allied to a lack of all sanitary or litter consciousness often makes 'popular' sites revolting.

Corsica is easy enough to reach with regular flights and some cheap bargains can be found. It is hardly worth flying only part way (to Nice, say), and a car is actually a mixed blessing. It was Corsica that freed me from the tyranny of a vehicle, even my much-loved, much-used camping car. You can take many local buses, trains and taxis before your bill passes what you've paid in car-ferry costs, petrol, servicing, insurance, documentation and the worry of having one's own car. Trains overnight down to Marseilles and ferries cross to Ajaccio or Bastia, the two big towns, and sometimes to other smaller places like Calvi. It is really no worse than reaching other remoter Alpine places — and there is a Mediterranean cruise thrown in! Ajaccio and Bastia are linked by a superb little toy train known affectionately as the *'Joliette'* which is both useful for access and fascinating in itself.

A small party of us was soon to be meeting up in Ajaccio. Because I had the car I'd brought all the camping and hill gear we would require. But it had broken down in France and now I had to leave the car to be worked on and somehow had to transport this load, by myself, to Corsica. It all worked out and the restful sea cruise was much appreciated. A flying boat landed across our bows as we entered Ajaccio. I also learnt that *Napoleon* was the last boat for some time, as after unloading, the boat was *'en grève'* (on strike — a new word for the emerging vocabulary).

There were expectant faces at the ferry's car-ramp as the team looked for the familiar blue VW — until I crept up behind them (via the passenger gangway) and wished them *'Bonjour'* — and could they come and carry the tents etc . . . *Bienvenue en Corse!*

The car lesson was learnt. It is now left at home. Without it I spend no more money and have far more contact with the real life of any country being visited. It is a fake convenience abroad. A backpacker should be able to carry everything he needs on his back, tent included, as we were soon to do in Corsica — a car encourages too much clutter.

We had one night at Ajaccio, the capital. The town was the birthplace of Napoleon Buonaparte and he has been transformed into a major tourist industry with the shops full of Napoleon souvenirs. We ate at the camp site as we had some reorganising to do and an early train to catch. The plan

plan was to base ourselves at Corte, at the centre of the island from where we would make different sorties. The run was superb, with Monte d'Oro (above the spinal tunnel) showing through the clouds and us sitting in comfort enjoying the views. It was a busy wee train. It goes under the Col de Vizzavona (1163 metres) then twists and turns madly down to Vivario, a perched, red-roofed hamlet dominated by its church, before just twisting and turning on to Corte. A taxi did two runs to the camp site which was set below the dramatic, cliff-top citadel. It was spick and span. The fields had just been mown so soup, curry and tea all tended to have additional roughage.

The morning was spent in the friendly old town seeking information and shopping. We were told it was a poor season for weather and that umbrellas rather than ice axes would be useful. I said we would be taking both! We packed in the afternoon and were tent-bound by rain all evening. However a taxi at 7.30 the next morning committed us to the wilds, regardless of the weather. It didn't take long to reach the wilds for two long valleys, the Gorges de la Restonica and the Gorges de Tavignano, debouch at Corte. We were driven up the former and the road was as nerve-racking as ever, a sort of single track without passing places. Our drive came to an end where a bridge had been washed away. It was stranded high and dry in one piece up a bank, where it had been dumped by an avalanche.

We tramped along with no risk of being run down, to our *howff*, the Bergerie de Grottelle. This proved quite a luxurious dwelling with tables and chairs and a roof high enough for lanky Martin to move about safely. The valley was deep-set between impressive walls which rose up into clouds. Lombarduccio was the resounding name of the nearest peak. The wet evening was passed round a fire of fir cones but a stutter of stars gave some hope of better weather.

Monte Rotondo (2622 metres) went surprisingly easily the next day even though it is the island's second-highest summit. The conditions were hardly summery and we followed our noses rather than any given route. The river was crossed by fallen trees and an hour of scrappy slope saw us onto a ridge bordering a corrie. A mix of alder scrub, snow and boulders lasted another hour but having outflanked things a bit to the Brèche de Cavaccioli (a gap on a spiky ridge) there was some modest scrambling to reach the Pta Galiera on the spine leading to Rotondo, which appeared as a fierce rooftop over a prow of precipice. We dropped down onto snow flanks and had a boggy tramp to the Collet Rotondo (2580 metres). It was a bit of an anticlimax then as the striking wall and roof could be gained easily 'from the back'. The central position of the peak allowed a good look round for, wonder of wonders, it had cleared. The descent was made mostly in one long bum-slide to the Lac de Cavacciole, a secretive glacier lake hidden in the octopus-arms of Rotondo. It was a fast, if wet descent. We just carried on down the corrie with no desperate vegetation ambushing us. By noon we were lying by the broom and crocus banks of the river opposite the hut, having enjoyed a good first walk.

In doubtful weather we set off to back-and-peak-pack, walking right up the valley to the Lac de Melo at its head. We left the tents by this circular lake and wandered on with our eyes on the Punte alle Porte but things went against our ascent. The scenery was given a wildness and loneliness by a fall of snow and our guide drawing of summer conditions did not convey the reality! We tried to gain a ridge above a higher lake but the gully up to it looked avalanche prone. The snow of the next gully slid off as we watched and very quickly clouds boiled up out of the Restonica so we were left cringing in flying snow. Even the easy flank had warning cracks on it. We retreated.

Our small tents were strong if not luxurious. I read up the guide by candlelight, looking for alternatives to higher regions. There was a storm overnight so the scoured landscape with its saucer of lake looked more like Scandinavia than the Mediterranean in the morning. By lunch time however the picture was quite different. The hot sun had come out and everyone was in shorts (the tents steam-drying over the Corsican pine branches), the air heavy with scents of flowers. We had spent the latter part of the morning tramping several miles down the valley, from the Lac de Melo, to the Grottelle Bergerie to the Tragone Bridge and up, up, a zig-zag path that fortunately kept to the shady side of a ridge. After an hour we found our eyrie and we were now lazing away a lunch break. A two-tailed lizard scampered over my legs.

Off again, we came on a stream resurgence, the Bianca

Fountain. I always find a full-grown stream bursting out of the ground an inspiring sight. What cold, clear drinking water it was too — and particularly welcome for a long uphill slope followed. This eventually led us not to a crest but to a plateau, an odd sweep of horizontals in a landscape of grim verticals. Most of the *bergeries* had been tidied up and were locked so it was obviously a popular beauty spot. You could tell that from the litter and the miles of ugly plastic water pipes running everywhere. The rain came on suddenly and hard, cutting off the song of skylarks and sending us scampering to the Bergerie de Cappellaccia on the edge of the Alzo plateau. We swept out a room and dined on the terrace with the evening clouds parting to reveal Rotondo as a fair imitation of Kangchenjunga. Cowbells and the splashing of water were the last sounds I heard before falling asleep.

Our descent back to Corte was memorable for we dropped steeply down to the Gorges de Tavignano and spent a day threading through their spectacular scenery. The path was decayed in places and a bridge across the river missing so it had its excitements. It also had its moments of bliss. Cistus, lavender and lilies made it a perfumed garden. The asphodel candelabras were at their best and huge saxifrages filled crannies in the rocks. There were so many flowers I just did not know them all. It was a contrast to come out of this rock-clasped world to the lushness of cultivation and then the bustle of Corte. Because it was Sunday there were seemingly endless carloads of noisy football fanatics.

We needed a day off to reorganise. Corte we liked very much and most of us used up more film there than on our walk. The citadel is perched perilously on rock and where at one corner the rock has weathered away, a tower hangs out over space — and over the camp site. Apart from exploring we spent several pleasurable hours in a favourite café planning our next walk from the Col de Vergio to the Asco Valley.

* * *

As buses were complicated we had to take a taxi up to the Col de Vergio. The driver was Corsican and cursed every stray cow and screeched round the many bends. We renamed it Col de Vertigo and were left there in a shell-shocked state. The col is 1484 metres high and the Porto–Bastia road is the only one to break through the mountains north of the road and rail line of the Vizzavona. South lay Rotondo and the Tavignano-Restonica valleys where we'd been; north, where we were planning to wander, weather permitting, lay Cinto, Paglia Orba, Tafonato and the Asco Valley, the biggest and best according to the books.

We contoured away from the col, glad to leave behind the messy signs of man (cafés, shops, chairlift, big wayside cross, piles of concrete or mechanical junk) but found the path was marked with yellow paint. This compulsive claiming of territory is one of man's less pleasant attributes; most animals leave note of their passing or possession — but much less obtrusively. The woods were splendid nevertheless: great pines below and birches so brightly green they looked newly painted and hung out to dry. We contoured round and down to pick up the Golo River, the main drainage to the east, which rose away up under Tafonato and Paglia Orba to the North. It was as delightful a valley as any with clear water and endless falls and many-hued rocks and took us to the Bergerie de Gratule. Here we found a convenient tree trunk jammed across the ravine, the stepping stones having been covered by the high water due to the melting snow. We crossed without difficulty and met up with the GR 20 which was clearly indicated by red and white marks.

The Vallon de Tula, as the Golo drainage was called, gave a grand highway into the big hills. It became progressively more snowbound as we steadily plodded up under our heavy rucksacks. There were huge areas bright with crocuses in flower. The Bergerie de Tula which we were relying on was a grubby hovel but there was a bedshelf for three and I slept on a pile of brushwood. It had been cloudy and cool, which helped the walk-in, but later there was a grumbling of thunder and it rained. The roof leaked so we re-laid its covering — a combination of plastic sheeting, old felt and a li-lo. We wandered off on our own for the afternoon and I went up a bump to the west to look to Porto and the sea. Ski tracks were not surprising, the upper valley had a Scottish glen feel to it — if you didn't see the twin bulks of Tafonato and Paglia Orba at its head, one on each side of the Col des Maures. We saw nobody, even in this more popular area, but few were daft enough to be out in such a period of unsettled weather or with the long-lingering snows. Fortunately most of us were quite at home on snow. I'd even say it improved things, for snow slopes are kindlier than scree slopes — as long as you don't slide off! The time we took protecting ourselves on snow probably equalled the time normally spent fighting scree or scrub.

It was freezing early, a pleasant change and we beat 'book time' to the Col des Maures. Paglia Orba is often called 'The Matterhorn of Corsica' for it has a huge point facing east (first ascended in 1919 by the English Finch brothers and a Norwegian friend — the first great route on the island) but the summit prow has a long cliff-rimmed plateau behind it which slopes west to the Col des Maures. In summer a gully of red boulders *('de tout calibre')* gives the easiest break up but today it meant using the rope, ice axe and crampons for a winter climb (on the last day of May), easier technically perhaps, but much more serious. There was a west top, then a hollow, the Combe des Chèvres (no goats today) before the slope up to the 2525-metre summit. It is quite a summit for, though we had ambled up the easy side we ended on a towering prow with a great deal of nothing all round it. North of us the crest is so jagged and steep it is known as La Grande Barrière. Beyond is the Cirque de la Solitude and the Minuta-Larghia-Cinto crest, higher and even more jagged in nature. The guide book seemed to have it right. Four German lads arrived, festooned in mountaineering gear and we assumed they had made some mighty winter climb, only to hear they had come up the next easy chimney along from ours!

Descending, we had a close view of Tafonato over the Col des Maures. Dare we try it? It is a high, thin, fin of rock with a big hole right through the middle and a frightful drop beyond. It is a spectacular, if easy climb rather than a difficult walk and we were not too strong a team with 'two oldies and one novice'. It would have to wait a bit anyway. Distant rumblings and blackening skies hinted at yet another storm. We hated going down so early in the day so traversed under Tafonato to gain the crest again for a peak called Capo Giargiole ('the gargoyle' someone suggested). This provided some good scrambling, reminiscent of the Cuillin but with several times the exposure, so the adrenalin flowed happily. Tafonato's west side was part of a west-facing world of towers and cliffs of impressive scale. Paglio Orba disappeared into cloud and we did not linger on our summit to become possible lightning conductors. We slid down a gully and were back at the Tula *bergerie* for afternoon tea. My last look out saw our col churning the clouds around while the *trou* of Tafonato was puffing out streamers in an odd fashion. An accentor hopped round my feet and a chough screeched through the clouds.

'The book says that in June a walking party might still be advised to carry one ice axe and a rope,' I read out to the other refugees.

We had had enough of our sordid bothy so decided on an easy peak and a descent to the Grotte des Anges (usually *'pas Anges mais Anglais'*) the historic camp and bivvy site with its view up to the 'Cervin de Corse'. We carried our packs up to the Col Triplex which lives up to its name, being a meeting of three ridges, and had an hour along to the Punta Licciola, an even better viewpoint than Paglia Orba, for Paglia Orba was in the view as well. (The real Matterhorn is the same. It is the best thing round Zermatt but *on* it, of course it is not seen!) The clouds began to boil up out of the valleys so after a snack on the Col Triplex we descended the other side. I think crossing a col to new country is far more interesting than simply climbing up and down a summit — heresy no doubt to some, but of much more ancient pedigree. The snow lay low enough to have covered the hedgehog willow so we did not have a struggle.

One gully merged with the next from the Col de Foggiale (the more usual one from the Golo) at the ruinous Bergerie Prugnoli and a path took us down to the big Viro river and the Grotte des Anges.

The *'grotte'* is a big bivvy boulder, used by generations of visitors, especially impecunious Brits, and beside it is a wooden shed. We opted for this and when a squall showed its roof was like a sieve we actually pitched our tent *inside* it. A bone-dry bivvy boulder up the hill sheltered me from another shower. I had gone off hunting caterpillars, the pine processionary being one of nature's curiosities.

It was Fabre, the great French naturalist, who studied them first of all and wrote the classic *Life of the Caterpillar*. There were quite a few 'nests' in the trees and I kept hoping to see a procession. The nest is a football-sized silken mass and may hold hundreds of caterpillars. You handle one only once for the web is full of hairs and these are an irritant (schoolboys' itching powder is made from them). The creatures themselves are poisonous. The notorious Borgias knew this and made use of them, birds know it and leave them alone. The caterpillars come out at night and go off, nose-to-tail, in a procession, the leader spinning out a silken thread along which they all march to forage and then follow back to the nest. So programmed are they that when Fabre enticed a line onto the rim of a tub holding a palm tree they marched round and round in an unbroken circle, for a week!

A London trio came and camped beside the wobbly shack. They were rather depressed at the weather and had had no successes at all so wondered at ours. We had to be fairly tactful in pointing out the difference lay in our rising a bit earlier in the morning! The weather had usually cleared by dawn to give a frosty clarity for a few hours and we had been up to use them. I left the others in the indoor tent and had a solitary night under my boulder. At first light a firecrest and a Corsican nuthatch were working up and down the pines outside. A woodpecker further off was knocking on the door of morning. For once it was a day of glory given. We were off at 5.30 am and only back at 3.15 pm but in between we stood on top of the island which meant, momentarily, on top of the world.

The pine processionaries were still promenading at the early hour of our start. We watched the light catch and slowly envelop the bastion of Paglia Orba. These golden early hours are hard to equal: the rich-scented woodland, the sounds and sights of little waters — it is a wholesome total made up of many delights.

We followed up the Viro river to its start but not far above the tree line it and all the 'foul screes' (*'pénible'* sounds even better) were happily buried under snow. Cinto is big rather than beautiful and toilsome rather than exciting so the snow was a bonus. We cramponed up under the red rocks and white snows of the Punta Minuta – Capo Larghia peaks, the most dramatic peaks of the area. Cinto is on the same crest but much further east and, jutting out from the crest between, was a radiating array of ridges falling to the south. This array was joined to the crest by a col, itself 2350 metres high, and on the other side lay a high lake with Cinto above it and draining down the Erco river. Only on reaching the

Col de Crocetta did we see Cinto. The Lac du Cinto was a frozen disc of ice, veined with cracks like a winter leaf. We gained the crest of the spine at a peak, the peak of the boulders (Pte des Eboulis) which, happily, did not reflect its name. It was back to Cuillin Ridge wanderings after that, interest eating up time, so we suddenly were standing at the summit. The Scotsman in the party grew quite loquacious: 'Nae a bad view at all' he conceded.

We could see much of where we'd been the week before. Rotondo was clear beyond Calacuccia and its lake, which lay down in the main valley where both the Viro and Erco rivers met the Golo. We all took photographs of Paglia Orba to impress our friends with casual 'Oh we climbed this peak too'. From Cinto it looked its fiercest — no need to mention the tradesman's entrance round the back. But what of Tafonato? Might we not try that tomorrow? The weather seemed to be staying clear this time. Success is such a spinner of optimism! We cheerfully bailed out sliding down the snow gullies into the Erco valley, which led us for several miles in the opposite direction to our base.

The Erco soon grew in size. We changed into shorts after a brew and found a path contouring above the valley. It crossed a bare spur with a *bergerie,* then became kindlier country after another ridge was passed and we were walking high above Calacuccia, west now instead of east. We were too high above any of the hamlets to try and shop for food or wine. A spring called for another picnic now that the sun was full in our faces, sizzling hot and quickly draining our energies. The Cinque Frati (Five Brothers) were jagged peaklets ending the last long ridge running off the spine and it took a long time, it felt, to shift it from being away ahead, to being above us, to being behind us. The traverse of the Five is a popular rock climb, but I would not have swopped it for our long day's tramp. What a difference the sun made — in more ways than one: you should have seen my nose! The sun set behind Paglia Orba as I was gathering bracken for another night under my boulder. We were growing short of food so blew the lot in a gargantuan meal. The pigs round the hut refused to eat our stale bread, so we toasted it and had it ourselves. The ants bore off the crumbs.

It was strange to set off up the Tula side again. There was a feeling of being owners almost, of possessing the landscape; it all seemed so familiar after just a few days.

Below the Bergerie Prugnoli we found a ten-foot line of caterpillars (about 120 of them) marching along their thread of silk. The trees were full of nests and some trees had been stripped entirely of their needles by the hungry creatures. They are not much loved by foresters. There was another area above the *bergerie* full of charred and gaunt skeleton trees, the result of a fire, caused either by a lightning strike, or by some careless human.

We followed the GR 20 paintmarks along the hillside up above the gorge to reach the Col de Foggiale after three hours of walking, then traversed across to the Col des Maures again. Some colourful figures appeared in the *trou* which indicated its scale nicely, but the thought of going up there was a bit intimidating. However, the good book told us that the *non-alpiniste* could reach the window 'with an ease hard to believe in such a world of verticality'. The actual hole is about 35 metres long and a third of that in height. It can even be seen from down on the coastal road between Calvi and Porto. We sat and worked out the route carefully, a change from yesterday when we went up and down Cinto without any book assistance. Someone suggested that here we had a 'mintin with a hole in it' and someone else capped that with the story of how, when the Royal Mint was shifted to a remote Welsh village, one of the London workers referred to it as 'the hole with the Mint in it'. We had something to eat as well but even procrastination had to end and we set off with just our cameras and the ropes.

The peak is clean, reddish porphyry (*à la* Buachaille) and a series of ledges criss-cross the east face, one conveniently entering the *trou* and continuing right on to the northern prow which is the route to the summit. Another ledge angles up to this one from the Col des Maures. We walked up it a bit then there was a bulge with a perched block which had to be stepped round. At once we were made aware of how the ground fell away. This feeling of 'exposure' (the technical term) intensified, for every step along was also a step upwards and as the ground below also fell away this also increased the tension. Yet it was easy enough. Only on the final prow did we rope-up.

The 'floor' of the window sloped, the view out was stupendous (to snowy peaks and a lavender-haze of sea) while the view down was such as one would normally have from a hang glider! We wended along to the prow where a small gap behind a rock thumb was filled with snow. The west side had much more snow so we tried to avoid it as much as possible. We gave thanks for Saint Porphyry as we scrambled up to the summit. It was, *sans doute*, the best of all the peaks of our two weeks of playing the Corse mountain game.

With lighter packs we headed out to civilisation in the afternoon. All too soon we were onto tarred roads but we cut corners and found old paths among the trees. Calasima, Albertacce, Calacuccia: the musical names led us back to the world of wine, fresh bread and honey, local cheese, cakes and coffee, before another scary taxi ride down the gorges to Corte. We had bought food while waiting so as soon as we were in we cooked another vast, but delicious, meal. It amused some of the other residents for we were living very much *al fresco* only having small tents. You can always spot the Brits on a foreign site by the state of chaos in which they live.

The site, and Corte, now felt like home to us and we hated the thought of departing. The fifteenth century citadel was Corte's symbol. Perhaps it was right that the champion of Corsican independence, Pascal Paoli, was born there. Boswell met him (and wrote his biography). We merely sat enjoying coffee and ice creams below his statue. A strangely sedate taxi took us to the station and we caught the toy train to Bastia and sailed overnight to Marseilles.

I collected my mended dormobile from the garage and as my AA credit vouchers neatly covered the bill I went on my way rejoicing. A tour in the Vaucluse, friends in Lyon, the bird sanctuary at Dombes, friends in Geneva. It took a week to reach the Channel. At the bird sanctuary there was one very English incident. A school party, all in uniform (caps, ties, short trousers and short haircuts) were admiring the mynah birds which bobbed and called out, 'Bonjour! Bonjour!' One kid turned to the teacher. 'Oh miss, aren't they clever. They can talk French.' Having bought several maps in Marseilles, there will have to be another Corsican visit (to justify that expense if nothing else) but there is plenty to fill many visits. My biggest regret was the minimal contact we had with local people on the island. The hills are not peopled and even the mountain villages are being abandoned for an easier life in the towns, or in France. Tourism is largely confined to the coasts.

So far I have never wandered in those southern ranges but the GR 20 calls and it runs through the Bavella landscape of pinnacles and over Monte Incudine so that will combine desires and no doubt lead to further dreams for further visits. Then there is Filitosa to visit, a prehistoric site with strange face-carved pillar stones and circles; there is Bonifacio on its undercut cliff-top, and how much more time I want just to look at birds and flowers. Oh, if one could buy time rather than thyme in the local market!

I don't know any place that can rival Corsica for musical names. There is an operatic ring to place names like Calacuccia, Vizzavona, Bastelica, Propriano, Vivario, Cucuruzzu. Just saying them is cheering. They sing of scented *maquis* and mighty mountains. Writing about them has made me restless in my northern eyrie. Maybe it is time to throw some gear in a rucksack and ring the local travel agent. 'Corsica? Yes sir, very pleasant place.'

It is indeed.

BIBLIOGRAPHY
CARRINGTON, DOROTHY, *Corsica, Portrait of a Granite Island*, John Day.
   This Corsica, Hammond, Hammond.
COLLOMB, R.G, *Corsica Mountains. West Col.*
FABRIKANT, MICHEL, *Guide des Montagnes Corses* (2 vols), *Corse* Michelin.
THOMPSON, I, *Corsica*, David & Charles.

MAPS
IGN maps at various scales are available. They are not as accurate or revised as sheets for alpine regions — so be warned! At 1:100,000 the island is covered in 2 sheets: Corse Nord, 73; Corse Sud, 74.

There is a 1 sheet map at 1:250,000 Corse, 1-16, useful for general planning. For walking the 1:50, 000 sheets are essential.

6

Ireland

ACROSS THE EMERALD ISLE

These are the things I prize
And hold of dearest worth:
Light of the sapphire skies,
Peace of the silent hills,
Shelter of forests, comfort of the grass,
Music of birds, murmur of little rills,
Shadow of clouds that swiftly pass,
And, after showers, the smell of flowers
And of the good brown earth,
And best of all, along the way,
Friendship and mirth.

(Henry van Dyke)

When I took Storm, my long-suffering dog, on a tramp from John o' Groats to Land's End there were many motives within the basic walk south through the British Isles. It was a mountain route for a start, keeping off roads as much as possible. In Scotland it played several games with the Munros (the listed mountains over 3,000 feet — still referred to in feet rather than metres) for we went from the most northerly, Ben Hope, to the most southerly, Ben Lomond and on the latter completed a sixth round of the Munros. (Not long ago a seventh round was completed in accompanying the dog round the last of *his* Munros — it's an infectiour game obviously.)

In England we walked down the length of the Pennines with a diversion to the Lake District to add the 3,000-foot summits there. Later we walked on westwards to Wales for its 3,000-foot mountains as well and so made a foot-link of the Three Country Summits: Ben Nevis, Scafell Pike and Snowdon. This has been done, occasionally, but as far as I knew nobody had gone on to tramp across to add the Fourth Country summit of Carrauntoohil in Ireland. Carrauntoohil

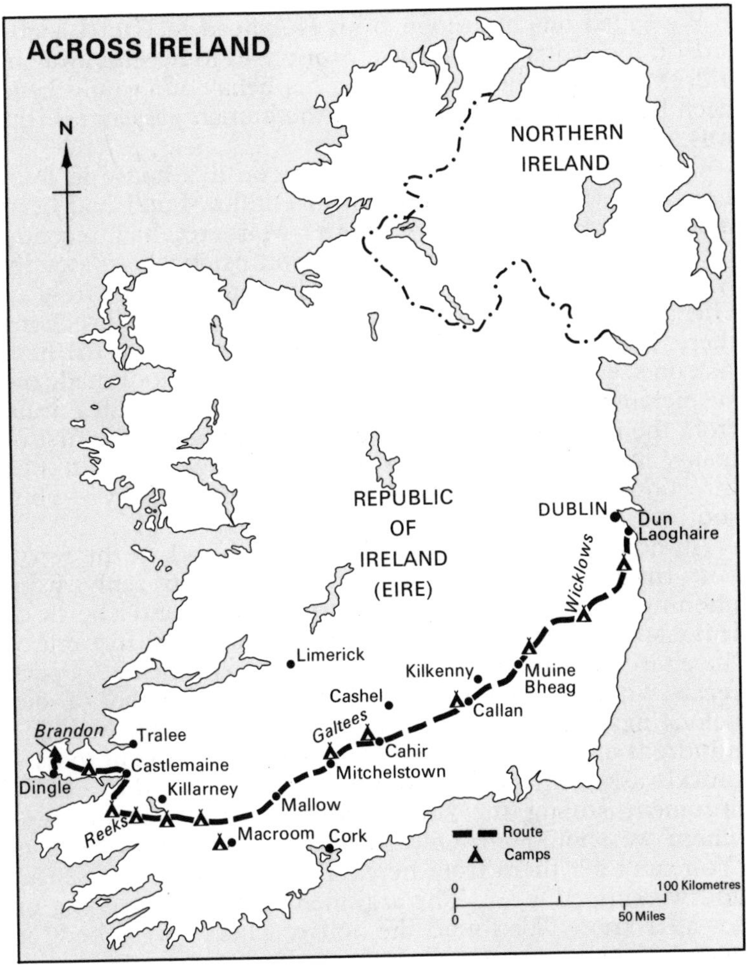
ACROSS IRELAND
N
NORTHERN IRELAND
REPUBLIC OF IRELAND (EIRE)
DUBLIN
Dun Laoghaire
Wicklows
Limerick
Kilkenny
Muine Bheag
Cashel
Callan
Galtees
Cahir
Mitchelstown
Brandon
Tralee
Castlemaine
Dingle
Killarney
Mallow
Reeks
Macroom
Cork
Route
Camps
0
100 Kilometres
0
50 Miles

(one of the Macgillycuddy Reeks) lies in Kerry, away in the west, while as far west as you could go is Brandon, also 3,000 feet. Two other Irish 3,000-foot summits lay nearer: we would add them all, on foot, in a grand hike across Ireland from coast-to-coast. Thus do we dream dreams and even put legs to them. There was a crazy logic you see in walking across Ireland even if it sounded daft in Killarney to say one was walking from John o'Groats to Land's End. The beginning was so very Irish.

We sailed one afternoon from Holyhead to Dun Laoghaire on the grotty *St Columba*. Storm had to be shut away in a deck cage for the crossing. As his behaviour would have been better than that of many of the human passengers this was a bit of an injustice.

Our immediate destination was a cousin's house in Dun Laoghaire, the ferry port south of Dublin, but I had been unable to contact her by phone. Margaret had recently moved house so there was some confusion about exactly where she would be — but as I had her new address in Glenageary I simply asked the ticket collector for directions there. He waved northwards, 'Just two stations up the line. Ask once you're there'. A hot tramp of half an hour made me suspicious as I knew the house was only ten minutes' walk from the ferry. We went in to a shop to consume the first of many ice-creams (an Irish speciality) and queried our directions. 'Sure, it's two stations from the ferry — but southwards!'

An hour after disembarkation we were back at the ferry: hot, tired and hungry. There was still no reply from phoning. I went in and bought a curry supper and a bottle of lemonade and Storm and I sat on the wall right in front of the church to eat and drink, glad to be rid of the heavy pack for a while. I had made the maximum spread of our belongings when the doors of the church opened and hundreds of people came out from mass and into our mess. I quickly asked directions again but this merely led to a lively argument among the congregation. Nobody could agree where we should go. One shrill voice produced the gem 'You can't get there from here!' I took a general consensus and we slipped away. The argument may still be going on for all I know. We found the house. There was nobody in and the neighbours knew nothing. Fortunately the people across the road did but it turned out that Margaret was away on holiday. We were ushered in and welcome tea was provided while they phoned the folk looking after and feeding Margaret's cat.

It took a few days to organise the trans-Irish walk. I posted parcels to several places with things like maps and film, spare clothing and food; I had a new stove to test, and Storm's 'Frolic' to break down into day-packs for the parcels. You don't just wander off if there is a specific route to follow and it takes plenty of planning and preparing. It is also vital for any big walking trip (or any other expedition) and many failures are due to inadequate preparations. 'If only I'd known . . . If only I'd done . . .' deserves little sympathy.

The Wicklow Mountains sprawl southwards from the very suburbs of Dublin and, as in Edinburgh, you can reach them along city bus routes. Storm and I however set off on foot and late in the day as it had rained hard all morning. We skirted the hills for 27 kilometres to a camp site at Roundwood. It was a beginning at least though we would have preferred to walk along the tops.

A dewy morning took us to Laragh and the Vale of Glendalough, a hidden valley of charm and historic interest, which is frequently buzzing with tourists — but not at 7.30 in the morning. St Kevin established a hermitage there about the year 619 and it was long a religious centre despite Viking raids, English interference and ecclesiastical squabbles. There are still some interesting ruins including a Round Tower.

A purely Irish architectural invention, these towers may have combined belfry with safety in raiding days for the doorway was always many feet above ground. No two are the same. I find them fascinating and later, having made this link of Four Country Summits on foot, I did a cycle link as well and took in the Isle of Man *en route* chiefly to see its Irish Tower at Peel.

There are two in Scotland (Abernethy and Brechin) and about 60 left in Ireland itself. Visiting them becomes quite a game too. In a hurry for the Holyhead ferry on one occasion a carload of us were determined to see Clondalkin Round Tower in the outskirts of Dublin first. We simultaneously hit dusk, rain and the rush-hour traffic and we had a poor map, but after much excitement we spotted the tower. After more excitement we reached it — only to find ourselves staring up at a factory chimney!

We wandered round Glendalough (its tower soars to 30 metres and has a conical roof), made tea by the Deerstone and saw ancient crosses at lonely Reefert church in the oak woods by the lake. Eventually we headed upwards to tackle the day's work. There was a rushing fall (Poll an Easa), and stands of big pines which gave welcome shade. Our track rose to nearly 650 metres to drop down to Glenmalure. Across this valley lay Lugnaquillia, the only 3,000-foot summit of the Wicklows, which we planned to reach by walking the rim of hills right round the glen. The quixotic one-inch map makes it look an easy matter. As contours are at 250-foot intervals it shows little of the landscape of bogs and braes and we took most of the day to round to the Lug. We met fellow walkers, the only ones of the entire crossing, and they asked us if we had walked through Bray the day before, 'We recognised the dog'.

The summit of Lugnaquillia, Percy's Table (3,039 feet), is a flat plateau. It was draughty so we wended on and pitched our tent on Slievemaan at the first handy water. We looked down the Ow River valley to an endless swelling of green hills, touched gold by the westering sun. A chilly night brought a cloud inversion which we came down through to the farmlands which surround all Irish hills. Beyond Hacketstown we passed the colossal dolmen of Haroldstown. Black horses careered round it in the blazing sunshine. Our route tended south of west after lunch so the roadside trees no longer shaded us. We sweated it out to Tullow and collapsed on the square with ice-creams. Every village seemed to sell soft ice-cream, a boon in that heat, and the heat brought a bonus in spilled ices lying on the ground. Storm became adept at finding these! In the evening, somewhere beyond the Fighting Cocks crossroads we camped in the corner of a field under a ruined castle.

The next day began as the previous one had ended: a pulsing sun punishing the pedestrians. Off the Carlow heights we had some clouds to give shade, but not for long. With hindsight, now, a longer route making much more of a swing southwards on hilly country would have given a more enjoyable walk. Between hill groups the Irish countryside is a maze of lanes, but hard on the feet compared to the higher wilds. In the intense heat of that day not even a Round Tower could tempt us off the easiest road westwards. We made it to Callan, an historical town but ice-cream took priority over ruins and a Paddy, served in the back of the butcher's shop ('Victualler' it said), was saddened by talk of the news of the day. The day before Earl Mountbatten and family had been blown up at Mullaghmore. I'd read this in a paper while crossing the River Barrow and was so stunned, walked past my turning to become temporarily lost. Women wept at the news and the feeling of outrage was profound. It could not but affect the day's enjoyment. We carried out our gallon container filled with water from the butcher/pub (I've met a bus-station/pub and even an undertaker/pub combination), bought a *brack* and pitched in a newly-cut barley field just out of Callan.

We had a third battering of sun. It was really just chance that this heatwave coincided with the longest section of Irish road-walking. It was still a long way to Brandon, never mind Land's End, and it would no doubt rain again, so we pushed on, by Fethard, dominated by Slievenamon of the Finn McCool legends to Cahir which means the *fort* and has one too. It was captured by Cromwell and has a typically bloody history but is well-preserved: ward within ward, battlements and towers, portcullis gateway, all above the quiet River Suir. We collected a parcel from the post office and had a brew by the river. Maps were re-parcelled and sent off and we pushed on, determined to be sleeping on the Galtymore Hills that night. Sun is best enjoyed by those sitting in the shade.

Even well up onto the hill slopes we could not find water. Every stream had dried up. A deep gully through an oak wood did eventually provide some seepage and we lingered in the cool depths, cooked supper and snoozed while the sun glinted silvery on myriad insect wings in the trees above. Storm found the energy to chase a red squirrel up a tree. The squirrel kept going but about three metres above ground Storm found the gravity barrier.

We carried water up above the tree line and camped with the sweep of plains below us. I could just make out Slievenamon in the haze. There was a real feeling of rewarded determination looking to that curtained east. There is no doubt that it is the hard roads that hurt for the next day was as long in miles and hours and considerably more in uphill footage yet, being over the open hills, we ended refreshed and strong. The sun was just as striking, but the heights were kissed by wind.

The Galtymore Hills rise abruptly on all sides. Galtymore itself is 3,018 feet, a weathered sandstone dome, the only peak to make the magic height, but there are plenty of 2,000 footers to emphasise the high promenade. The view is all downwards, to a patchwork quilt of green fields, stitched together with wild hedgerows, spotted with white farms, from whence the turf (peat) reek could even be enjoyed on the tops. The laughter of children floated up through the haze. I do like the Galtymores, known from many stays at Ballydavid Wood hostel at their foot (on the Tipperary side) but this was special; to range them from end to end, on a day of sunshine.

The going was rocky early on with vast new plantings on the flanks and a seemingly endless succession of bumps ahead till the cone of Galtymore appeared in view. O'Loughnan's Castle stood as a squat, square tower until, as if by magic, it disintegrated on approach into a crumbly conglomerate outcrop. Galtymore summit (3018 feet) is sandstone as was the Lug and as would be the Reeks and Brandon. Lyracappul, Slievecushnabinia and Temple Hill were all over 2,500 feet so the walk west kept the dramatic feeling of height. The inadequate map, the clinging haze and forest plantings made our descent line a bit of a mystery tour but I knew that when we hit any road it would take us in to Mitchelstown, our next post call. In Ireland they are now felling forests which have never been delineated on the maps. It does make for interesting navigation.

A stream proved to be dry and I groaned at the prospect of searching for water again (was this Ireland, I ask you, where even the cows have webbed feet?) but as we went down the gully we *heard* water and came on a bubbling resurgence of the vanished stream. Perhaps we were on the limestone country that has formed the famous caves just to the south. The weather pattern changed with dramatic speed and we fell asleep to the pitter-patter of million drops of rain on the thirsty earth.

The walk went from the sublime to the ridiculous the next day, the last in August. Having won our fight with the moating forest we lost a round on the road when a bull disputed our passage. In the middle of the square at Mitchelstown we sat in the usual state of re-organising our belongings (you fight every ounce of the way) when a garrulous drunk asked what we were doing. Eventually I explained I liked doing my Christmas parcelling early — an explanation which quite satisfied his enquiry. Two women then came along. One was blind and her sighted companion asked if I would allow the blind girl to touch the dog, 'so she can see him'. Storm, an eye-catching Sheltie, played up as a flattered dog can, while the delicate hands ran over his face and fur. 'Lovely, lovely' she quietly muttered. Storm licked her nose in return. It was rather touching.

Our route was forced back onto roads and the roads soon became rivers as the weather went from 'soft' to hard-soft. It was nearly thirty-five kilometres to Mallow by which time the rain was in the very marrow of my bones and Storm had become an untouchable. We went in to drip-dry in a pub in the friendly town. There was no camp site I was told and we walked on when there was a lull in the weather. While standing in the wet again by the Race Course a farmer offered us a lift to Millstreet or Macroom. When I explained our self-propulsion rules he said, 'No bother. No bother. I can give you a lift back tomorrow morning.' You don't look a gift horse in the mouth.

Millstreet had an International Show Jumping event the next day and so as beds would be difficult to find, we crossed the hills southwards to Macroom where we were left at the Castle Hotel with a return lift promised for eight o'clock the next morning. The hotel comforts were enjoyed and some good singing from the bar lulled me to sleep. I woke at two o'clock, conscious of a bell ringing on and on. It was not loud but it was quite irregular, utterly persistent — and damnably sleep-destroying. It was still ringing at five o'clock. I'd hardly slept and, when I did, simply wove nightmares round the insistent sound. Was I going mad and imagining it?

I slipped on some garments and set off to investigate. It was a bell behind the reception desk grille that was ringing. Was it an alarm? Why had no one appeared? My puzzlement was interrupted by a banging on the door. After a muffled cross-questioning I opened it to let a man in. 'By the saints you took your time,' he complained. 'I'm only a guest here,' I retorted. 'Ach, and so am I' he smiled sweetly and trotted off upstairs, quite sober as far as I could see. Storm wagged his tail at the fiend.

The eight o'clock lift back failed to materialise so I had breakfast and set off to hitch. A lift eventually took us to Millstreet. Its streets were packed with people, horseboxes and Range Rovers but there was no bus to Mallow. After an hour a reporter picked us up and we were dropped off at the spot where our overnight capers had begun. Then we set off — to walk to Millstreet!

We abandoned the direct road as one horsebox tried to knock us into the bramble hedge and I ambled along reading a book. At the top of the pass above Millstreet we discovered

127

the Boggeragh mountains were well-named. We struggled through plantings (not on the map of course) to gain bleak yellow moors which were blowing mists like the aftermath of a battle. Turf-cutting trenches and pools of water added to the effect and the rain came down in the heaviest deluge I was to know in the six-month walk. The hand holding the compass went numb with cold. We pitched the tent in self-defence. Rain sounds quite different from the warmth of a sleeping bag with a mug of tea cupped in one's hands.

It cleared later and I hung out the dog's towel to dry (I carried a towel for him but not one for myself). A brief stroll ended by climbing up Mullaghanish (2,133 feet) — having been nicely foxed as to scale by the summit TV mast. If legs ached, the heart danced at the explosive view west to The Paps, Crohane, Mangerton and the Macgillycuddy Reeks themselves. *'Thalassa!'* I yelled and raced the dog back to the tent.

The Clydagh river led us down but we diverted to climb Caherbarnagh which at 2,239 feet was the highest of the local hills. The descent was delightful. The air was pungent with the scent of bog myrtle and the roadside walls, taking on the wildness of Kerry, were thick with brambles and blaeberries. As I picked the upper levels, Storm was busy with the lower berries. The glen descended under the Paps ('the breasts of Dana') but the peaks we had been up were not mentioned in any book I looked at later. We had a break by the deep gorge, flood-noisy, spanned by Poulgorm Bridge before going on by Loo Bridge youth hostel, which is a converted railway station. The signal still stands by the platform to give it character. We camped some miles on, buried deep in a forest near a cheery waterfall.

Mangerton Mountain at 2,756 feet is really a sprawl of hills and the deeply-cut Glenacappul with its three paternoster lakes is perhaps only surpassed by the similar splendours of Brandon. We battled out of the forest onto the hill slopes but a coffee-break there was shortened by midges arriving as the wind dropped. Mist blew in but we went on to Stoompa over a landscape that was as rough as anything in Sutherland before it blotted out the spectacular land-scape. We followed the rim of Glenacappul. It ends at a neck beyond which the Devil's Punch Bowl bites in from the other side. A bearing over a tundra-like plateau led us to the summit cairn of Mangerton.

I was once told a tale about an incident by that cairn. An Irish lad reached it bang on two o'clock as he noticed from his watch. A couple of minutes later a plummy-voiced Englishman arrived and asked the lad the time. He put a finger to his lips, paused, peered all round the horizon, held up a moistened finger, patted the soil and then said, 'It will be two minutes past two by me reckoning.' The visitor turned to another arrival. 'Have you the time please?' The new arrival looked at his watch. 'Two minutes past two.' Re-telling the story later the Englishman said, 'I know they live close to nature in the west but that was fantastic. Telling the time so accurately!'

We navigated carefully down out of the clouds and the day took on a sunny cloak. Triangle Lake was turquoise blue and the mountains of the Reeks reeked till they cleared and lay sprawled among the many ranges of Kerry. Our delight was soon ambushed by the descent of Galway's river. It was a frightful landscape of tussock, bog and water. No step was safe and in fierce sun and a cloud of midges we found the easiest route was down the slabby river itself. It was worse than the Rhinogs, a roughness of route I'd only recommend to my best enemies.

When we hit the road we walked along to Ladies' View, a Trossachs-like 'honeypot' looking over the Lakes of Killarney. A sandwich and some liquid was welcome before we scrambled down to the Upper Lake. Ahead, and above, Carrauntoohil was catching clouds out of the blue sky. I began to feel unwell and a squat among the rhoddies convinced me my sandwich had had some unwelcome additives. We crawled along to the stream draining Lough Googh, set high on the Reeks, but failed to make this objective. Most of the night passed diving out of the tent. It was a vicious dose of the trots and rather spoilt one of the finest sites of the crossing.

I forced some food down to regain some strength, which would be needed for the traverse of the Macgillycuddy Reeks, though there was no urgency as I had gained an extra night's food supplies. The cloud was right down as we began zig-zagging up the steep flanks of the Reeks. We took it slowly with plenty of rests and kept on stuffing in rich foods. It worked. We gained strength as the day progressed, the clouds eventually broke, and Ireland's loftiest summit was a high point after all.

The Macgillycuddy Reeks are as interesting as the name would suggest. They would appear in any Top Ten list of fine days on big ridges to be enjoyed in these islands: a cross perhaps between the Mamores and Crib Goch. They present a big corrie to the west, cliff-girt, with a watery 'pair of spectacles' in the hollow and rimmed with the highest summit. Running east from this is the Ridge of the Reeks proper: an undulating array of steep-flanked summits, grassy walking over much of them, but ending in a double sweep of narrow rocky ridge.

Our slow ascent to the ridge brought us to the dip just before this trickier eastern end. I was thankful to dump the rucksack and rest awhile. The clouds began to tear apart. Loch Googh, now far below, gave the impression it was rushing along the hillside. The Reeks are a big barrier and in the prevailing westerly weather they catch all the weather the Atlantic cares to blow. They set me the problem of both climbing them all and journeying on beyond them. A big walk requires some "pacing". The Reeks were tackled so as to give the least amount of effort.

We set off to scramble along the narrow ridges to Cruach Mhor, one of the 'interesting' sections, which we then had to retrace back again. I know the Reeks well (so does Storm) so the route-finding was easy but the strong wind and my relatively fragile state meant the dog was often romping ahead and mocking my slow progress. The gritty sandstone gives good footing and later in the day we saw fossil wave ripples in the rock. St. Patrick's Cabbage (London Pride/Nancy Pretty) grows here in its wild state and we saw the giant butterwort and Kerry slugs among other interesting things.

Cruach, the end 3,000 footer, has a big cairn, or shrine rather, on top so it is unmistakable. It was back in 1969 that a school party of mine arrived out of the mist to find an old man up a ladder working on it. He had brought up ladder, cement, paint, water, everything. We debated whether this was intense devotion or a penance! He on the other hand thought we were all crazy and saw no point in walking in the hills. One of the boys joked that it was my job so I was paid to do it. 'Ah, that makes it all right then.'

We kept to the crest all the way back to the rucksack. In one place the ridge narrows to a mere blade of rock in thickness. Puffing under the rucksack weight we took on the rest of the Ridge of the Reeks, very different in character, being grassy underfoot. It is grass with the minimum adhesion however and plenty of divots showed where others had gone flying. The flanks plunge down steeply on both sides and small 'eyes' of water are set in the sockets of the deep corries. It is grand walking. Several summits are over 3,000 feet. At the col before the final cone of Carrauntoohil there is a gully, the Devil's Ladder, which descends to Hag's Glen; this is the tourist route to the top of Ireland — definitely a penance!

We considered camping as there is a good spring high on the final cone of Carrauntoohil but it was still very windy. We brewed instead and continued round the narrow rim to the Caher peaks of the splendid western corrie, then came back to the rucksack and up to the cross on top of the highest summit of all: 3,414 feet. We raced for it but just failed to beat the arrival of cloud. We collapsed in the lee of the cairn. A few minutes later the clouds broke all round and above, but not below, so it gave that brilliant effect of flying over a sea of clouds. You could have heard my whoops of joy back in Dun Laoghaire!

Beenkeragh (3,314 feet) Ireland's second-highest summit, jutted through the clouds so we chuntered down the face to the col and tackled its chaotic ridge of sandstone structures direct (they can be flanked), enjoying the scrambling and the glimpses down through the clouds to the lochans below. Beenkeragh was the third big hill round that corrie but we continued round the rim to take in all the 2,000-foot summits as well. The wind was sheeting the water off the lochans but we swung off towards Killorglin and somewhere under Skregbeg found a breezy but not too breezy knoll for the tent. It was a midge-free evening and I enjoyed the eyrie-like view down to the sea and the hills running out along the Dingle Peninsula to finish at the bold shape of Brandon. Beyond Brandon the next land is America.

The exposed mountain site caught the wind when it rose to a gale in the night so I had another night of little sleep and set off rather blearily, for Killorglin — the first place of any size we had seen since fleeing Millstreet. We ate our way down a brambly turf track. At one stage a cow blocked our way so I gave it a whack. It politely stood aside and it was only looking back that I saw it was in fact a bull.

At Killorglin we picked up our last parcel. A packet of muesli had punctured so things were a bit dusty. It was good to pull out the last map of the crossing. We walked round to Castlemaine at the head of the estuary of Dingle Bay so perhaps the actual coast-to-coast ended there but, with Brandon, perhaps my favourite mountain, still ahead, a last 3,000-footer of all those outside Scotland, that romantic summit was my planned ending. The Reeks had kept back a great torrent of cloud all morning but this eventually spilled over and the afternoon turned misty and wet — 'moist' was the local comment on it. Rather than traverse the Slieve Mish range, the backbone of the peninsula, we kept to the quiet road below the worst of the weather. The hedges were often composed of tall fuchsia bushes and the verges were of montbretia. In Murphy's Bar the locals were speaking Gaelic. We really were in the west.

Inch Strand juts out at right angles from the land: six kilometres of dunes onto which the Atlantic surges in splendid rollers. We camped after a search for water, and there was no difficulty sleeping that night with the surf lulling us to sleep, just as it does at home. I liked the spot so much that we took a day off just to relish the setting, a barefoot day of bliss for me, with Storm racing about like blowing bracken as he chased sanderlings along the edge of the foam. We walked to the end of the Strand and back. On a wall someone had scrawled: 'Dear Inch must I leave you? I have promises to keep. Perhaps miles to go to my next sleep.'

Suddenly I was aware of another ending. Brandon was not far away now. Soon I would be racing (if Irish buses and trains can be accused of anything so uncivilised) back to Dun Laoghaire and the ferry, to pick up the John o' Groats to Land's End walk on Snowdon. The length of Wales (Snowdonia, Rhinogs, Cader Idris, Plynlimon, Rhayader Hills, Brecon Beacons, Black Mountains, the Wye Valley) and the surprising South-West of England (Mendips, Quantocks, Brendons, Exmoor and great coastal walking); all that still lay ahead, most of it new country to me.

The familiar has an altogether different hold on the affections. The Dingle landscape of the magical west was loved of old. Must we leave it indeed? West, west, where the best dreams lie? I did not want to finish the walk across Ireland at all.

It took several weeks before the last sand vanished from our camping gear. We left Inch in an ominous calm, with sky, sea and even land pastelled in shades of grey. The forecast was for 'occasional showers'. The fuchsia hedges on the coast road were three metres high in places. We swung inland to Anascaul and the surprisingly named South Pole Inn. Tom Crean once owned it and he had endured polar adventures enough. He was awarded the Albert medal for saving 'Evans of the *Broke*'; he was in the party that recovered the bodies of ill-fated Scott and his companions and he was one of those who made the boat journey with Shackleton (also Irish) which is one of the greatest survival stories of all times. As we left the village the morning milk was coming in by ancient donkey-cart and modern mini-tankers. Shy children on the way to school could have been those of Winthrop Young's poem *Brandon Bay*. The very air smelt of sea. The walk was all but over.

We reached the heights by Lough Anascaul to discover a big area of quite dramatic hills (some day we will return to walk their full length) with the bonus of that vast seascape round them. We climbed one or two peaks as we wended towards the Conair Pass, a hill road that cuts off the Brandon peaks, as it claws its way from Dingle town to Cloghane. It is overtopped by big cliffs so I was keen to reach it before the weather broke. With one hill to go the rain began. It did not stop for sixteen hours. Nor was I helped by the vital section of map being erased along a fold. Somehow we made it down the precipitous slopes to the road, but the peaks leading to Brandon direct were inadvisable in the wild conditions. We flanked down and round to the Owenmore Valley to reach the great eastern corrie of Brandon where we would camp. I optimistically thought we might still have a sunset view from the summit. The furze-bright fields were saturated. The 'shower' went on as if determined to wash Brandon away before we could climb it. We squelched up above Lough Cruttia 'the harp lake' hoping for an anti-midge breeze. There wasn't one. Up on the next shining level, near Lough Nalacken 'the duck lake', a clear stream among red boulders and a sea view to the strand at Ballyheige were irresistible. 'Camp here Storm!' I yelled. 'Five hours of rain is enough for man, dog or ducks.'

We pitched the tent slowly and carefully in case there was

a storm later. The tea came to the boil while we did so. I took off my soaking boots, then the blessed Berghaus waterproofs that had kept me bodily dry, and dived inside. As I set about demolishing tea and cake I began to feel stinging bites. It was not midges this time; we had erected the tent on top of an ants' nest! They were soon swarming over everything. There was nothing for it but to re-garb and set up camp all over again a few feet away. The rain rained. All evening. All night. Did I say Brandon was my favourite mountain?

Pushed to have a favourite hill in these islands it could well be Brandon despite the frequency with which it throws the distilled Atlantic at its devotees. It is such a romantic mountain as well as being a spectacular one in various ways. The west means so much in Celtic lore and this is the most westerly 3,000-footer of all. On a clear day they say you can see America which, given Brandon's weather, is perhaps difficult to gainsay. More historically it was from Brandon Creek that St Brendan, Brendan the Navigator, set out, long before Columbus or even Erik the Red, on a journey that took him to the continent of America. His spirit pervades the place. It is his mountain. He had an oratory on the summit (you can see the ruins to this day) and the easy ascent from Ballybrack is still called the Saint's Road.

St Brendan was born near Tralee (at the inland end of the peninsula) in 483 and founded monasteries at Ardfert, Brandon and Clonfert. His monastic rule lasted virtually till Norman times and he made evangelical journeys to Brittany, England and the Scottish Hebrides. One of the vanished churches on St Kilda is named after him and there is a Brendan Creek in the Faroes. Ireland was a beacon when Europe was plunged in the Dark Ages. The Romans never crossed the Irish Sea to settle and much of Irish history has been the continued saga of trying to be free of outside interference. History is largely the past painted up as propaganda. A walk through a country is a useful education.

The Brendan Voyage by Tim Severin is a fascinating account of their reconstruction of the sort of boat Brendon would have used, and their successful voyage in it to America. The romance continues.

'Showers, of a continuous nature' was a term I once heard on the radio. I now knew what it meant. The rain only stopped at 8 am — a sixteen-hour 'shower' I suppose. My sodden bank-notes were dried out during breakfast and both Storm and I were amused by a wagtail landing on the tent. We watched a tracing of little footprints through the fabric but eventually the bird found the slope too steep and slippery so went slithering down in an undignified manner, swearing something awful. Apart from keeping a few items to nibble during the day we finished off every bite of food for breakfast. A brief lull in the weather let us see Kerry Head and Brandon Bay but the day soon reverted to being wet and wild.

A more dramatic path to the summit begins at a shrine at Faha above Cloghane and skirts round and into the innermost corrie, then toils up the headwall to gain the rim just ten minutes below the summit. We joined this Pilgrims' path after traversing along above the cloud-hidden paternoster lakes. In the corrie the wind was so violent that it sent me sliding along the glistening slabs of rock yet the headwall was calm, every nook bright with flowers. The climb up is brutal. Motoring-style warning notices were in evidence: *Aire — cnoc gear* (care — dangerous hill), which one of my kids suggested meant 'engage low gear'. The wind caught us up again as we gained the rim and I struggled up to the summit leaning at an angle. The dog did not seem to be affected by the gale.

Brandon is 3,127 feet. We crouched in the ruins of Brendan's oratory for a snack. An ugly cross made of what looked like scaffolding was definitely a twentieth-century structure. Several mounds are probably the remains of beehive huts from the saint's time and there is a choked well. On May 15th, St Brendan's Day, pilgrims still ascend the mountain, though I doubt there are many as the 20,000 reported in 1868. We saw nothing of course on that storm-blasted summit but I could recall other days: an April frost-magic ascent; an October heatwave, swimming from lochan to lochan; a September traverse ending on the great cliffs of Brandon Head, *curraghs* tiny dots in the silver glitter of sea three hundred metres below our perch. I could recite a litany of names of places about us: the Three Sisters, Smerwick Harbour, Ventry Bay, Mount Eagle, the Blasket Islands, Dingle . . . I gave Storm a portion of chocolate. Brandon was Brandon and if the weather had to be imperfect then it was all the better that it was all the worse.

Fine hills deserve big storms. 'Dog, you are well-named! Shall we call you Monsoon now though?' Storm just grinned. He is very hard to live up to.

We descended the Saints' Road to Ballybrack and walked into Dingle. It was the weekend so we had to wait till Monday for a bus to Tralee and the train to Dublin and the local train to Glenageary, two stations *south* of Dun Laoghaire. That night we went to a play at the Gate just to add a crazy contrast. Then it was only a ten-minute walk to the ferry. I refused to return Storm to the flea-ridden cages and sneaked him into a quiet lounge instead. 'Sure, but he's a gorgeous fella.' He's a natural diplomat too. On hearing what we'd been doing the steward just said, 'Do you tell me that now?' in tones which hinted at doubt if not disbelief. 'You don't meet dogs taking a walk across the country every day. You'll be having to write a book about it.'

Well that happened eventually and two chapters of *Hamish's Groats End Walk* tell of the Irish days. It is retold here because, with longer hindsight, it was one of the most varied and enjoyable big walks I've ever done. It was so characteristically Irish. Doing it again I would keep south from the Wicklows to the Blackstairs Mountains, Carrick-on-Suir and the very fine Comeragh Mountains and so come to the Galtymore Hills by the Knockmealdown Mountains and, of course, follow all the hills out along the peninsula to Brandon. May or June would be the best weather months (it occasionally rained on Storm and me you'll have noticed) and east-west is the most rewarding and romantic direction to travel. The combination of fine hill country and such friendly, hospitable, human places between makes for much of the enjoyment. You can't help enjoying Ireland.

You may never manage Nanda Devi, or even St Kilda, but this is only a ferry trip away. If you try it you'll find Irish miles are smiling.

Page one: Castle Campbell above Dollar with the Ochils beyond. These were the hills where one boy discovered the adventuring that lay in walking.

Left: The Old Man of Storr on the island of Skye, perhaps the strangest place one can walk to in Scotland.

Above: Sandy by Loch Morar on the first day of the Ultimate Challenge crossing, a wilderness that surprises many in crowded Britain.

Below: In mountainous Corsica looking to Paglia Orba.

Above: The Macgillycuddy Reeks in Ireland with Hamish's dog Storm who accompanied him on the walk from Dun Laoghaire to Dingle.

Right: The first view up the Quebrada Santa Cruz on the trek round the Cordillera Blanca.

Overleaf: Nanda Devi seen up the Rishi Ganga gorge on the spectacular walk to the Sanctuary.

Below: Norway: on the ascent to the Svartisen ice cap just north of the Polar Circle.

Previous page: The Cascade d'Ouzzoud in the High Atlas mountains of Morocco — one of the most varied and scenic landscapes for long walks.

Above: Mullach Bi on St. Kilda.

Below: Dunkery Beacon, the highest point of Exmoor on the Somerset–Avon walk.

BIBLIOGRAPHY

Ireland has an incredibly wide-ranging literature. The following are just some practical titles of use to walkers and a few of the books I consult most frequently on related topics.

BROWN, H. M., *Hamish's Groats End Walk*, Gollancz and Granada paperback.

HARBISON, P., *Guide to the National Monuments of Ireland*, Gill & Macmillan.

IRISH WALK GUIDES: A series of six regional paperback guides to the major areas.

1. *South West (Kerry)*
2. *West (Connemara)*
3. *North West (Donegal)*
4. *North East (Mownes)*
5. *East (Wicklows)*
6. *South East (Tipperary/Waterford)*

(Outline maps and descriptions)

HAYWARD, RICHARD, *In the Kingdom of Kerry/Connacht/Where the River Shannon Flows/Etc.*

KILLANIN, LORD & DUIGNAN, M.V., *The Shell Guide to Ireland*, Ebury Press.

LYNAM, JOSS (edited), *Irish Peaks*, Constable.

MOULD, D., POCHIN D.C., *The Mountains of Ireland*, Batsford.
Ireland from the Air, Batsford.

MULHOLLAND, H., *Guide to Eire's 3000-foot Mountains*, Mulholland

PRAEGER, E.L., *The Way That I Went*, Methuen.

MAPS

An index of maps can be obtained from The Ordnance Survey, Phoenix Park, Dublin. For walking these will be either Half or One Inch to the Mile. They are often well out of date and inaccurate. John Bartholomew also produce maps which can be more useful for general travelling.

7

Norway
A TOUR THROUGH NORWAY

There is no satisfaction so intense as victory over some of the savage forces of nature. Better for the moment than vice royalties or garters or millions is the joy of making the first ascent of some hard peak, or sailing a boat through a tempest.

(John Buchan, *A Lodge in the Wilderness*)

It has been my good fortune to visit Norway on several occasions and my better fortune to have enjoyed more than the normal ration of fair weather. Being of the north, Norway's weather can be wet and wild, the all-too-brief summer 'topped and tailed' by winter snows and darkness. As an enthusiast for the northern isles of Scotland it is not surprising that Norway is so attractive: it is our north magnified, our grandeur glorified, our small tunes given the splendour of Sibelius.

The country impresses in so many ways and forms: colour, company, wildlife and the people have all contributed to my memories being pleasant ones. There are shocking contrasts of jutting verticals and sweeping horizontals; the colours of summer are boldly displayed, then they burn in the fires of autumn and grow subtle under winter's power. This tough land and sea scape has bred a vigorous people who live in the remotest corners and whose boats ply the furthest fjords. In Norway we see the wildest north of Scotland exaggerated: the glaciers are still gnawing into the mountains, the rivers are mightier, the sea lochs grander, the forests more extensive.

The most convenient crossing to Norway is from the Tyne and we have usually travelled by car ferry from there to Bergen. Scandinavian countries are all shockingly expensive so we have always taken tents with the dormobile — and laden the poor wagon with food. The roads are

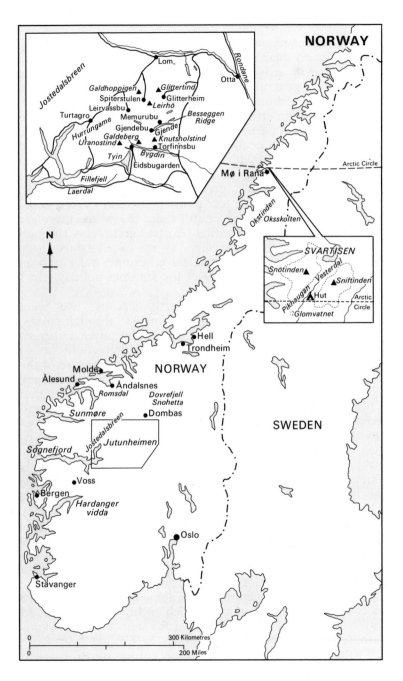

NORWAY

Jostedalsbreen

Lom

Rondane

Otta

Galdhoppigen
Spiterstulen
Glittertind
Leirvassbu
Leirhø
Glitterheim
Turtagro
Memurubu
Besseggen
Ridge
Hurrungame
Gjendebu
Gjende
Galdeberg
Uranostind
Knutsholstind
Torfinnsbu
Bygdin
Tyin
Eidsbugarden
Fillefjell
Laerdal

Arctic Circle

Mø i Rana

Okstinden
Oksskolten

SVARTISEN

Snøtinden
Vesterdal
Sniftinden

Pikhaugan
Hut

Arctic
Circle

Glomvatnet

N

Hell
Trondheim

Molde
NORWAY
Ålesund
Åndalsnes
Romsdal
Dovrefjell
Snohetta
Sunmøre
Dombas

SWEDEN

Søgnefjord
Jostedalsbreen
Jutunheimen

Voss

Bergen
Hardanger
vidda

Oslo

Stavanger

0   300 Kilometres
0   200 Miles

139

sensational (many are unsurfaced) but there is relatively little traffic on them so motoring is an interest rather than a necessary evil. All camp sites are immaculate as is the landscape in general (a contrast to Corsica) while ferries, mountain huts, shops, garages, everything one uses in fact, seems to function efficiently. Many people speak English so it is possible to make more of the personal contacts. There is a touch of Swiss neatness in the farmlands and, as in Switzerland, every useable acre is seen as a precious asset for much of the country is rock and water, ice or trees. (The area of water is actually greater than the area cultivated.) The wildlife is northern too: many of Britain's rarest birds abound in Norway, reindeer still roam the wilds; there are arctic flowers. The Polarcirkel (Arctic Circle) cuts through the country two thirds of the way up its elongated 1770 kilometres. To reach that magical milestone and climb an ice-cap was a major objective of the summer holiday trip I describe.

The walking was varied, partly because we were frequently heading up to summits as well as through passes, and we met, as in Corsica, with a belt of vegetative nastiness: thickets of willow and birch scrub which could be as impenetrable as the *maquis*. The forests though were of the north: spruce and pines and birch and great open plateaux of arctic-like appearance. Frequently it was views *down* that astounded and it is no wonder that the sea became, and remains, the easiest highway. There are 33,800 kilometres of coastline. The valleys are usually gouged U-shaped examples of glaciation's work in the past and hanging valleys make it a country of waterfalls. To build roads at all is remarkable but there are a surprising number toiling across this landscape of mighty ups and downs. The lack of tarmac seldom matters for the roads are well maintained. As they may be under snow from November to May it is economic and practical to have them without a surface. It is not really fun on a cycle for the ups and downs never stop, tyres cut into the surface or, if the roads are dry, dust becomes a problem. There is a lot to be said for Shank's pony.

We had a 'secret weapon' which helped to ensure we had a successful trip in a summer which most people reckoned had been a poor one. We lived by our altimeter-cum-barometer: when it began going back we headed down from the wilds and motored on to the beckoning north, when it began to rise we stopped in whatever range was nearest and enjoyed good treks and climbs. It worked a treat. There were five of us in the big-hearted, overloaded camping car: two Davids, one mercurial Ian, one quiet Stuart and the old man.

★　　★　　★

An overnight sail took us to Bergen. When we came on deck we discovered we were passing granite reefs which lay like whales with, here and there, a fur of vegetation and the holiday weekend huts of the fanatic outdoor people. Water in summer and snow in winter, the Norwegian is still a great outdoor activist. Everyone seems to have a *hytte* (hut) on the islands, or on the *fjell* or both. I remember once skiing on the far side of the Hallingskarvet, north of Finse, and feeling very much like a polar explorer, when suddenly I was overtaken by a family: mother, father and three kids, the youngest being towed on a saucer-like sledge. They soon vanished into the glitter ahead and I only caught them up because they had stopped to use the shovel that had been strapped on mum's pack. In that waste of white they were digging down at a very particular spot — their *hytte* lay there. It had a trap-door in the roof. 'We come most weekends' the seven-year-old boy explained. 'Everyone goes *langlauf* in Norge.'

I tried (without success) to think of neighbouring families at home who would consider such an activity as a casual weekend pursuit. The other extreme surfaced as we lined the rail after our filling *smörgåsbord* breakfast.

The others went off to see Bergen's famous aquarium while I went to photograph the *Statsraad Lehmkuhl,* a full-rigged ship now permanently based there. To my nautical joy I discovered the lumbering *Amerigo Vespucci* was also in port. This looks like a cross between the *Victory* and *Cutty Sark* and has a crew of several hundreds of Italian apprentice seamen. After a coffee by the fish and flower market near the Hanseatic houses of the old town we paid a quick visit to Grieg's home. Trollhaugen was interesting as it let us see a house interior: it was all wood, the great building material of Norway. Grieg's studio was perched above a fjord and must have been a pleasant place to work. The composer was small and to reach the keyboard of his piano sat on a thick book. It was still there: Mozart's piano sonatas. On the way out we also stopped to see the Fantoft *stave kirk*.

Stave churches are like the Scottish brochs or the Irish round towers in that they are a unique architectural structure, characteristic of the one country. Even they are of wood, which is partly why only 30 remain from an original 800 or so. They are small, for construction depended on the length of tree trunks available. Four massive posts (staves) were set at the corners and on this the pagoda-like structure was raised. Everything was wood, even tiles and nails. Christianity was new when they were built and the older pagan designs were incorporated on doors and walls (entwined beasts and flowers), while fierce dragons' heads jut from the roof tops. The interiors were richly painted and many of the altar pieces especially have survived in museums. Norway is full of museums, parks and sculpture. The people *show* their delight in where they live. Bergen, though the second city, has a cheery grace to it. The Fantoft made us *stave kirk* collectors. It was fascinating. David noted the church was not on its original site — which lay some days to the north. It had been taken to bits, transported, and set up again at Bergen. Oslo, the capital, has a stave church from Gol. 'Just like playing with Lego!' Ian commented.

We had to use two ferries to spend that night at the Vike camp site on the Romarheimsfjorden. The second ferry comprised a half-hour sail in the pale evening light (in high summer there is hardly any real darkness) through typical fjord scenery: islands and cliffs, cheeky patches of cultivation and clouds and snows high overhead. We had chosen a fairly quiet route rather than the popular one to reach the Jotunheimen, our first area for walking and climbing, and were rewarded with a delightful landscape.

The geography is hard to convey. Nowhere else is like it: so wildly complex, yet lived-in, and criss-crossed by road, rail, water and foot communications. While we had come for the last, the others proved equally interesting. The fjords are both barriers and aids to travel. South of the Bergen–Oslo railway is interesting but less spectacular country with a heavier-populated southern coast. North of the railway the next big feature is the mighty Sognefjord — 183 kilometres long! A branch of the railway line descends to the fjord at Flåm, a route which is a must for rail enthusiasts, being the steepest track in Europe, while off the main line lies popular ski country. North of the Sognefjord lies the Jostedalsbreen, Europe's biggest ice-cap while, eastwards, really in the heart of the country, is a continuation of many waters and mighty mountains — the Jotunheimen.

East again, beyond these mountains, the landscape relents and road and rail communications sweep up north-west from Oslo to Andalsnes on the Romsdalsfjord. Between the Jostedalsbreen and the Romsdalen is the heart of the fjordland: a jigsaw pattern of water, quite bewildering in extent and with so many superb places one could explore. Norway's drawback is man's shortage of years. It needs several lifetimes of exploration. After several visits I still have to drag out maps any time I try and recall episodes. The thousands of -*dals* and -*fjords* become quite confusing. Even the maps are not too accurate but to map the country at all is an achievement. Norway comes back to me in a series of vividly-coloured pictures so it is these kaleidoscopic memories that are described, rather than any guidebook attention to detail. It is probably the most rewarding trekking ground in Europe. Our first camp site, a small field tucked in below the cliffs, looked out on a smatter of islands in the fjord. There was a white-painted wooden church. Some blond children came round selling strawberries. As I lay listening to the drum of rain that night I was already renewing my delight in being back in Norway.

The next day we had to use four ferries, simply to work up to the head of the Sognefjord. To reach the first we made an early start with a 500-metre pull up a valley (all misty heights with water gliding out of the clouds), several minor fjords to motor round and then a wait as we were too early. Ian tried to fish off the pier. Some fish were brilliant blue and others were gold-spotted. They were quite safe. We crossed to Lavik on the north side of the Sognefjord and turned eastwards for the rest of the day. When the road could no longer cope, despite hairpins, tunnels and being built over the sea, a ferry would portage us a few miles along, or even swop sides. We ended up at Øye at the foot of Lærdal. On the most southerly of the fingers of water the Sognefjord reaches into the heart of the mountains. It is all mountains. There are no gradual approaches, no foothills, no mental preparation; precipices rise sheer out of the sea and when the clouds moved there was usually a hint of snow visible on the heights.

Lærdal in the sun was a mix of crags, gorges, trees and waterfalls. One fall called for photographs: then we had a coffee stop to see the Borgund *stave kirk,* perhaps the best of them all. It is a fascinating place. Six roofs with wooden tiles rise, tier on tier like a pagoda, and from the corners the crosses and dragons' heads arch up. The proportions are so right that it is difficult to judge the scale.

After the road from Gol joined ours we swung up onto a real *fjell* landscape (the Fille-fjell). It was speckled with snow and the greens were spring-bright. Craggy noses of rock separated many blue eyes of tarns. The world was clean-gleaming and scented. We had arrived in Slingsby country: the Jotunheimen.

One of the great classics of mountain literature is W.C. Slingsby's *Norway, The Northern Playground.* His first ascent in 1876 of Store Skagastölstind (2406 metres) one of the country's highest and most difficult summits was an historical event. His daughter, married to Winthrop Young, made a centenary visit in 1976. Slingsby by himself more or less created mountaineering in Norway. For Norwegians climbing is a minority game to this day. If you live and work there, mountains are part of life, so climbing them for fun is unnecessary. Mountaineering is really a form of escapism for country-deprived urbanites. Most of the early exploration of the Jotunheimen, 'the home of the giants', was the work of botanists — a breed even more foolhardy than mountaineers!

It was the poet Vinje in 1857 who coined the term covering these mountains, an apt one with more than 200 peaks over 2000 metres and scores of small glaciers and lakes of all sizes. It was Slingsby's high praise of the area that brought us in to the Gjende – Bygdin – Tyin lake country rather than to the western Hurrungane of the Storren. Walking and easy peaks rather than climbing was our plan. In a landscape that combines Lake District, Iceland and Yosemite there is plenty of scope for all forms of activity. We had a long lunch break by Tyin's blue waters. Massive crags fell into it beyond. I wandered about in a glut of bird and flower spotting. Ian and Dave thought Uranostind looked like the Matterhorn. 'Maybe we could climb it.'

Someone read from an old guide: 'fearsome precipices on both sides . . . west face considered unassailable, ' but it had been first climbed by Slingsby. It went on the list.

The road went on through and down from Tyin to Bygdin, ending at Eidsbugarden hamlet which was busy being developed so had everything from tidy hotels to hovels with odd tents and decorative flagpoles. There was a bust of Vinje, the poet. We camped on a great area of a heather species which only grows in one place in Scotland; our door faced along the lake. We traced the map on the hotel wall and planned a three-day trek in best Slingsby style. The weather however deteriorated so we shifted to a quieter, no-fee, spot by Tyin ready to abandon the area or go as the barometer hinted. A walk locally produced alpine catchfly, bistort, roseroot, butterwort, cassiope, azalea, catsfoot, sorrel, cloudberry, gentian, mouse-ear, and dozens of others. I didn't mind the rain.

The barometer changed dramatically so we were back at Eidsbugarden early to make sure of sailing on the *Bitihorn*. It was a bit like the *African Queen*, with an awning and a big, fake, funnel. It had a great turn of speed and sliced along the upside-down mountain reflections in style. About 18 kilometres along the lake we landed at a jetty — Torfinnsbu — and *Bitihorn* sped off for the east end of the lake. There were a few huts, no people, and an ambushing sense of overwhelming solitude. Our plan was to cut through the hills northwards to Gjende by the Svartdalen (Black Glen) and then return direct to Eidsbugarden, a triangular trip, with one side already accomplished by the sail.

It was warm work in the sun as we breasted the slopes and ridges to gain the pass but we were rewarded with a route as fine as any, anywhere. I described it in my log as a cross between the Lairig Ghru and the Llanganuco. Beyond the long, level central section rose Knutsholstind (2340 metres), sharp and shapely, while on the west side were ranked chunky hills with glaciers embedded in their flanks. We made a dump of our gear, brewed, and set off for the pointed peak. It was not a hard nut to crack: the initial slope was like trespassing on a garden rockery, then there were bands of slabs, wet from melting snow patches, before we came on the waymarks of the normal route. It is comforting when one's chosen route turns out to be the proper way. A good rocky crest led to the exposed summit. The north ridge was jagged and the east side held a big glacier. We had found the one chink in its armour. When I noticed the height I realised we were on one of the biggest peaks in Norway. 'This hill's in the Top Twenty' I said. The weary Davids didn't doubt it.

The biggest hills of Norway lay north of us while west, like cloud on the horizon, lay the ice of the Jostedalsbreen. A piebald world of rock and snow lay below us; with the turquoise lakes we were linking the only real colour. Ian shot off down fast so there was tea ready at our cache. We had soaked dried vegetables while away and forgotten all about them. 'Has beans?' suggested Ian. Paths, while clear, are not 'made' like stalking paths so the walking can be rough and wet. There were mosquitoes to discourage dawdling. I jotted down my feelings: 'An arc of terminal moraine clearly seen. The path kept up left so the descent, when it came, was brutal. A birch forest was full of warblers and noisy rustic bunting. The flora unwound again — you could gauge height by the flowers. A redshank bleeped at us from a lochan. A wobbly bridge and wet meadows landed us in the true heart of the area, Gjendebu. A bliss of cool shade. We pitched our two tiny tents by the path to the jetty. Dave hobbled in just in time for supper. His boots were hurting. Ian suggested that with two Daves in the party this one should be 'Boots'! We drank pints of tea each, before, during and after the meal. It was a 10.30 pm bedding. Quite a day.'

A cuckoo woke us at the late hour of seven o'clock. We had needed the sleep and voted for some more that day. The Veslådalen gave us a gentler exit, with many a look back at the lake ('next time'), and near a tarn on the watershed we pitched the tents in a sunny nook for a lazy day. I read much of the time to work out our future programme but joined Dave for a stroll up Rundtum, the nearest hill. With a name like that, it had to be climbed! Reindeer were lying on snow patches to keep cool.

The view along Bygdin from Eidsbugarden is dominated by the peak of Galdeberg, so we set off at 5.30, minus David Boots, to climb this. A valley led to a frozen lake below its north side and we were able to scramble up a ridge onto the bouldery summit plateau. The view was as dramatic as we'd expected with Bygdin directly below us. We reversed the ascent route and a yell from a great way off ensured Boots had tea ready for our arrival. We, not Boots, enjoyed the walk through a lunar landscape to the sudden lushness of the lake again. We threw everything into the waggon and drove from Eidsbugarden back to Tyin and along a smaller track round its north end — aiming to camp as close as we could to Uranostind. The Koldedalen was a delight but all too soon the road was blocked by snow so we pitched there beside a stepped waterfall. The pool below it glittered like fish scales from the low back lighting of evening. It was a site of perfection, and that is a description I seldom use. If walking and climbing is good, the stops between can often be better still.

It rained in the evening but we pinned our faith in the barometer which was still high. My alarm woke me at 2.30 and it was cold and clear. I roused the others and began breakfast work. We roused Ian again and were off at 3.30. The road was well blocked though this was mid July. The season for the hills is really just July and August with perhaps a bit before and after in good years. We rather liked the late-lying snow. Our early start allowed us to tramp up on its frozen crust rather than squelch through bogs or fight scrub. David Boots finally conceded defeat 'at the hands of his feet' and retreated, saddened at missing such a walk and worried at the price of new boots — if we could find some. (It was trips to Norway that turned me to the light, comfy, completely waterproof footwear that most Scandinavians use. They are like mini-wellies and after an initial outcry Bogtrotters and such are now used in gentler Britain. They must have saved much agony and many tons of Elastoplast. For years I became 'wellie-boots Brown!') We came to an area of tarns and a corrie which led us up to the tongue of the Uranosbreen. The glacier had receded since the map was drawn and the then snout was now a growing loch, one to add to Norway's million others.

It was a 'dry' glacier which meant bare ice, visible and firm, rather than dangerous snow which may cover crevasses. We donned crampons and wore them to the summit. The glacier gave a long, gentle plod till we were passing under the twin peaks of the mountain, an east flank, which caught the sun, and had softened. We went right round to ascend the north ridge, keeping on its west side as long as possible, but the last 1650 metres was an exhausting flounder in sun and soft snow. The summit was reached along a thin ridge with exposure such as the others had never met before.

We had some food but didn't linger for the sun would be working on the snow all the time. We floundered down off the summit cone and then bumslid a short cut down onto the flanking glacier. Avalanche debris had fallen to cross our up-tracks and we hurried slowly down the glacier, then did a round and down, still on snow, to valley level, at Uradalsvatn, a lake which was still frozen. It was desperately hot walking back to the VW; Boots made lashings of tea and we flaked-out for a couple of hours of sleep. The perfect site then produced mosquitoes. We fled out to Tyin and on and on till we found a camp site that was not too busy. We washed sticky clothes and had a swim last thing. The sun drove us out of the tents by seven the next morning. As there seemed to be a high stuck over Norway we decided to have a look at the other end of the Bygdin-Gjende lakes.

A rough track took us to the east end of Bygdin and we photographed 'our' Galdeberg and then the *Bitihorn* as she sailed in front of the peak of the same name. A stiff *up* and a long run *down* in the car took us to Gjendesheim at the east end of Gjende. The place was packed with cars and a boat stood at the pier. When we heard it was leaving in twenty minutes we wiggled and barged into a parking space and had a mad packing. The *Gjende* gave an idyllic sail up to Memurubu, passing under the Besseggen Ridge, the scale indicated by tiny coloured dots of people. Memurubu was a Slingsby base. What would he make of it now we wondered? We booked in to the tourist hut and had a room of clean, fresh wood, so typical of its kind. This area in particular has many huts, linked by marked trails, and it was our poor-Brits status rather than anything else that kept us camping most of the time. Many of these huts (as good as hotels in many cases) are run by the Norwegian Mountain Touring Association (DNT) or by some thirty local associations with reciprocal rights. They are rather like the Austrian Alpine Club Huts in operation, some providing full board even, while others are spartan, but welcome, bothies. There are also some well-placed youth hostels so one's own hostel association and the DNT may be worth joining if making extensive walking tours. My day at Memurubu went in flower-hunting. There were so many new Alpine or Arctic species. I added thirty to my list and, incidentally, met a bluethroat, wheatears, wagtails, dippers and plenty of waders. The gravel by the shore was sheeted with catchfly and the willows were big woolly bushes. I followed a busy trail of wood ants for 200 metres to their metre-high nest. A paddle across the river was icy, but supper called! We ate to repletion and sat in the sun over coffee. The last boat came and went. The hut book had surprisingly few British names in it. Martins nested under the eaves and the wood of our room radiated heat long into the night. It was a pleasant spot. 'Why do we bother walking?' Dave asked.

Breakfast at seven o'clock was one answer. The usual Norwegian table, laden with breads, cheeses, meats and fish, had us eating to capacity (and Ian beyond it) so we had to have some exercise. Gjende is dominated by Besshö and we climbed this in the morning, a rather Ben Nevis type of plateau with big cliffs on one flank. The sky turned grey and we almost welcomed it as a relief from the smiting sun. We collected our rucksacks again and followed a track along, 700 metres above Gjende to the Besseggen ridge. At a col, the Bandet, another lake (the Bessvatn) abuts to the north so there is water on both sides and you teeter along a Crib Goch-like ridge between. It was wild and dramatic. The Bessvatn looked like Loch Hourn, even to the curtain of rain sweeping across it. *Gjende* on Gjende looked like a toy boat. The scrambling led to the Cairngorm-plateau of Veslefjell from which we raced the rain down to the waggon at Gjendesheim. The rain won by ten minutes — and then we found the car was boxed in.

We looked at the barometer. As it was down (a long way) we motored north. As the weather stayed very mixed for some time we ended up motoring right up to the arctic circle, a journey we originally intended making by train. David bought boots in Otta on the great north road, the E6. We were sad to leave the Home of the Giants but on the way back we ran west from Otta to Lom and then south up the Visdalen to Spiterstulen, a site between Galdhöpiggen and Glittertind, peaks which take turns at being Norway's highest mountain depending on how much snow covers them! (They are both on 2470 metres.) We took the latter in on a round walk using the Glitterheim DNT Hut which lies a day's walk north of memorable Memurubu. Store

Memurutind, Leirhöe, Styggehöe, Store Smörstabbtind and other hills were also climbed so we did not do badly out of the Jotunheimen.

A day or two later, with a rising barometer, we prepared for a two or three-day trip in the Dovrefjell to take in Snöhetta (2278 metres), for a long time thought to be Norway's highest summit. It is still the highest in the country, outside the Jotunheimen. Its gentle lines arched into the blue west of the E6, not far from Dombås, where the Romsdal-Alesund road heads off. It had been just visible from the Jotunheim summits. It once had a reputation for remoteness but a five-hour walk-in now leads to a hut, the Reinheim, which we planned to use. We would climb the peak and walk out then, or the next day.

As soon as we pulled out of the birch woods by the main road (Siberian jays, nuthatches, nutcrackers, treecreepers) the view became huge with distances. It was almost African. We picked up the Kaldvella glen for a while but then had to cross its river where a bridge had been washed away to take the Stroplsjodalen to Reinheim. A couple of *saeters* with cows or ponies were the only signs of man. Glacier-gouged tarns were attractive. The Reinheim Hut wasn't. Madame in charge had no English, no smile, no welcome. She might condescend to see what she could do if we came back at nine o'clock that evening. We went to brew but she shrieked at us for this so we crossed the nearby river to eat and plan. It was only 11.30 so we decided Snöhetta was the important item, a five-hour round trip we had read.

It is a very easy walk with the way marked with big T symbols in paint. It was a bleak and barren landscape with miles of boulderfields and, here and there, a dash of vivid blue water as if the lakes had fallen from the sky. Nearing the top, crowds of scantily-clad Norwegians were coming down. Perhaps the hut was full. It was the first ascent where we'd met other people and an elderly man on the summit was not too polite about 'the old witch' in the hut. Boots grinned: 'I thought it was maybe us.' He was delighted to be walking in comfort again. 'Skint, but skipping!'

The summit was cluttered with a weird army building but the view was vast. We enjoyed recognising Jotunheim summits to the south, while to the west lay the massed might of the Romsdal peaks. There and then we decided to visit them on the way south. Some day too, I would like to walk through to them, from this area, which would give a five or six day tramp, finishing in the 'Yosemite of Norway'. The Romsdal is a mighty climbing area so even if the walking is harder than usual it is worth the effort to see such splendid peaks as the Romsdalshorn or the Troll Wall, the highest precipice in Europe; or to walk and sail the dramatic Eikesdalsvatn; or go up the Trollsteig road with its eleven hairpins and a skyline of the chessboard peaks of Bispen, Kongen and Dronniga; or to visit Ålesund, the 'Venice of the North'; or perhaps take a trip, as we did, in a Cessna seaplane and view it all from above. As there is an English-language guide to the Romsdal I'll skip our days there. It was near the end of August by then and we needed candles at night and set off with gloves and balaclavas in the morning. The summer is brief. Meanwhile it was a long way to the Polar circle and even a long way back to the road off Snöhetta. We decided it would be pleasanter not to become one of the Rheinheim dwarfs.

The descent was helped by sliding down all the snow edges and patches we could find. At one stage we nearly shot into a startled reindeer. This time we remembered the peas we'd left soaking and these together with instant potato and a tin of tongue, soup, and apple flakes made our supper. After coffee we set off on the five hours out. We set off a bit too soon after eating so all had stitches. The sole of my left foot was smarting and a plaster went on the blister. We had one stop to photograph a group of ponies and foals. They took to Dave for some reason and our best shot was of him surrounded by the creatures, wondering how he could escape. When the Stropla River joined the Kaldvella we had a brew stop. There were baby bluethroats and pipits and a ptarmigan family about. Cuckoos no longer called. Insects by the million glittered in the sun but, fortunately, they were non-biting!

I dealt with my raw sole: a rim of swabs and a dressing over it all. That relieved the pressure and for the five kilometres left we sang through a list of songs without repeating any. We came down in the evening, tired and content with our 50-kilometre walk.

Trondheim filled the next day. Its ugly suburbs were forgotten as we found a town of many good things. I went to the Maritime and Natural History Museums but everything seemed to close at 3 pm. The cathedral (begun in 1066) had some of the brightest and best stained glass I have ever seen. We left by an old mechanically-lifting bridge and stopped for the night in Hell. Hell was wet. I've a slide of Dave in Y-fronts cooking breakfast under a brolly. I don't remember much of that day as I drove virtually non-stop from 7.30 am to 3.30 pm, a strain on the bumpy roads, but it took us into Norland and added 425 kilometres to the journey. (The total was to prove 4025 kilometres as we returned far south to Oslo on the way home.) We knew we had gained the north because the mosquitoes became man-eaters.

Fed up with the E6 we turned east and spent the morning heading northwards in Sweden rather than Norway. Soon after re-entering Norway we turned off on a rough 45-kilometre side road leading to a remote hut under the Okstindan, whose highest summit, the Oksskolten, is the highest in northern Norway. Its first ascent was made less than a hundred years before, an indication of the remoteness of the area. It is a small ice-cap and was a good preparation for the Svartisen which was to come. We went to bed with mixed hopes of success as it was cloudy and wet. Having slept in, I discovered a clear, cold morning at six o'clock. We shot off, even though the barometer stayed pessimistic. The instrument was right of course and eight hours later it was quite foul but, by then, we were up and down, well inside the book's nine hours. A thunderstorm can lend wings to the weariest feet!

A waterslide came down into the valley from our peak's northern glacier and by going up the edge of this, or on it, we avoided the clawing birch scrub, even if we had some slippery excitements instead. At the top instead of a glacier we found an area of piled up rubbish and a lochan: the snow had retreated considerably since our map was made. We put on crampons for the ice and went up the edge and then right across under an icefall to use its newly-bared lateral moraine as an easy ascent line. Once above the icefall we were on the ice-cap proper and went up it on the bouldery edge. We just failed to gain the summit ahead of the clouds but could peer down a big north face or out over the snow dome with odd *nunataks*. It suddenly felt like an arctic world which made it new and exciting for most of the party. 'Let's get to Mø tonight,' Ian pleaded.

Mø i Rana had been a magical name to us. It is the major town just south of the Polar circle and from there we would launch our main trip into the grim-sounding Svartisen (The Black Ice), the largest icefield in Arctic Norway, which was as far as we'd get towards the north. A third of Norway still lay beyond, the genuine 'land of the Midnight Sun', the North Cape, the border with Russia. Mø was an uninteresting place but the friendly tourist office had maps and information to help our scanty home-grown information. We drove out to a camp site and packed in hope. The weather had been poor all summer so maybe we would have to walk *through* rather than *up*. The Svartisen is divided into two separate sections by a deep valley, the Vesterdalen, and to gain this was our first task.

A succession of dirt roads took us into the back of beyond and when the last track petered out at a farm, we walked. The farmer could speak no English so we left a note on the van. It was grey and cloudy and the route gave a good imitation of a steamy tropical forest. We had a haul of 8 kilometres up to a lake, which was desperately hard work. I can't recall ever sweating so much yet no skin could be left bare or it was pounced on by mosquitoes. The Glomsdals-vatnet outflow suddenly vanished into the ground, the only evidence we noticed of this being a famous limestone area for cavers. Later we must have passed the entrance to a system which has been followed for over 2,000 metres. I bet cavers don't have to suffer mosquitoes.

After rounding the lake we lost the path in the jungle and floundered before finding it again. It went brutally up from a *saeter* to round the prow that guarded the end of the Vesterdalen. The valley had two levels so to speak with the river down in the basement and a long ledge giving a sort of balcony for our purgatorial promenade. This shelf was the Pikhaugane on the map but became Piggygane to us. (It was a swine of a walk.) It was strange to see purple saxifrage still in flower and a white-tailed eagle patrolled overhead. Ian suggested it was really a vulture waiting for us to peg out. When we came on a tarn with a hut we decided we must brew before anything else. The Pikhaughytta was occupied by two English lads who were still in bed. The hut was furnished and pleasant so when they declared they were departing we were glad to move in. It would be the perfect base — and safe from insects. The afternoon was wet but an evening clearance allowed a quick recce to a spur above the other end of the tarn. It was strange to stand on limestone features and look over a world of glaciation. The hut book was full of English names, all there for the caving, apparently the best in Norway. The night was crisp and cold. We were staying all of 300 metres inside the Arctic Circle, one ambition fulfilled.

It was an up at 3, off at 4 start to a day which was to yield a sixteen-hour hike, the hardest of our travels, but we returned with the scalp of Snötinden. All we had to go on from the guidebook was this bald statement: 'On the main glacier lie Snetind (now Snötinden) (1599) Sniptind (1591) and Istind (1577), which are the highest peaks. They have all been climbed, but there are no reports.' Our ignorance yielded some adventurous bliss. Luckily we had bought a newer 1:50,000 map in Mø. Our older 1:100,000 did not show a lake, over a mile wide which lay in the middle of the valley and was its dominant feature. It was quite impassable on the west side as cliffs fell into its waters and a glacier snout pushed down to deposit icebergs in its blue waters. We had to round the lake on the east and somehow break up onto the snow dome of the western ice-cap. It looked desperate, and dangerous, with defences of cliffs and hanging glaciers and even before that there were the rivers.

A mile on from the hut a whole series of streams came down into the valley. One had a fine fall and all gave tricky crossings. We then battled down birch and willow slopes to the bouldery edge of the big lake, the Björnefossvatnet, and round to where the Vesterdal waters poured into it in a braiding of four separate rivers. We managed to hop across one river, forded a second but the next two were serious and called for the rope. We were very glad to have practised the specialised techniques of river crossings beforehand, last Christmas Day, in the River Carron below Gerry's famous hostel at Achnashellach. A deluge had produced a waist-deep spate there and clad in little but our waterproofs, we worked out the systems. Launching someone on the end of a rope is disastrous if he falls over: he is then held under! A continuous loop is used so whichever man is crossing is held above *and* below and can be fielded quickly. (E. Langmuir's *Mountaincraft and Leadership* is one of the few books available covering this topic.) We stripped off and had a good tussle with river three but number four only needed a handrail rigged up. In Ian's phrase they were 'brass-monkey deep'.

An iceberg was grounded offshore and had been so undercut by waves that it looked lke a blue mushroom. We scampered up the moraine deposits beside the Björnefoss in an effort to warm ourselves again. The river, after all, was just melted ice. The hard uphill work began after that, giving perhaps the best of mountain fun, the choosing of a line up unknown territory. It 'went' which was the main thing. We cairned much of it as we dodged along rakes or up granite steps. We ate our lunch below the final slabs across from a cold, blue snout of hanging glacier and actually saw a chunk break off and crash down the cliffs into the valley. A long traverse took us onto a rock ridge that curved up onto the ice-cap. We had won through!

A snow dome led us safely above the glacier we had been dodging. Its summit was a *nunatak* (a rocky islet as it were, in a sea of ice) and from it we looked out over the snowfields of the ice cap. It would be twenty kilometres across at least. With the signs of a front coming in from the sea we pushed on over an intermediate *nunatak* to the bigger snow dome of Snötinden. It was well crevassed and even the lively Ian was silenced when he put a foot through the snow above the depths. The summit was a shock for there were boxes of buildings and piles of aerials, batteries and such like for some new construction. Nobody was there and we assumed it had been carried in by air. Our devious route had taken eight hours and it took as long to return even without going astray down all the slabs, ridges, rakes and gullies.

We cut down more directly to the river above the *foss* and where boulders split the flow, had another full-scale roped river-crossing. Stuart managed to go under but his clothes were well wrapped inside his rucksack. The river was waist deep and flowed with impressive force. Boots didn't think this would do his cold much good. We dispatched Ian ahead to start supper and followed as fast as weary legs allowed. The slopes down to the lake were heavily scented with blossom. We hoped we could cross all those streams where they merged into the river but it was too dangerous and we had to haul up the jungly, insect-ambushing slopes. Feet were wet and tongues dry when we stumbled back to the 'Piggy-hutta'. Someone had been in and tidied the hut during the day — even cleaning our dixies. The weather was reverting rapidly and we fell into bed with no thoughts for the future except sleep.

We enjoyed twelve hours of it. Dave managed to go a full twenty-four hours without leaving the hut and during that time we met some Norwegians camping nearby. Ian went off with their girls to do some potholing. As the others resorted to bridge I took to *Kenilworth* and finished its 444 pages before bedtime. Strips of dried skin peeled off the sole blistered on Snöhetta. It was still rather dreich the next day and Stuart and Boots opted out of a walk up to the top of the eastern half of the Svartisen. They went potholing a bit with the locals, and chatted to a helicopter pilot who flew in while searching for a missing jet. The valley lower down was due to be dammed. The remoteness is none too secure. We had an enjoyable climb over Kamptinden to reach Sniptinden. There were no desperate river-crossings either. It took three hours to walk out back to the vehicle next day. On arrival I wrung out my shirt, but at least I'd only received two bites in the jungle. It only remained to drive the old waggon up the Dunderlandsdalen (sounded appropriate) so it too could claim being north of the Polar Circle. It was a wet night so to have succeeded with three peaks (and four wheels) beyond that dotted line was quite good. It felt a long way from home.

Half of our six weeks in Norway had gone by then so we rolled south again to play the second half. When we left eventually the statistician of the party declared we had walked, scrambled, or climbed 28 summits in what was regarded as a wet summer. Both on and off the hills we had enjoyed ourselves mightily.

BIBLIOGRAPHY

Bergen, Oslo and other towns have many books about Norway *in English* so a bookshop visit on arrival is useful. Guidebooks do change and buying locally can ensure information is up-to-date. The following are particularly recommended:

HOWARD, TONY, *Walks and Climbs in Romsdal*. Cicerone Press.
Mountain Touring Holidays in Norway, Norway Travel Association.
PRAG, PER, *Mountain Holidays in Norway*, NTA.
SLINGSBY, W.C., *Norway, The Northern Playground*.
STYLES, S, Mountains of the Midnight Sun. Hurst & Blackett.
Three in Norway by Two of Them. Longmans Green & Co.
Weir, T, *Camps and Climbs in Arctic Norway*, Cassell.

MAPS

The sheet 3-4 'Midt Norge' of the Cappelen 1:325,000 map covers most of the main areas and is essential for motoring. There are sheets at 1:250,000 covering areas like the Jotunheimen, useful for overall planning. For walking the largest scales available are recommended as the maps are not always very recent or very accurate. Ask suppliers for a recent list.

ADDRESSES

Norwegian Mountain Touring Association, Stortingsgt 28, Oslo 1.
Norwegian National Tourist Office, 20 Pall Mall, London SW1Y 5NE. (Wide range of informative leaflets on all topics.)

8

Peru

A WALK AROUND THE CORDILLERA BLANCA

Though sluggards deem it but a foolish chase,
And marvel men should quit their easy chair,
The toilsome way and long, long league to trace,
Oh! there is sweetness in the mountain air,
And life, that bloated ease can never hope to share.

(Lord Byron)

Before doing anything in the back-of-beyond in South America you have, first of all, to reach it. Even the flying out was not to be straightforward on this trip but then international flights are sordid at best and airports the most exasperating, boring places invented. The sheer volume of jokes on the subject proves this.

There is Bob Hope's crack about 'having visited almost as many countries as my baggage' or the pseudo advert boasting you 'can breakfast in New York, dine in London and have your baggage in Cairo, all in the one day'. As we intended a mixture of walking, climbing and seeing the best of the country, all in one month, we too had a certain pre-occupation with luggage. We really did our homework and organised things as thoroughly as possible before setting off. This was a decade ago now but Peru was such a memorable experience that it remains fresh in memory.

Beryl Griffiths in London had organised a body called 'The Andean Society' in order to gain charter rates under the rules of the time. All she had to do then was fill the plane — which she did. There were about seven mountaineering parties besides archaeologists, butterfly-hunters and straight tourists. You could tell the first as they clanked as they walked and electronic security devices went crazy over them. 'Do you usually wear a belt of karabiners?' asked an incredulous official. 'Only when I'm wearing my big boots and duvet.' How that overloaded plane ever left the ground is a mystery. Perhaps the butterfly-hunters did not have much in the way of heavy equipment.

The weight-saving by wearing everything was bearable, just, in London in July. In Bermuda it was unendurable. The blue waters at the end of the runway proved irresistible. Everyone was down to pants and bras and splashing about. In the air again I recall the stewardess walking up the gangway muttering 'Knickers! Knickers!' — for every seat seemed to have the improvised swimsuits hanging up to dry.

At Antigua we had another stop-stop-stop. We taxied to the end of the runway ready for departure only to come back. Engine failure. When we were told they would try again, but one hour later, five of us hired a cab to run into St John where it was carnival time. We had a wild dash to be back on time, but made it. Everyone was on board waiting for us, and had been for half an hour, so we entered to boos and hisses — rather lost on Colin, who was deaf and merely thought everyone was grinning at him. We taxied to the end of the runway, ordered drinks, but again had to return to the terminal — this time in a decidedly jaded replay. The engine still wasn't right so everything was off-loaded and the plane flew off to Trinidad for repairs.

Some hours later what appeared to be a spare VC10 suddenly became ours so we all trooped on board again. We had only been on the go twenty hours by then. A blur of bad sleep, food and bad sleep and we reached Lima, at 2.30 am local time. We set the echoes ringing through the empty airport. There were plenty of forms to fill in and *soles* to purchase with our pounds, but no real delays. An announcement for our party over the tannoy had us whisked away to the BOAC offices. There our pre-arranged shopping was stacked up. Barclay (one of our team members) had contacts with the Salvesen family (Peru's main sardine fishing operator) and Andrew, their man in Peru, had a girl friend in BOAC. Andrew kindly put a flat at our disposal in Lima and helped in many ways like arranging most of the expedition's shopping.

It was strange how we were to find contacts between Morocco and Peru. Barclay and I had been together in Morocco several times and when we walked into the monastery of St Catarina in Arequipa we simultaneously gasped 'Morocco!' — the Moroccan (Moorish) style had of

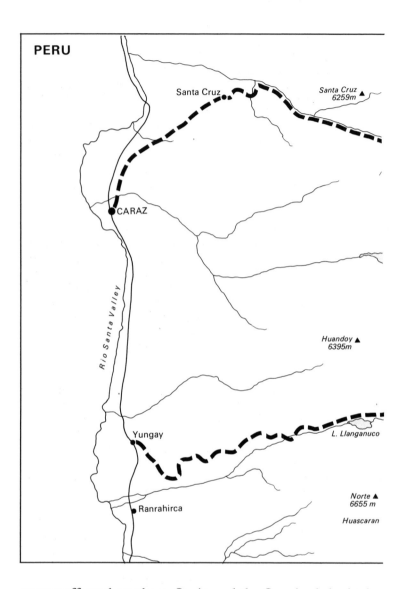

PERU

Santa Cruz

Santa Cruz
6259m

CARAZ

Rio Santa Valley

Huandoy
6395m

Yungay

L. Llanganuco

Norte
6655 m

Ranrahirca

Huascaran

course affected southern Spain and the Spaniards had taken
it round the world to Peru. Sardines, being cheap, formed a
large part of our diet in the Andes (as they did in the Atlas)
and came in various flavours from lemony to peppery. Over
one tin I commented, 'These are just like the Moroccan

160

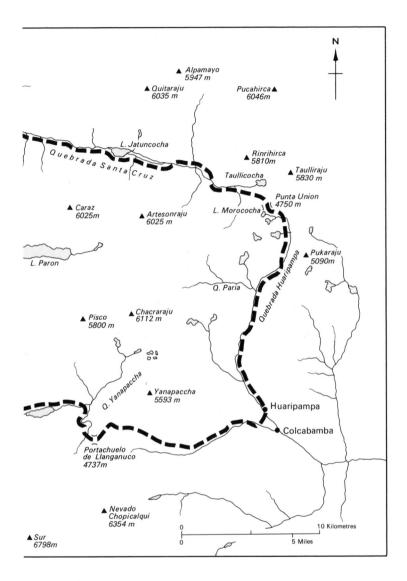

N

Alpamayo
5947 m

Quitaraju
6035 m

Pucahirca
6046m

L. Jatuncocha

Quebrada Santa Cruz

Rinrihirca
5810m

Taullicocha

Taulliraju
5830 m

Punta Union
4750 m

Caraz
6025m

Artesonraju
6025 m

L. Morococha

Pukaraju
5090m

L. Paron

Q. Paria

Quebrada Huaripampa

Pisco
5800 m

Chacraraju
6112 m

Q. Yanapaccha

Yanapaccha
5593 m

Huaripampa

Colcabamba

Portachuelo
de Llanganuco
4737m

Nevado
Chopicalqui
6354 m

0   10 Kilometres

0   5 Miles

Sur
6798m

"piquant" sardines' and then saw 'fabriqué en Maroc' stamped on the tin. Talk of coals to Newcastle!

Dawn at Lima airport was hardly inspiring nor were the bald tyres on the beaten-up Peruvian Airlines plane which whisked us off for Cuzco. The hostesses, in brilliant orange uniforms, were dazzling and cheerfully put up with our dashing from window to window as we flew by snowy summits into the Andes.

Cuzco was having a gala day so the main square was packed with troops and armoured vehicles, and various military and ecclesiastical dignitaries made interminable speeches. The town seemed run down and the people listless. Even the vendors simply sat before their wares. The streets stank of urine. Our Hotel Colon (Columbus) was seedy. But we spent two days of enjoyable sight-seeing. We had all read John Hemming's fascinating book *The Conquest of the Incas* so burrowed into all sorts of places on and off the tourist track. Inca stonework is fascinating and when the church of San Domingo, built on the old Temple of the Sun, was largely destroyed in a 1960 earthquake, the lower, Inca, walls survived intact, stones so firmly fitting together that, in cliché terms, a knife blade could not be inserted between them. Yet the Incas built without mortar and with no knowledge of devices like the wheel.

Above Cuzco, at Sacsayhuaman, stones of over 3,500 kilograms have been used in this three-tiered fortress of zig-zag walls. In Cuzco, in the largest remaining Inca wall, there is a stone with twelve angles to it, each dovetailing into neighbouring stones. Who were these builders then?

The Incas, according to legend, were descended from the sun and came down to earth on an island in Lake Titicaca. In the fifteenth century they suddenly exploded to found an empire which took in much of modern Ecuador, Peru, Chile and Bolivia. It was a conquest which created a remarkable system of Communism — with the Incas as a ruling class with their god-kings. Human sacrifice and other rites were performed. They built stonework structures which have withstood earthquake and pillage. They wore magnificent robes of feather and gold. Their empire was unique. In the early sixteenth century it was split by civil war — and Pizarro arrived. Unhappy conjunction.

His small force of men and horses (a terrible unknown beast) boldly marched into the inhospitable land, captured the king, ransomed him for a room filled with gold (priceless artifacts all melted down by the freebooters), then strangled him, descended on Cuzco to its destruction, and within a short time pushed the last resistance back to the edge of the jungle. The Cross had won the field.

We puffed with altitude to visit the large figure of Christ on a hill above the city (a gift from Palestinian Arabs in 1944), where the children were flying kites. They at least were bright-eyed and lively. Spinning tops were the current toy craze, and *The Prisoner of Zenda* was on at the pictures.

We made the journey to Machu Picchu by train, as the present trail had not been created then. It has only taken a decade for it to be made and spoiled — what a shrinking world we live in. The train left by shunting back and forth up a succession of zig-zags, higher than the Christ figure, to gain a wide valley. There seemed to be no exit but we suddenly swung right and plunged into a gorge down to the Urubamba valley. Machu Picchu was never discovered by the rapacious Spaniards, and lay buried in the jungle till found by the American explorer Hiram Bingham in 1910.

It is perched between sugar-loaf peaks which rise from the entwining Urubamba river, a tributary, eventually, of the Amazon. It is the epitome of ruined cities: beautiful in itself; mysterious in that just who built it and why is not known; and in a setting which is unique — a panorama of jungle, hills, and gorges with a running horizon of snow-capped mountains. So well known from photographs, it still left us gasping.

It was one of the forts built by the Incas from which they fought a rearguard action against the Spaniards. The last 'rebel', Tupac Amaru, was executed in 1572 after which time these strongholds faded from memory and were overgrown by jungle.

Upstream from Cuzco lies the Sacred Valley of the Incas where there are several ruins, and terracing which is still cultivated. It is a fertile area, overshadowed by snow peaks. The fort of Ollantaytambo is another marvel. It proved impregnable. Its temple contains a construction of six blocks of smooth red stone, weighing 50,000 kilograms which were brought from a quarry 650 metres up the hillside opposite — no one knows how. To those brought up on G. H. Henty (that dates me) it was easy to imagine the conquistadors and Inca warriors locked in combat on the terraces of Ollantaytambo.

The Spaniards, for all their unforgivable destruction of a unique civilisation, in turn have left some fine monuments. Even Lima, a horrible city of two million inhabitants, has colonial houses and churches of architectural beauty.

Perhaps the most notable Spanish town is Arequipa, an hour south of Lima by air. Like all Peru it has suffered the toil of repeated earthquakes but still has preserved many fine carved frontal doorways on the various churches. These are built of volcanic stone called 'sillar' — for all the world like Camembert cheese in colour and texture.

Behind Arequipa is El Misti, an almost perfect cone of volcano. Though it towers 4,000 metres above the city it looks a mere afternoon's walk. Balancing it, an even higher chain of peaks runs north. To reach Lake Titicaca the railway has to break through this barrier, which it does in about four hours. Then it runs several hours more through vast upland plains with wandering herds of llamas or alpacas to Juliaca — where we spent an evening bargaining for rugs and pullovers, ponchos and carpets, all made from the wool of these weird beasts. Beyond lies Puno and the lake, 4,000 metres above sea level.

We had hoped to sail across the lake into Bolivia but that country was having its bi-annual revolution and the boat did not sail. There are two boats: the old *Yavari* which was built in England, carried up on mule back, and rebuilt in 1862 and the *Ollanta* (2,000 tons) which was brought up by rail in 1930.

We did, however, chug out to the floating islands of the Urus — a sad place, for the race has declined and the few hamlets hang on at subsistence level, the swamp life ensuring chronic rheumatism. A floating school has been built, not of the usual reeds but of the ubiquitous corrugated iron. Our uncontrolled approach ended with our ramming it.

The last place we visited before returning to the clammy unpleasantness of Lima City was Sillustani, 35 kilometres from Puno, away into the middle of nowhere. Perched on a promontory jutting into a lake were a series of round towers of the almost expected perfection of stonework. They bulged out towards the top slightly and were hollow inside. These were tombs of successive cultures again. Even their date is uncertain, though pre-Inca.

From there one looked over an almost empty landscape: old, forsaken terracing, a small hamlet, a reed boat on the lake. The glory has departed.

All this travel and looking at sights was purposely done at the beginning of our visit. Many of these places are at considerable altitude and the longer we spent at height the less chance there was of sickness when we did walk off into the blue. Only in the Himalayas will you find a mightier range of mountains than the Andes. They are not to be treated lightly. Pulmonary oedema is a very real hazard. Medical assistance is not available and the remedy of losing altitude quickly is often impossible.

The Andes run for thousands of miles, parallel to the Pacific coast of South America. In Peru's Cordillera Blanca they reach the largest grouping of high mountains. The Blanca lies about 100 kilometres inland from the coast but is the continental watershed. Less than a dozen passes break through this chain and by combining any two of these you create a circuit with some of the most spectacular walking and trekking in the world.

The mountains are relatively accessible, for you can be in their midst just half a day's walk from a major road and, though they are big, snowy mountains, long *quebradas* (deep glacial valleys) lead into them so there is no need for walkers to cross glaciers. The eastern side of the watershed is greener but very remote, its waters facing a 6500-kilometre Amazonian journey to the sea! Most of the Cordillera Blanca is part of the Huascarán National Park and visitors are asked to treat it with respect. It has not been over-waymarked and indecently promoted so the feeling of wilderness is real — something ever more rare these days.

Those going into the Cordillera Blanca must register with the park authorities in Huaraz or elsewhere. As the first couple of days are likely to be in Huaraz anyway and knowing how conditions or regulations can change, it is probably easiest to call at the office there. They can help in many ways. Huaraz (pop. 50,000), is the only major town, so complete the trek's stocking-up there.

Most of our preparations were made in Lima where we had a few hectic days organising things. At a supermarket we ended up with a row of trolleys, to the consternation of the girl at the checkout. Our bill was two metres long! Somehow everything was done and at 4 o'clock one morning we were off in three *colectivos* up the Pan American Highway northwards. *Colectivos* are large American cars which run along set routes, like buses, or can be hired entirely, as we did, for a specific run. It is a hair-raising form of travel but less so than going by truck or bus. The 300 kilometres from Lima to Huaraz is done in the day with the road reaching 4,100 metres on the Conoccocha Pass. From it we had our first view of the Cordillera Blanca with Huascarán, one of the mightiest peaks (6,768 metres) seemingly huge and near, but still 50 kilometres away. The pass breaks over the snowless, barren Cordillera Negra, while between the ranges the deep Rio Santa valley forms the romantically-named Callejón du Huaylas. Huaraz is the capital of this remote province of Ancash.

Huaraz, on our visit, was a mess of rubble and rebuilding following the great earthquake of the year before. We had a night there before a three-hour journey down to Caraz on an overloaded bus. Caraz was cut off for several days following the *teremoto* as helicopters could not fly through the dust cloud and it took a month to repair the road enough to let trucks through. Yungay, the village where we would come out of the mountains at the end of our circuit, had been wiped out by an avalanche of unimaginable size. The avalanche was turned by the Rio Santa and poured down the main valley for 16 kilometres to Caraz and far down the valley beyond.

At Caraz we had a pleasant hotel built round a courtyard. From the balcony we were level with flowering shrubs which were attracting jewel-bright hummingbirds. We spent some time with the friendly police chief and the Prefect and Pedro Mendez Mendez was appointed our chief *arriero*. As he needed a day to round up thirteen *burros* and a couple of assistants we had a fairly sociable stay. The Sub-Prefect took us to see the refugee accommodation the Germans had provided — practical, cheap, indestructible 'igloos' of plastic. Pedro came in to say he would be there at seven, *mañana*.

He was too, along with the beasts, and Fidel and Benedicto the idiot *arrieros,* who managed to lose their first *burro* within a couple of hours of our departure. We lost one member of our gang too and he turned up just in time to miss a search party who had gone to look for him. The loads began falling off the mules. It was hot and dusty. In other words it was a typical start to an expedition!

We soon rose above the clearly-demarcated valley cultivation to follow old trails up the prickly hillsides; the modern road is happily avoided by the beasts. Some of our luggage was damaged by a rope pulled tight across it and a large stain spread on one of the kitbags. Eggs and oranges were obviously suffering. We had lunch at a cafe in a village (a white flag on a pole indicates a liquor-store), surrounded by children, puppies and strings of maize drying in the sun. We demolished their remaining stock of beer and *Inca Kola* (a pleasant urine-coloured beverage), knowing it would be our last extravagance for a long time, then our cavalcade moved on and upwards as it did all day. There were 7 *gringos*, 3 locals, 11 mules loaded with our gear and 2 with theirs.

The route through the gorge into the great Quebrada Santa Cruz was blocked with earthquake debris so we toiled up a zig-zag track beside it, our feet sending up clouds of dark blue butterflies. A condor lazily swung overhead. Someone estimated twenty minutes for the slope ahead; it took two hours. At three o'clock we found a pleasant meadow with a clean mountain stream and declared it our camp site. Some pitched tents, others made tea and Barclay, brave man, tackled the messy contents of the kitbag containing the melted butter. There is always plenty of sorting out the first night or two but being a gang of old hands we soon shook down into an efficient routine that left the maximum time to relish our surroundings. The three locals kept to their own fire but helped to demolish the vast dixie of soup we had made from damaged tomatoes and other vegetables. We were in bed by eight o'clock, writing up logs by candle-light, while the moon flooded down the Santa Valley and left the Cordillera Negra opposite like a black Cuillin cut out against a lemon sky.

Being wide awake at 5.30 I lit the stoves to begin the new day. Barclay, Alastair (who had been sick several times in the night) and I set off at about eight and we had a good bird's eye view of the loading pantomime from above on the zig-zag track. 'Colin really seems to have the knack' Barclay commented, at which moment Colin stood back to boot one *burro* in its rear! Several of the beasts took off for home with Benedicto flapping after them. It was nice not to be on loading duty that day.

We were all together again at the end of the long haul up the zig-zags. There was a profusion of flowers, to which we could not put names, a frustration that was with us throughout our walk. Our rest period was one of excitement for we could now gaze up the huge trench of the Quebrada

167

Santa Cruz. It sliced its way through the mountains like a knife cut. Great white scars, all the way up, showed the work of the *teremoto*. A granite tower faced us.

Like the Grand Old Duke of York, having marched up the hill, we immediately marched down again — over a slabby, rocky slope where the zig-zags were so tight that each mule in line faced in opposite directions. We prayed no loads would come off for they would bounce a long way and be irretrievable. When one beast shed its load (onto the path rather than over the edge) we were all well implanted with thorns before we caught the culprit. Pedro was ahead with seven *burros,* in good order, but the other two *arrieros* seemed incapable of handling the rest without considerable help. There were some stern words once we were safely down into the valley. Pedro dismissed them as 'Indians who are only good for drink'.

The valley gave easy-angled walking and if the scale was a bit overpowering there was a great variety of detail. There were many avalanche scars, some were from the collapse of huge granite buttresses which had tumbled 650 metres and fanned out their white debris onto the floor of the valley. We came on some huts in a small area of cultivation and waited for Alastair to catch us. There was a lake, the first of several, with Andean pied geese and other birds we could not recognise. What looked like yellow-bright woodpeckers I knew to be oropendolas, as these were on some bird stamps in my collection. A less overgrown lake followed and we watched the mist clearing off Quitaraju and other peaks up the valley. It felt almost unreal to be walking so casually among great mountains such as climbers dream of in their most exotic dreams.

The beasts struggled through a big slope of shattered boulders. (We could admire their abilities if not their natures.) A dozen ponies galloped off from the next lake. Colin and I helped Pedro through an area of maquis-like jungle to reach the last long *pampa* of the day. We arrived with twelve beasts and no *arrieros* — so unpacked and pitched camp. Pedro in fact had gone back to rescue number thirteen which had baulked at a shaky bridge and ended belly-deep in the mud, despite having two attendants. Tea was welcome.

We were only in at 5 o'clock so the meal went on into darkness. The *arrieros* built their fire directly upwind so we had a smoky evening. A hired tent (no doubt given as aid for the refugees) was large enough for the seven of us to squeeze into for eating. It became bitterly cold after dark. Periodically there would be stonefalls, which sounded rather like waterfalls, but having filled our twelve-hour ration of daylight with walking, we were soon sound asleep. 'An earthquake would hardly have shifted us,' was someone's ill-chosen comparison in the morning. We had passed some big fissures during the day.

Two nights were spent there and we went off on various local walks on the 'free' day, some of us climbing up to the 5,000-metre mark on a ridge of Nevada Santa Cruz in the hope of views, but it never cleared and a chilly wind kept us on the move. Some plants seemed to be made of flannel and we found weird caterpillars and stick insects as we descended to a textbook terminal moraine that held a green lochan in its curve. 'Lochain Uaine' I called out. 'Aye, but it's a far cry from Ryvoan,' Alastair replied.

We took less than two hours from rising to departing, from cold moonlight to cool brilliance. The peaks soared to their ice-creamed summits, white cones on a blue backcloth, a vast spaciousness rendered in heraldic simplicity. We wandered up one *pampa*, then scrub and trees led to a second level, from which we looked up a side valley to a churning of clouds. Suddenly the clouds dropped and an elegant pyramid of mountain stood clear, its ridge flanked by pleated crinolines of white. Hardly a rock showed. Alpamayo, 'the most beautiful mountain in the world'.

The beasts caught us up while we were admiring Alpamayo and we became involved with managing them across a stream. That bit of fun ended with Barclay and I with nine *burros*, Pedro with three recalcitrant brutes and the two twits with one, which had lost its load. Not long after a knolly strath proved to be riddled with bogs into which the *burros* would stray. One collapsed. I could not bear to watch and went on a bit to sit looking up to Artesronraju, wrote up my log, and doctored Graham, who was being sick. We were suffering the after-effects of civilisation. I had a filthy cold. Delight and despair so often go hand in hand.

Some Indians were camped on the last *pampa*. The women wore bright red skirts and sombre 'top hats'. We could look right up to Taulliraju, the peak that closed the valley head. If Alpamayo had a queenly grace that made it feminine, Taulliraju was all brute male. It was incredibly ice draped, with just an occasional black crag bursting through the white coating. To the right it fell steeply and then rose in a small horn of a peak below which lay our escape, the Punta Union. In the other direction lay Rinrihirca.

We had planned to cross the pass but Graham was too poorly to push on and we had discovered what someone called a perfect campsite, in a nook sheltered from the cold winds off the glaciers; a tawny grass area overlooked by granite walls and with a truly fabulous array of peaks all round. The Indians came on with their pack ponies and by the time they were up the pass we could hardly see them. We kept being impressed by the scale. Our *burros* arrived. Robert Louis Stevenson, wise man, contented himself with one donkey. Thirteen was a decidedly chancy number.

It was only midday so we had an enjoyable rest day: doing nothing much and resting afterwards. Nobody wandered far for the glory was all about us. We made a big supper which we ate leisurely and read before the cold drove us into our down bags. At sunset the peaks seemed to catch fire, with flaming clouds pluming off the summits then, mere minutes later, the stars were out, the wind died, and the night crackled into icy darkness.

Graham still had a temperature of 102° so we had to mark time for another day. It began with Scottish dreichness but we still set off in various directions, mostly upwards, to expand the view when it came. I went bird-watching up to a bump opposite but the bump was the end of a ridge so I followed it to a big spike below another dramatic peak: Curicashanja. The peak could be skirted but beyond lay a chaos of impossible snow structures. I was level with the Rinrihirca-Taulliraju col so was pleased to feel fit despite my cold.

There was one tent more when I reached camp: it belonged to two New Zealand lads who had crossed the pass and were glad of some English-speaking company. All nine of us squeezed into the 'Refugee Tent' and blethered happily till after ten — a late night on the trail. Graham was much improved.

The pass of the Punta Union is 4,750 metres high, almost as high as Mt Blanc, the highest *peak* in Europe, yet it is such a well-graded ascent that its crossing was a relished experience rather than a toilsome grind. Our acclimatisation had obviously paid off. We were given the bonus of a fine morning.

Never steep, the path periodically zig-zagged tightly, in places built up into man-made steps, at others crossing natural, angled slabs, so blending in, that it was difficult to see the path line from across the valley. The Taullicocha, another moraine lake, right at the head of the valley, only came in sight when we looked down on it. The glaciers fell directly into it and at one stage an avalanche of ice broke loose and crashed down into the water. Pucahirca, another of the giants appeared through the col left of Taulliraju, which still loomed over us in fantastic powerfulness. We lifted metaphorical hats to Lionel Terray who first found a way to its summit.

Both my cameras ran out of film so while I changed them all the mules and humans passed on through the neck of the Punta Union and the resulting silence in that awesome place had the hairs on my neck tingling. I was loath to leave the white wonderland on that side but the gap in the pass suddenly framed Pucaraju, a kindlier peak which might even tempt us to climb its 5,090 metres. The way ahead always wins!

The upper slopes below us were dotted with small, bright blue lakes and there was a green lushness we had not seen before. The waters draining before us fed the Huaripampa, which flows down to the Rio Marañon, one of the Amazon's largest feeders. The path descended by a tortuous twisting staircase of skilled construction. This path is often given an Inca attribution but was constructed at the turn of the last century. To think it is Inca work is quite a compliment! There was a peony-like flower which Pedro called 'Rima rima'; it is believed to help backward children: if the flower is passed across the child's lips, the infant will then talk. Another beautiful flower was the blue *Gentiana prostrata*. The poor donkeys had a beating in one boggy place. Taulliraju stood on its head in a reflecting pool of a tarn, our last view of the giant. We contoured and dipped down to the Quebrada Huaripampa where we camped at the crossing place, the only spot not completely covered by big grass tussocks.

The hot afternoon encouraged some washing of clothes and bodies. I went through the food and commented that we would not starve for a while. Supper that night was soup (with the last of the beaten bread from Caraz), tinned frankfurters with fresh potatoes and asparagus, peaches and earthy local coffee. The only fly in the ointment, if that is the right metaphor, was midges, a home element we could have done without. We covered all skin areas and crowded into the tent to eat. A bonfire and darkness dispelled them. We rose at four o'clock to go and climb Pucaraju. It was out of sight but we were dominated by a huge, shattered pinnacle. 'I hope that thing stays up for another two days,' Graham commented. Up a side valley, Chacraraju, the ferocious 'Matterhorn of the Andes' had us shaking our heads in awe. An endless succession of bad conditions stopped us not far off the summit of Pucaraju: time was out and energy going and the weather failing. We reached camp as the rain started at dusk. The thunder banged away and the stream was soon a torrent. The tent leaked badly and we soon fled it, pitying the three who had to sleep in it, but when the temperature dropped it froze so the discomfort was not so great. In the morning when we lit the primus it all thawed of course! The burros did not like their white world of snow and the locals had the ear flaps of their headgear lowered. It was not an efficient departure. The conjunction of snow *and* midges was unusual.

It turned out to be a pleasant day's walking down the Huaripampa: the snow soon faded and there was a succession of flats *(pampas)* with wending streams to test crossing techniques. There were ducks on a tarn and the birds became brighter and noisier as we descended into more jungly vegetation. There was a feeling of utter remoteness and the shut-in feeling of the Santa Cruz days had gone.

Fidel and Benedicto managed to embed one *burro* with all its legs down separate holes and their remedy of simply beating the beast was more than we could take. We told them to unload and help the brute. When the saddle was removed we found a saucer-sized sore on one shoulder where the harness had been badly-fitting. Pedro had called them 'Abajo comida de condor' (food for the condor) and we heartily agreed. We could have been happier with Pedro alone.

We came down to cultivation again. One of its first signs was a football pitch, one where kicking to touch (on one side) was to be discouraged: a 300-metre drop to the river. Houses were of stone and were thatched. The village dogs were docile. We found Huaripampa, the main village, a charming spot, clean and with geraniums brightening the courtyards. The river here begins to swing off eastwards on its marathon journey to the sea. Huaripampa is at an altitude of 3,700 metres and 300 metres downsteam at Colcabamba village the river comes in which we would follow to our pass back over the watershed of the Andes. We did not go down to Colcabamba, a busier place (now quite geared-up for tourist parties), but doubled back to cross the Quebrada Huaripampa and then climbed up to cut out two legs of the triangle. It was a brutal ascent through forest in which tiny fields had been hewn. One patch was being ploughed with oxen and a man staggered past with a huge bale of barley. Eventually we twisted out onto more open land, spacious uplands with peaks all round again: mountaineers' country. Yanapaccha overlooked us and rather than go on up to the lake-studded level below the pass (akin to the Punta Union) we camped where we were below the snow level. It was the most demanding day of the walk around.

An Australian couple, Alistair McArthur and Ann Dechaineux, came down from the pass and they had heard news of us even in Lima they said. He had been in Antarctica and worked at Glenmore Lodge in Scotland, so we found plenty of people and places in common. It was another sociable night in the tent. It was my birthday too I realised rather belatedly.

The same evening we had a complicated planning session as we split into those determined to climb one peak at all costs and those who preferred to keep moving and see more of the country. In the snowy conditions I inclined to the second group, being hopelessly restless anyway, always wanting to see what lies over the next horizon. We all met up in Lima for the last couple of days (meatless days which rather cut down gastronomic celebrations) and heard how they fared. They had a 'mule rolling down the hill with feet in the air' sort of day after we left. Nevada Pisco Este was tried as a day effort but failed so a camp was set up at the col and one pair reached the top though Colin was not well enough. They in turn split up with some going off to Chavin and trekking through the Punta Yanashallash (4,680 metres) to Huaraz. Alistair and Ann went over the Punta Union but

Ann was struck down with pulmonary oedema and Alistair had the agonising experience of having to leave her, alone, and go for aid — a two-day effort — before she was lifted out. She was very lucky to survive. We met them, hale and hearty, in Lima later on.

The Portachuelo de Yanganuco (4,767 metres) was the resounding name for our pass back over the Andes spine. We had woken to a frosty world which attractively decorated all vegetation in white hoar but set the tents stiff as boards. It was a slower departure with several ploys to organise instead of our regular routine. The cloud rolled in and it began to snow, the path was muddy and Pedro's voice echoed among the crags as we threaded a route through the tarns: following the dainty slots of the *burros'* footprints and the sprawling tyre-sole treadmarks of Fidel and Benedicto. Pedro, tall and dignified, we liked very much. The two *arrieros* were sad, incompetent youths with whom we could establish no relationship. An Indian family came down, singing one of their haunting refrains, garbed in brilliant colours as usual, and we noticed the mother had a dog instead of a baby tied to her back. The col itself was bleak and only yielded a half-view downwards. But we saw Huascarán, high, and lifting its chunky twin summits above the clouds. The 6,768-metre North Summit is the highest point in Peru while, in the Americas, only Aconcagua and a few neighbours are higher. We walked with giants: Chacraraju, Pisco, Huandoy ranging along the north side of the Quebrada Yanganuco, while Chopicalqui and Huascarán hemmed in the south. The spelling of names and peaks and passes can vary from map to map but is usually recognisable. Yanganuco is often Llanganuco for instance, but has not jumped to Wales.

The path zig-zagged down, contoured, then zig-zagged again as we came 'down to a temperate valley . . . smelling of vegetation . . .' We deserted the main valley to turn up the Quebrada Yanapacha, the cirque below Pisco, where we found a hidden shelf under the peak and set up our tents. Dusk, supper and rain came together. The drips from the roof of the tent tinkled on the plates sitting on the floor. We squatted in the squalor quite contentedly — till a larger patter of drips landed on the candles. The overnight occupiers waited till everything froze-dry before rolling out their bedding.

The morning rings its excitement in my brief log entry: 'Wake to frozen calm. Out to a staggering view of the great, castellated Huascarán: the South Peak a bridal train of snow, the North Peak a plastered keep of warm rock and white battlements. Chopicalqui lies edge on, improbably steep, while on this side of it the mists boil over the pass of yesterday. The snow is almost down to our level, so we just crossed in time. The Pisco peaks appear like white flames above us. Later the sun touched everything with gold . . .'

It was our coldest start. Every pan of water had a disc of ice in it. Three of us were heading down, four upwards. It was odd to lie back and hear someone else give the orders of the day. We shook Pedro by the hand and turned to the descent. All too soon we were onto a motorable road which now reached up to the head of the deep U-shaped canyon of the Yanganuco but the *burros* and pedestrians rebelled against using it. We kept to the old ways, a track which wended by the two larger lakes set in the valley. Past the first lake was a colossal stone avalanche, from the 1970 catastrophe. Below its debris lies the fatal camp site of fifteen climbers from Czechoslovakia. The second *laguna* was noisy with ducks, gulls and an osprey. Red-barked *quenual* trees gave a Cezanne-like touch but the gentleness vanished abruptly as the trail wound down, much too steeply, to try and cut the corners while, overhead, rose sheer rock walls and prows of granite on a scale none of us had ever seen before. The Huascarán side was a succession of massive buttresses. After a final twist down, the country opened out before us, patched with fields of barley, a rich landscape of yellows, purples and browns. We came on the great avalanche and its overwhelming visual impact and stopped to eat simply to break its hold. Oropendolas, hummingbirds, the blue butterflies — it was like rewinding the start, except for the mark of the *teremoto*. We walked for miles with its scar beside us.

Across the valley it looked as if open-cast mining had been operating way up into the clouds on Huascarán. This sterile sweep cut off trails and cultivation with sharp brutality, the deadly work of the 31st May 1970. We were there in August, the year after. The Cordillera have a long history of earthquakes but this disaster was unprecedented. The earthquake killed over 80,000 people in the Callejón de

Huaylas and left another million homeless. Ninety per cent of Huaraz was destroyed. It was the biggest human disaster in the history of the Americas.

High on the North Peak of Huascarán a granite buttress collapsed in the quake and fell westwards into this valley. The forces and figures are hard to grasp: 10–15 million cubic feet of rock and several million cubic feet of ice fell, mixing together (and with the soil) to form a concrete-like mass travelling at 300 kilometres per hour. It fell 4,000 metres and travelled 14 kilometres before reaching the Rio Santa near Yungay, turned down past Caraz to finally stop after a total distance of 65 kilometres. Yungay was simply wiped off the face of the earth: 18,000 people perished, 240 survived.

Our walk down into Yungay was an emotional experience. An inestimable sadness seemed to haunt the bare, concrete-bare, slopes. Only a few straggling plants starred the wastes. Rough wooden crosses had been erected all over the place and we passed one or two black-dressed women here and there, kneeling before these markers of lost homes, lost families. They told their beads and the tears fell down their shocked faces. In passing we could only turn to them our own tearful eyes, a brief bond in the bleak misery of suffering. Yungay had been protected from previous avalanches by a 200-metre high hill ridge but this gigantic avalanche simply swept over it and down onto the town. The debris lies four metres deep over everything. The few who survived were able to run up a hill to the cemetery. As we descended we could see how the flow lapped up to the statue of a Christ figure, arms outstretched, leaving just that tiny island of safety. Four scrawny palm trees marked the town centre — the only living things to have survived the crushing sludge.

It was not the ending we had envisaged but it was an unforgettable one. The name Yungay can still bring a lump to my throat and I look back on it as one of the most moving — and influential — experiences of my life. The world, sadly, is full of Yungays, all crying out to shame our soft, self-indulgent, affluent society.

We had wandered down alone but found each other by the roadside. The *burros* found us. The baggage was unpacked. We bade farewell to Fidel and Benedicto. After an hour a *colectivo* picked us up and we joined a laughing lady with her hens and market goods. A *colectivo* which had not stopped for us was soon overtaken. Its axle had broken. Ours did not have a third gear. We added a fat mama while her children sat on our laps and somehow two more adults squeezed in as well. The next day we left Huaraz for Lima and other wanderings. I wrote in my log at Huaraz, 'A journey over — and a chapter opened'.

★ ★ ★

The dozen years and more since then have led to considerable changes of course in Peru, in busy Huaraz and even in the Cordillera Blanca. The country has not had an easy time and life is more difficult for many. Huaraz has grown again, to be ten times its previous size (now 50,000). A new Yungay had sprung up, on a safer site nearby. Many trekkers now visit the area and it is more organised for visitors. (The Bartle book mentioned below gives all the practical details and is essential reading.) Whatever the changes the mountains remain: aloof, grand, and breathtakingly beautiful: an irresistible lure for restless hearts.

BIBLIOGRAPHY
BARTLE, JIM, *Trails of the Cordilleras Blanca and Huayhuash.* (The definitive guide with maps, glossary, etc.) Available, in UK, from Cordee Books.
BRADT, H & G., *Backpacking and Trekking in Peru and Bolivia.*
HEMMING, JOHN, *The Conquest of the Incas.* Macmillan/Penguin.
MURPHY, DERVLA, *Eight Feet in the Andes.* Murray.
PORTWAY, CHRISTOPHER, *Journey Along the Spine of the Andes,* Oxford Illustrated Press.
RICKER, JOHN, *Yuraq Janka, A Guide to the Peruvian Andes,* Cordee.

MAPS
The 1:100,000 *kamkartes* in the Ricker book would be adequate for trekking. The Schneider map at 1:200,000 covers the whole Cordillera Blanca, but can be difficult to find. Bartle has an inset map too. Blueprints at 1:100,000 are available at the Ingemmet office, Guzman Barron 582 (Centenario), Huaraz. (2 sheets for the C Blanca) and the Santa Cruz to Llanganuco circuit is well described in other local productions.

9

India

TO THE NANDA DEVI SANCTUARY

She has a rainbow in her heart
And quiet beyond the moon
She is earth, hill, water, cloud,
All faith-kept things.
Treat, oh treat her well, for we
Soon leave the secret room.

It would really take a book to cover in detail our varied doings during a visit to the Nanda Devi Sanctuary one autumn a decade ago. We were 'a mixed bag of the middle aged' as someone said: Donald was an architect, Charles was an insurance inspector, Stephen a physicist, Frank a surgeon, and I had not long stopped being a school teacher. Later we added two younger members, Peter (in computers) and Ian (engineer) but basically this was a trip planned as a special venture before years and responsibility curbed the freedom to roam — though Charles and I, being batchelors, still wander the world. Nanda Devi did indeed prove special, certainly the most adventurous walk any of us had experienced.

We all knew each other from various shared trips to mountains in Europe and further afield so there was a wealth of experience in the party. It was planned meticulously and if the hard work ensured success, the rewards were none the less. The Nanda Devi Sanctuary is beautiful beyond the singing of it and the approach walk is astonishing. We had read so much about it that of all the places in the world this was where we wanted to go. The gamble of weather in the spring, with the chance of the monsoon creating serious problems and the demands of serious expeditions on porters at that time, made us prefer to go during the unusual period of autumn. It had the precedent of Shipton and Tilman of course. As for much of the time since their day the Sanctuary has been 'out of bounds' or impracticable, it had the magic lure of being almost unexplored while, set in it, ringed by 70 miles of peaks, rises the ethereal, majestic peak of Nanda Devi, 'highest peak in the Empire' as it was once described. Like the Matterhorn or Alpamayo or Everest it immediately

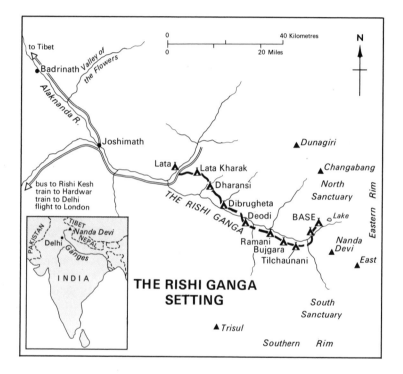

conjures up a distinctive image, a sort of romantic vision glimpsed through a mist of legend and history.

The mountain is a goddess to the local people (a manifestation of Parvati), and guardian demons *(rishis)* protect the approaches. Badrinath is one of the most sacred places of pilgrimage for Hindus, the Alaknanda River being one of the sources of the Ganges, and into it drains the seemingly impenetrable Rishi Ganga. W.W. Graham and his guides in 1883 wandered through the area almost in

Shipton-Tilman style and found a route in to half way up the gorge. Nobody went any further till 1934 and the next visit, in 1936, saw Nanda Devi climbed so the urge to further exploration slackened. Then the War came along, and then politics made it a forbidden area. When we decided to go in the 1970s it had only recently been 'opened', so we leapt at the chance of following in the footsteps of some of our own legendary heros.

For this visit to India I not only kept up my usual daily log book but wrote a whole series of aerogrammes home for more general consumption. You would need several incarnations to even begin to explore or understand India. Westerners are simply overwhelmed by their first visit. Having been born in Colombo and brought up in the East I felt strangely at home but was as fascinated and enthralled as ever. Everything you hear about India is probably true — and so is the opposite. (It is enigmatic and religious for instance, and also basic and materialistic.) Our walk in the mountains only occupied part of our time in the country and I wrote home far more about the non-mountain days. Everyone has to find their own India.

We were lucky in being made 'at home' in the home of Peter and Chloë Greaves in Delhi. Delhi in the monsoon is pretty wearisome and being spoilt by kindness went down very well. It is odd how things work out. Early on we had decided it would be advisable to have a medical member in our gang and I said I'd try one or two people I knew. By an odd slip I sent our plea to the wrong person but when he (Frank) wrote back, it was to say he'd jump at the chance of visiting India. The Greaves were his friends!

I arrived before anyone else and the very next day flew with the Greaves to Kashmir. That took several air letters to describe. So did our eventual gathering and packing in Delhi before the 'Musoorie Express' bore us off to the Himalayas. Donald's wife Christine joined us for our training days and Frank's wife Wendy arrived to join him after the trekking. Frank and Ian were left behind to try and free the medical kit from customs; its retention was a typical bit of crazy Indian bureaucracy. Even changing a cheque could take three hours and several Nanda Devis of paperwork — and that in 100°F temperature and 100 per cent humidity. Welcome the hills. 'He who goes to the Himalaya, goes home.'

The following account is from my letters to the UK, with any additional comments being given inside square brackets.

6 September: Joshimath

We are just back from a six-day acclimatising trip which was more like what we have come for, even if the monsoon gave it an atmosphere akin to Glen Coe when it decides to be wet. When dry and sunny the scenery was brilliant, quite stunning in the contrast. We hired two porters: Sher Singh and 'Red Pants', the former quite a dynamo whom we've invited to stay with us in the Sanctuary as base man the latter a drooping weed of a long-haired youth.

As the bus departure went from 6.30, to 8, to 9, to 11 we took the alternative — and walked. The route began with an 800-metre drop to the Alaknanda (Ganges), here a river of fantastic power, deeply down in the improbable gorges. The bus failure was explained by a landslide. A big boulder was blown up as we arrived. How the echoes rang! It is a pilgrim road so after several miles we were able to enjoy tea in a pilgrim shelter before crossing a swaying suspension bridge to land in the wilds. A sign indicated 'Velley of Flowars'. We tramped up for several hours through jungle and camped at the first water available. A day of waterfalls. Joy to be on trail, feet set 'on curves of freedom'. The next day we just went on and on to camp on an alp at 3,000 metres. A gang of Sikh pilgrims had their children carried in basket-chairs on porters' backs (looked most uncomfy) and turned out to be from Sheffield, so they had a local blather with Charles. All stood, brollies in hand, and it could have been a meeting outside the Crucible rather than a jungle track in the Himalayas. Their turbans are kept dry by plastic covers! Camp sites are all delightful, despite the monsoon.

The next day we travelled through a gorge into 'The Valley of the Flowers' proper. This was the title of a thirties book by Frank Smythe (one of his best and worth reading) and the name has stuck. The Byundar Valley has a ring to it as well though. The flowers passed their best a month ago but were still prolific. Seeing *mecanopsis* in its real setting alone is worth the journey. There are whole families I can't even recognise, others are thrilling for contrasts of site and colour: a blood red *ranunculus*, grass of Parnassus, a mint of powerful scent, thyme, edelweiss, asters, vetches, geraniums. I hope I can find a book to sort out the puzzles. I squatted under my brolly (to Christine's amusement) making notes. Peter came in with an armful of rhubarb. All the party are food-conscious so we eat well — off real food: chapattis, dal and rice are so much better than the western dehydrated rubbish. The jungle gave way to pines and finer, open, country. Shepherds, under a boulder were smoking a water pipe. Their handsome dogs came walkies with us! We soon made a comfy camp in a meadow: boulders to sit on, tea on the go always, and 'home' for a day or two. We had a resident hoopoe and heard choughs crying out of the mists.

Our day in the valley was a dream. The clouds broke after a night of deluge and we could see up to the walls of glacier and rock. There were hills after all! Rataban was the peak that rolled into eye above the valley-head but it is out of bounds as it is on the border with China. We turned back from the upper glacier at 4,000 metres. Wee birds were bathing in the water held in rhoddie leaf bowls. Brollies for sun in morning, and rain in the afternoon. Christine, under hers, cooked a good supper. The shepherds live in birch-bark roofed *howffs*. The porters went off to a village but strolled in at 7 am for our exit expedition: a 1000-metre haul up to the Kunt Khal (3280 metres on altimeter), a tiny pass but it gave a breathtaking view up the Valley of the Flowers in the ration of dry next morning. It was raw cold so our breath steamed the air. The porters slept under a groundsheet only — a hardy pair.

New snow fell to just above camp level. In the crispness whole ranges of mighty mountains rose above the mists. We went camera-crazy. Sher Singh went chapatti-crazy. (His are twice the size and half the thickness of ours!) We were off at 8 am and the descent took till 4 pm — a 2000-metre drop of complex way-finding; difficult and dangerous. Stinging nettles were added to the flora, being discovered by being well stung. Seldom gentle enough to dispense with hand-holds and footing never easy. Waist-deep, wet, vegetation, torrents, gullies, screes, cliffs (one traverse on a lip was hairy), an alp pock-marked with fallen boulders, bamboo thickets: we had the lot. A boulder blocked the route with river on one side and a climb on the other. Sher Singh climbed along and down in bare feet and Peter followed. Donald and I lowered the gear (and Christine) before abseiling off. It was a scruffy gang that rolled into

Hanuman Chatti. Rakshi was produced. The bottle was marked 'Govt. of India Excise', a nice touch for the home brew. Buses came so we bundled out the tea house and into one (50 folks in a 20 seater) for the 3 miles to Badrinath.

That was some run. The road had 22 hairpins and is literally carved into precipices and the 9,000- and 10,000-foot markers slipped past before we plunged into the overcrowded, overwhelming holy pilgrim town; such a contrast after the days of solitude. We had a huge meal in a hotel boasting it was 'the best and nearest to the "holly" places'. We all relish the many-spiced foods. Sleep poorly as a result no doubt but at 4.30 a temple loudspeaker gives an hour of scripture readings before a choir passes and the un-soundproof hotel comes to life. It was Lord Krishna's birthday. We celebrated it in the steaming hot springs. We were filthy, lacerated and rope-burnt from our epic descent. The place teemed with pilgrims of all kinds. Fascinating. Some have *walked* from the south to India. An afternoon bus returned us, with acceptable excitements on the way, back to Joshimath.

Ian and Frank had caught up, having finally wangled the First Aid Box out of Customs. They 'went to Agra to buy brollies and see the Taj Mahal'. At Hardwar they had fun changing trains: they arrived at Platform 1 and were told Rishi Kech left Platform 4 so humped all the gear there. The train came in on Platform 1. They madly fought back there only for the train to 'leave' and then return — to Platform 2. They made a quick trip to the Byundar Valley and wondered how we had managed to vanish.

Wonder how long it will take to be off again?

8 September: Joshimath

Nearly ready to leave Joshimath, we hope! Quite a packing operation. A Cambridge gang has been in the Sanctuary and provided useful information and we scrounge all sorts of things off them. An Australian group for Changabang is waiting for their Liaison Officer from Delhi. Quite a lot of social life among the toil. Donald and Christine went off to Lata to see about porters (we need dozens) while Peter sat like a buddha among the roomful of sacks and boxes. Each of us has a private kitbag/porter on top of all we need for wandering and camping in the Sanctuary. Christine has become chapatti-maker on a

183

permanent basis. Sher Singh referred to her as 'very good man'. I had a whole day sewing loads in hessian covers, a foul job. My mosquito net is a boon. I don't slap and scratch. It is stuffy in our cell of a room so we leave the door ajar and, for security, had a bucket balanced on it and tin cans here and there so a touch would create a real clatter. Stephen proved its efficiency! A big Japanese party has hired all the available porters so we are stuck anyway for a few days till they exit. Christine is going off for Delhi and Bombay so takes mail. [Not feeling too well she had a check-up and was discovered to be pregnant! Young Jamie made the hills at a tender age.] We have a big meal out, a 'Nanda Devi of rice' with endless side dishes. Bananas are only a penny each. We eat well and are all disgustingly healthy. This brief scrawl just to say a lorry is ordered for tomorrow. We may be off!

9 September: Lata Road-end

The five Australians, eight of us, an Indian L.O. (liaison officer) and all our gear made quite a load on a lorry and we actually were off on schedule. We stopped at Tapoban (mentioned in W. H. Murray's *Scottish Himalayan Expedition*) for Aussie shopping and Pommy eating. We are now immune to hair-raising roads and only shut our eyes occasionally. We were dumped on a verge, in the middle of nowhere it felt, above the Dhauli Ganga. (Lata is half an hour above the road.) There we camped, a tarpaulin over our pile of gear, and tents or brollies sheltering us from the rain. It rains about half the time but is a vertical, well-behaved precipitation, not at all Scottish. The Aussie L.O. is a pleasant climber and not a military shop steward. The day went in sorting out porters. They dribble in from the Japanese trip but Lata (or rakshi) is a bit too handy. We will need goats as well. They carry porter food so this avoids the porters for porters Catch 22 situation. The river runs grey and powerful and, with the waterfalls, crags and everything else makes the home scale so puny. A popular climbing cliff at home, with its guidebook, would vanish in the vastness here. At the cafe in Tapoban Stephen came up and asked 'Have you looked at the lorry tyres?' to which Peter, mind elsewhere, replied 'Yes please, but no sugar in mine'. Log and this start of a letter are done by candlelight. The river roars.

There were no vital hold-ups. The porter food was repacked in 6-18 kg panniers for the goats. 'Goat-man' is quite a character. His beasts behave better than the bipeds. We all wended up the hillside in haphazard fashion. Through my binoculars I saw plenty of Lata stops and was glad when a porter caught me up at the Bhalta camp site. It would have been annoying to overshoot. Loads arrived over many hours and we grew impatient waiting for that day's food box — only to find it was there already! I stoked a wood fire and we cook a meat, veg and spiced macaroni dish. Chapattis with cheese and/or jam and good coffee saw dusk slip into stars. The porters' fires wink among the trees. Goat bells tinkle. It hardly rained all day. Perhaps the monsoon was over we suggested. Sher Singh thought not. 'Monsoon finish two days.'

That first day we only climbed 650 metres, a third of the initial uphill but doing the lot in one is not advisable. We were astir by 5.30 and soon left the glade to the crows and smoke. The climb was steeply upwards all day. 'Vertical mud' someone called it. Huge pines were draped in Spanish moss: a vertical Mila Dorcha! The rain returned for much of the day — and night. Lata Kharak was an exposed ridge and sordid in the extreme. My tent was in one of the last loads to arrive. (I'll carry it myself in future.) Hours crouching under a brolly tend to pall. As I was rigging a shelter to cook under, all the tent sites had gone, so I was perched on a platform built of kitbags. Donald was ill last night and came in weak but recovering. A goat is slaughtered — to propitiate the Goddess of Weather we hope. Bed at 7 pm was bliss. It rained all night.

It rained for the seven hours of march the following day too: a double stage. My porter arrived ahead of me and my 30-lb load felt every ounce of it, but I did stay in my tent till ready to go. At the end of the day it took time, inside sleeping bag, inside tent, to warm up and dry out a bit. We suffer because of wanting to be *in* the Sanctuary for the maximum good weather time, while the walk-in is equally, perhaps more, important aesthetically. We are not seeing the fantastic scenery. [We were to see it in the crisp colours of autumn on the way out.]

We climbed, endlessly, to a pass at 4,252 metres (thank goodness we are acclimatised and fit — a real sweat) then kept up and down at that level on a path which felt as if only glued to the cliffs by mud. A strain as always precarious. Some of the porters are in bare feet or old gym shoes. Maybe it is as well we didn't see the drop below: 1650 metres to the gorge of the Rishi Ganga. It was long thought impenetrable and a big 'curtain' of cliff added to its defences. Our long haul up was to gain the height needed to outflank these problems. We thought of Shipman and Tilman, early heroes, recent acquaintances, with ever-growing admiration.

Dharansi, at 4,145 metres was passed, the site the porters were keen *not* to use under monsoon conditions. They have neither tents nor sleeping bags and survive under tarpaulins in remarkably cheerful fashion. A col beyond was 4,237 metres and on a bit we suddenly plunge 1,000 metres down a slope to forest level and camp at Dibrugheta, 3,499 metres. A moating torrent from Dunagiri was crossed by a bridge consisting of a solitary log. The goats filed across quite cheerfully! Having cooked the night before I retreated to tent comforts. It was an eerie site with smoky fires and voices muffled among the dripping trees. Nobody seemed very cheery and supper was tired-looking pasta and corned beef literally floating in a gravy of rainwater. Only Charles, Ian and I could be bothered making chapattis and coffee. [That squalor was a remarkable contrast to the stop there on the exit, though it produced its own excitements.]

Everybody dried or singed things over fires in the morning and it was 11 before we set off for a short 3-hour stage. The rain had only turned off at 6 and we kept expecting more. The path took us briskly up for 300 metres and then contoured up and down and in and out — good horizontal progress for a change — till we came back to the Rishi Ganga itself and crossed it by a doddery bridge to camp on the other side (Deodi, 3,292 metres). It was a joy to wash and eat well again. Tents and clothes hung from the birch trees. The porters sang. They also slaughtered another goat. The victim's belly is slit and a hand rips out the heart which sits beating on a plate thereafter. Frank, a surgeon by trade, was full of admiration. A porter came and daubed my brow with red powder. We had 'cheuchy' goat for supper.

Today's weather was actually good. The sacrificial goat worked! Or Sher Singh's weather sense. The monsoon appears to be over. We can expect cool clear days now until winter comes. Today's route was a real yo-yo one: up, down, up, down, 300 metres each time. A valley came in from the south, from Trisul, climbed by Tom Longstaff in 1907, the first-ever 7,000-metre peak to be scaled. Even he didn't find his way into the Sanctuary, though in 1905 he'd made a col on the Eastern Rim and looked into it.

We had another up, down, to where the Ramani River comes in from the north. The mighty side of Changabang (recently climbed by Bonington *et al*) lies that way. The gorge becomes sheer beyond and camp is a small level area held between cliff and torrent. My door is on the edge (mustn't sleepwalk) and the noise colossal with the precipices acting as sounding boards. A familiar enough sound but the scale again is just so big.

I'm finishing off this airletter as we have a postie. The Aussie L.O. has been ill and Frank is worried enough to suggest he makes a rapid exit in case of pulmonary oedema. Goat man takes his beasts back from here. One animal got on the cliff and knocked a stone down on a porter's head. Sher Singh grinned. 'Only head. Duralam Singh thick skull. OK.' — but he'll go out too just in case. The porter carrying the First Aid Box is suffering from a strained back! Donald, Stephen and I went on to get photos down on the camp. The track is suddenly very exposed as it teeters up the overhang above the gorge — a mere dent in 600-metre crags. Rhoddies and birch make welcome handholds but some bits are really scary. The fun is about to begin. It feels as if we are regrouping and preparing for action — sending the wounded out and writing letters while we can.

All the sites are rapidly being fouled. The porters rip down wood to burn, ground is churned to mud, hygiene minimal and litter left everywhere, even on the edge of a pounding river. [The Sanctuary is now closed to allow it to recover both from human despoilation and from the ravagings of the goats. This spot had, for generations, been as far as man and goats had managed, but the locals found a way in and grazed the Sanctuary to death in a couple of seasons.] Tomorrow is the 'official' ending of the monsoon so it is just as well the weather has started to settle. We have had an easy enough mud-walk through the outer defences and tomorrow starts the real challenge of penetrating from Outer Sanctuary towards the Inner Sanctuary. We have had tantalising glimpses today of Nanda Devi, India's highest mountain, (7,817 metres), locally a goddess, very beautiful and aloof. It stands in this secret place ringed round with near impenetrable peaks and drained by the mighty Rishi Ganga — up which we slog for eight days to gain entry. It is one of the world's fabulous places and the walk-in is memorable already. Wonder what I'll be saying in the next letter you receive?

17 September: In the Sanctuary

Some time to actually write a bit. The last letter went off from the Ramani camp. We thought we had had some impressive walking by then, and so we had, but the next two days just overwhelmed us. 'Mind-blowing' is a horrible phrase but accurate of the double-day we did from Ramani. I have never been so scared for so long at a time, ever. It left us exhausted from mind to toes! Our admiration for Shipton and Tilman reached new summits. They broke through here the year I was born. [They had been enthusiastic about our planned wanderings in the Sanctuary and looked forward to seeing our photographs but, on return, we found Shipton had died and Tilman had sailed off and vanished *en route* to the Antarctic.]

The day began early (fires flickering into life at 5 am) with a 7 o'clock departure. We began with a brutal 600-metre grass slope which shrank the river below to near-silence. From a spur we had a fabulous view of Nanda Devi, framed in the vee cleft of the Rishi Ganga, the summit setting a plume across the bright blue sky and the new snows reaching far down into the shadows.

We wended on with a continued supply of awkward wee places to deal with (the track was just made by passing feet), on slopes that were never less than very steep (VS in rock parlance, XS lay ahead). I have the drawback of a vivid imagination. There were places with fixed ropes. On a walk! [Since then I have talked to several famous climbers who have been in for new routes on peaks like Kalanka and Changabang and it is the *walking-in* that draws their comments and superlatives. One expects the spectacular, the difficult, when climbing — not walking! This was comforting: I thought I was the only chicken.] We wound in and out and up, higher and higher, till we came to a nasty gully with a drop of 1000 metres to the river, with muddy slabs beyond. The remains of a piton and rope hinted at the dangers but the porters with our ropes had romped ahead! On e of the Aussie porters lost his load of flour. It went tumbling down, visually and audibly, all too like a human falling. Thank Nanda it was not a porter. They are amazing. Awkward boxes or sacks are simply carried on backs and held with ropes. They have a sort of emergency ripcord so at a tug can drop the load. I think the porter did that here to save himself tumbling off. Lucky too it was a load entirely of *ata* — it could have been all their ice axes and other such irreplaceable and indispensable items.

The famous Tilman Slabs followed but they were decently tamed by fixed ropes. The last place of slabs had none and was quite an effort, with the equivalent of two Ben Nevis north faces under one's heels. Technically it is easy enough but when every step of the long hours had to be safe it became a bit of a strain. It is hard to describe as there is nothing comparable. The opposite side of the gorge is simply sheer cliff for thousands of feet, choughs minute specks on it and big waterfalls appeared as tiny spouts. A few tent-spaces dug out on the slope indicated Bujgara site but we walked on past its spectacular setting. The bluff beyond was edged by a track only as wide as our feet, impressed into the steepest vegetated slope I've seen. It rose and fell from the path in staggering scale and I've photos to prove it I hope. (Stagger was the one thing you didn't!) Ahead loomed more prows and bluffs, one the "Pisgah" of Shipton/Tilman, so called as from it you could view the Promised Land. We lost about 300 metres to round one spur and at once doubled back to toil 300 metres up, traverse under the next wall, go down a rake, scramble up to the next — then, far from the route being low, we turn up again on wet slabs, vegetation, a gully bed and a haul out to the crest of the final barrier. Ian, far below, heard my yell of relief and glee from Pisgah top. It felt as if one could reach out a hand and touch Nanda Devi. It was no longer away ahead, a remote, framed beauty. It now filled our world: a stark, bold, intimidating mass of black and white. Full frontal. The new snow was down to the moraines just above where I stood. Just 200 metres ahead a pillar of smoke rose in the still air. This was Tilchaunani camp site. I was soon clasping the most wonderful mug of tea in the whole world.

It was an unusual camp spot. The tents were pitched on

slabby platforms cut into and built out of the steep hillside. It was split-level living. Eight porters had simply dumped their loads and shot off back for Ramani for a second carry the next day. They whooped past us at one awkward spot. What men! (Goat Man and his charges, the injured porter, the sick L.O. and one fit porter to help had returned from Ramani, so some doubling-up was inevitable.) Water was scarce and a porter made a spout from a rhubarb leaf to catch the drips. Exhaustion won over excitement. We were abed by seven. I had one pee visit in the middle of the night. It was breathy-cold and there was an extravagance of stars. Nanda Devi, so ice-white by day, was a black, blank, recognisable shape in the silver sheen of stars.

The exit from Tilchaunani was by fixed ropes over another band of slabs. We were able to look away past the mountain into the Northern half of the Sanctuary — right to the peaks of the Eastern Rim. This, the Uttari Rishi, is now our home till winter comes. Being on the south side of the Rishi Ganga gorge we had first to cross to the other side, but as we began losing height we saw, or rather didn't see the river, for it is so deeply-cut as to be invisible. We would have to cross the river draining the Southern Sanctuary first, then the Northern one. It looked like an interesting day. It was.

[Nanda Devi towers between these two draining rivers, each fed by mighty barriers of peaks, but you cannot walk round behind the mountain for it is attached to the Eastern Rim by cliffs soaring far up to 3000-metres. The peak is climbed from the southern half of the Sanctuary. The northern, which Shipton/Tilman described as one of the most beautiful places they had ever seen, was much less visited: the lure for our trek.]

Donald and I were off first and Donald almost at once went for a slither on the slabs — fortunately on the fixed ropes — so we treaded like Agag thereafter. There was a huge gully to cross and it was the first of many ins and outs. We rested on a spur after a bouldery bit and had a neck-craning view up to Nanda Devi, then it was mostly a long, descending traverse. We just about died when two turkey-sized Himalayan snowcocks went squealing off from our feet with the suddenness of grouse but the noise of pigs. We found the skulls (with horns) of two burral. Down in the gorge there were snow pigeons and a pale gentian stared between the grasping birch. A cave would have made a pleasant bivouac — but work lay ahead.

The Aussies had chosen a quicker line from camp (crafty Pommies!) so already had a pulley system across the gorge. The whole drainage of the Southern Sanctuary roared through a cliff-girt gap half the width of a country road. A good long-jumper had made it onto a big boulder from which a high step onto the cliff on the other side was possible. They had just rigged up a pulley system from cliff to cliff and it was soon busy as dozens of people and dozens of loads were hauled across. The humans slipped a loop under their arms and held on to the karabiners snapped into the pulley-wheels (we had come prepared, Shipton and Tilman would have thought us quite decadent) and were yanked across. The pegs all held! As up to four loads of 56 lb plus, crossed at a time, they had been well tested.

It was only after I'd done my share of work at the crossing and was wending on up onto the ridge between the two rivers that it suddenly struck me that we were actually *on* Nanda Devi. Quite an emotional realisation! [A new air letter began here.]

We went on along rotten crags to where the valley opened out and a high bank would do to anchor a rope to slide down and across to the other side. Porters began to arrive but, naturally, the ropes were at the rear this time. Donald, impatient as ever, went on to cross on the glacier snout upstream. It was an infuriating wait, especially as the river was only just too dangerous. Peter arrived next and it was all pretty shambolic with the three sahibs yelling at each other, the roar of the river and the milling mob of porters who mostly refused to cross as camp was only going to be 300 metres away on the other side. As the money was across it spoke loudest. The ropes sagged and had to be held aloft overhead at both ends by several people. It always seemed to go slack when an unpopular lad was halfway over! (We usually agreed with their choice of victims. No sahib was ducked fortunately.)

I withdrew to prepare supper at the temporary site while others ferried loads and haggled over paying-off most of the lads. Stephen and Frank opted to go round by the glacier snout rather than risk a wetting but they left it too late and had an unscheduled and uncomfortable bivvy when frosty darkness caught them. It was eight o'clock before I pitched my tent. Only time to scrawl in the log but not a day to be easily forgotten. Our missing pair turned up for breakfast (and had their supper as well). They had reached the glacier but instead of taking Donald's easy crossing line below the snout they had gone onto the ice which was hopeless in the falling dark so they retreated to shiver the night away in a small cave, retreated at first light, and crossed the fixed ropes anyway.

Some of the good porters roll up with loads doubled from Tilch. More will come later. We brew with them again. Righ Singh is a real character in a tartan tammy. He has been up Trisul, the Devistan peaks and to Camp II on Changabang with Chris Bonington. Sher Singh is his brother. These two, Donald and I, carry hefty loads and go off to recce for our permanent base camp. The Aussies are to be based at a tarn beyond the white, granite-covered, snout of the Changabang Gal (glacier) but it is a bleak spot and we settle for a grassy slope before their glacier where there is a spring of delicious water and an abundance of dead wood for the luxury of fires. [We only used a tenth of the paraffin so laboriously carried in, as we cooked on wood and could even heat water enough to take semi-baths out of a bucket!] The others went back to the first river crossing to help with the last loads and ensure everything is over the rivers today if possible and up here tomorrow. We should manage with the porters available. Sher Singh spots the porters descending from Tilch. We could hardly see them, even with binoculars. We were back at the temporary camp to meet the gang arriving. Without 'Braggart' Singh, the ineffective, blustering 'head' porter, yesterday's shambles was avoided. Most cheerfully splash through with just minimal rope aid, treating it as a big joke if one sat down in the foam. Some of the Aussie porters stopped for the night, after we roped them in for an afternoon's work: six of us, seven porters (everyone — except Frank — cooking) took a 56-lb load up to the Base Camp. Our choice seemed to meet with approval. We had a cheery night round a fire after a tin of UK ham and spicy rice, while Righ Singh showed his chapatti-making ability. [The dough is slapped from hand to hand rapidly to form a thin 'pancake' which is then baked on a special metal dish — slightly hollow — which is oiled with *ghee* first. It is an acquired knack which was to become a big part of our life in the next weeks.]

Sher Singh decided not to stay with us. He'd be too lonely I suspect and we can't afford another bloke. (We'd love to keep several, for they are delightful folk.) There is a pow-wow going on now about our date of exit and which porters are to come for us. To make doubly sure a letter in English can be taken to the Lata school-teacher to translate and read to them. The Rishi Ganga under snow is not a trekker's idea of fun. Nerves are only easing now and our spell of idyllic camping and wandering about should be bliss before we have to return to the gorge. I try not to be involved and scribble away to get these air letters off with the departing porters tomorrow. Our only loss coming in was a karabiner falling into the river yesterday. So much for the dire warnings. Our chosen Base Camp is 4,500 metres yet we are able to load-carry and romp about unaffected by altitude and we sleep like babies. Much as we enjoy the gregarious porters (and ourselves) the best is about to start: the bliss of solitude, in one of the world's most inaccessible and beautiful places. We all have our small individual tents, plus a couple of snow-line ones, so can do just as we like — quite the antithesis of an 'expedition'. Shipton and Tilman would approve!

Everyone has now retreated to tents. Candles glow and odd conversations are muted by the river. I wouldn't be anywhere else in the world. I'm falling asleep as I write so must stop. Goodness knows when or how the next letter will reach you.

18 September: Base Camp

The seven porters carried loads to Base while we breakfasted. We then carried our tents and gear up while they descended for the last seven loads. Their tarpaulin makes a kitchen shelter with a wall of tins and boxes, all very organised. [We generally ate outside and cooked on a trench fire rather than primus or gaz stoves. The cookhouse was the spot where Frank seemed to write home every night. As he'd begin 'Dear Wendy' the cookhouse was thereafter 'The Wendy House'.] There was a great shaking of hands with the seven (all due to return for the exit: one each for us, plus a couple of extra for food, etc), and we took photographs of them perched on a boulder. *Namaste!* Sticking this — it will be posted in Joshimath sometime. Love to everyone. *Namaste!*

193

[Life in the Sanctuary was all we hoped it would be. When we later met the Aussie's L.O. in Delhi (fully restored to health) he asked if we had 'had our hearts' desire' — which is what it had been for a gang of respectable middle-aged characters! Donald, our main driving-force, was ironically to drown in a Highland stream a few years later. Others have hardly been abroad since, as job and family commitments have taken priority. It was the walk of a lifetime — and you can't repeat such things. Someone had Orwell's *The Road to Wigan Pier* with him and quoted 'In order that one may enjoy primitive methods of travel, it is necessary that no other method should be available. No human being ever wants to do anything in a more cumbersome way than is necessary.' That led to some commenting.

Not many letters were to be written (though I kept a log book going) but I'll quote a bit from what there was just to give a flavour, and then more on the exit — the Rishi Ganga walk, in reverse. We enjoyed sparkling weather as we had hoped but it grew steadily colder, autumn tinted the vegetation in colourful fashion, the snowline crept down and it was time to go. We hoped to make a trek up from Ramani on the way out to see the startling tooth of Changabang (the face to be climbed by Boardman and Tasker) Changabang and Kalanka were the dominant features above Base Camp.]

19 September

We go up to the Aussie camp for afternoon tea! Rumour had it that the lake was hot. It was very cold, but not frozen, so we had overdue baths. On rounding to their camp we were told it was their drinking water! Their site a bit of a slum from other gangs. Ours has never been used, a strange feeling.

20 September

We wander up to 5,500 metres behind camp and from the edge of the Changabang Gal see the cathedral-bold peak and Kalanka next to it. Study the Aussie route and wish the youths well! It was the other way that most impressed. Nanda Devi still soared 2,300 metres above us, shapely and fluted and draped in white, quite indescribably beautiful.

21 September

Three of us go off to stay in the innermost corner of the Sanctuary where an arm of glacier curves round to end at the wall that joins N.D. to the Eastern Rim. A foul, bouldery glacier to cross, then miles of meadow to a cirque surrounded by ice cliffs of over 2,300 metres. An avalanche high up growled like thunder and we watched it fall, slowly turning to dust which just faded away. The scale is mind-boggling. We sit on a flowery knoll, calmly drinking tea, watching the wagtails and reading books, quite ordinary activities, but every now and then the eyes stray and the disbelief floods back.

1 October

It is a task writing the log each day. The Aussies go out in a few days and will take mail so I'll complete this air letter. We feel marvellously isolated here. Time flies, yet we fill the days very contentedly. I've finished making a stack of chapattis for Ian (back from a 48-hour trip on his own) and Frank (joining me next for a trip to one area we've not looked at). The rest are up by the Rishi Kot Gal. We've all been there. Charles and I went on the glacier a bit, probably my highest-ever at 6,400 metres (higher than Kilimanjaro) and came 'home' by a high traverse towards a small peak above camp. We went to go up it, a puff at that height, but at 5.30 the top proved to be 100 metres of tottery towers and spires away. We had no gear, no torches and camp was 1800 metres below us. It is dark at 6.30. Stephen and Donald heard our yells in the night so brews and food were waiting. The cooking fire looked like a fallen star. A moon has waxed and waned. It is cold and clear always: freezing at nights, sunny during the day and windy in the afternoons. A very restful existence. We read a lot. It is light at 5.30 and we are up not long after — as soon as the sun shines on our camp. I'll take this up to the Aussies tomorrow and have a night by the lake to have a dusk and dawn of bird-watching there. Back to my book now for an hour: Montaigne's Essays (Frank's).

[The books carried by the party were an extraordinary mixture, ranging through David Niven autobiography, Arthur Ransome, Priestley, John Masters, Alan Bullock's study of Hitler, Barrow's *Robert Bruce,* and Herodotus — his *Histories* being by far the most read of all!]

195

3 October
We were entertained by Garry at the Lake Camp. Charlie has gone up despite a bad ankle. Garry has a 6,000-metre 'ceiling' he has discovered. Their big push is on now so he can only wait. Frank and I camp on the other side of the lake and it snowed on the tent overnight. Things left out were mere snow-lumps in the morning. Yet an hour or two of sun made it all vanish. Frank had a rough night so we change plans and he goes 'home' and I go up the glacier edge till 1 pm (instead of overnight) and back to Base as well. All the tents pitched so quite a reunion. Onions led to a disturbed night so I took a tablet which brought on vivid dreams. In one I recall trying to stop an endless stream of porters to have them dig down to hidden water which would then gush out to become a great pilgrim spot — but they wouldn't stop.

5 October
I was still in bed when the eight Aussie porters arrived. They have tea and Frank, Garry and Andrew (who arrive from different directions) have coffee — which John Masters suggests is 'the Raj's revenge on India'. Andrew at once gave Frank a frostbitten hand to deal with. He had a big burn blister too as he had no feeling to notice anything hot. They failed on Changabang. Really just ran out of steam and sensible enough to call it a day. The one bit of bad weather caught them too — just below the summit. (I wouldn't swop any big hill needing a treadmill slog for our time of freedom to wander.) The lad who was hit on the head at Ramani was one of their exit porters. There were *Namastes* and they set off after the other three who'd passed before I was awake.

7 October
Wash some clothes after breakfast and spend most of the day going over food, dividing it into exit-needs and sanctuary-needs, etc. Some chicken meals vanished in the night but we'd brought some gash food from the Aussie site. We are not short! Far too much dehydrated rubbish which we just don't use. We'd rather cook rice, chapattis, etc., and carry that on trips. Last of the local dried apricots for supper: wee, scruffy things with a flavour unknown at home. I was going to sleep in the Wendy House to see what

it was that was raiding us but when I noticed the size of the paw prints I changed my mind. I didn't fancy a big cat gnawing my nose while pinned like a mummy inside a sleeping bag. Every night is colder now. Camping up the Changabang Gal we could see the Plough: made me homesick. Afternoons cloud up more now too. Winter is not far off.

9 October
The marauder scattered raisins about last night, left his signs on Charles's karrimat and went off with some coffee! The thrill of the day was to see a wallcreeper when across the glacier on Nanda Devi's flanks. N.D. always glows like a torch going out, long after everything else is in darkness. The last of our egg powder went on breakfast omelettes. It was duvets-on for the afternoon as mist and snow blew through. Finished 599 pages of Herodotus in bed. A clattering of stones and can just see 16 chamois-like beasts tiptoe past across the glacier.

10 October
After a couple of days alone we are suddenly all seven in camp again, full of various doings. Celebrate with a big meal ('We can't carry it out — so let's eat it!'): soup with chapattis, an Australian chicken and mushroom meal with vegetables, Christmas pudding, fruit salad, coffee . . .

11 October
A lazy morning of recovering. With a few days to go there is a mix of feelings: to be lazy or go off on one last wander? Lots of tea is brewed and jam chapattis consumed. The wood pile takes a hammering as 'baths' became popular in the morning sun. Some of us were sitting doing nothing much with a view to resting afterwards when we heard voices. In our Sanctuary? In trotted Goman Singh (another of Sher Singh's brothers) and four porters. They had come several days early because they feared winter was closing-in and it was imperative to be out before the big snows came. Their weather-wisdom is not to be questioned (the monsoon ended when they said it would), so we go tomorrow!

This was a real bombshell. We just hated the idea. Our self-indulgent activity would end, our plans were suddenly all changed and hurry-hurry introduced to our timeless paradise. The day was spent in frantic packing. Items, precious in this spot, suddenly had no value — like 10 gallons of paraffin, sealed and brought all the way from Delhi. Before supper time Sher Singh, Righ Singh and the others rolled in. In face of their cheerfulness we could only cheer up ourselves. They brought us a *real* treat: a bag of fresh apples and newly-harvested potatoes. They also brought mail from home which dispersed the sahibs to their tents after supper. I moved in with Donald so Sher and Righ could use my tent. The other porters sprawled in the Wendy House or just sat and talked at the fire all night. Donald said Christine had had fun escaping from Joshimath as avalanches had blocked the road. She had met cockroaches in the pilgrim place . . . By candlelight I finish off this bitty-bitty letter and wonder just where I'll post it. The present will so soon be parcelled off to be stored into dreams.

14 October: Dibrughetta

Taking the chance to fill a last letter on the last night of the walk-out. If it is more of a scrawl than usual it's because thumb, forefinger and pinky are covered in plasters. We have all acquired deep cuts, which grow from tiny nicks, and catch on everything in an uncomfy way. Frank, surgeon and violinist, is quite worried and feels he'll need medical leave for hands before he starts cutting up people again. [Alas, no extra leave; once out our hands recovered in a few days.] Dry altitude the cause probably. Our *only* medical complaint. Base Camp was higher than Mont Blanc too — but we took care, as oldies, and had good porters, good food and good weather helping. We are only now recovering from the advanced departure date and already we are nearly out.

Charles and Stephen insisted on staying for another four days and two porters waited for them: we have mixed feelings about that, now, and hope they exit safely. [They did but have been reticent about the journey so it must have been rather traumatic.] They had food enough to stay the winter we felt (35 man-days because of the early departure). The porters all carried 60 lb or more as they scrounged jerrycans and other, to them, useful objects. They were all cheery and there were no hassles at all. They even understood we were poor Brits and most of the gear going out had to go home with us. Gifts of duvets and equipment, were not on!

We set off about 8.45 on the 12th and avoided the river by using the glacier and its snout. So often the path relaxes only to spring new nasty features at us; it did here too as we romped down by the river — suddenly it was cliff and we had to squeeze below or across it before reaching our crossing-spot. Rocks in the water were ice so it would have been a nasty crossing. We found a rope in place over the next one. Sher Singh crossed somehow by dangling in a sling from a krab and hauling! Odd bits of cord, even nylon bootlaces, were joined to make a pulling line (the rope was in the rear!) and an uncomfy bosun's chair affair. I preferred to jump, a method only one porter cared to copy.

Tilchaunani had no water but we were only passing through anyway. From it we could see the bright dot of the lone tent at Base Camp — now many miles away. Everything is dry and brown compared to our arrival following the monsoon. The fixed ropes had gone (rope is precious to the locals) so we had a dicey crossing to the site. We went on for Bujgara (sadly omitted coming in), just a third day rolled into that one! A Japanese expedition's porters were leaving as we arrived and are suspected of being the rope-removers. 'Reni-men' our 'Lata-men' said scornfully.

Having pulled up we set about losing height again. The rocky start was all right but the frozen slopes of tussocky grass were unpleasant. The scree, so demanding before, was run down in a flash. Stumps of fixed ropes were infuriating as we simply didn't have the rope to rig new security. Some of it was shockingly exposed and we tried neither to look down nor think about it as we staggered on with a hefty pack. At times we climbed down, facing inwards, so 'path' is a relative idea. Part of the shock of the porters' early arrival was having no time to psych ourselves up for the Rishi Ganga. Our mad rush out hardly gave us time to think. 'The porters are not just superhumans but psychologists as well', I commented that night.

We toiled up a rake beyond the bluff and then there was a long mainly-down switchback. At one place we crawled along a ledge on a cliff face. Devil Donald threw a stone off and began counting. It fell so far we did not hear it bounce.

Bujgara was very welcome: a swallow's nest under the eaves of Nanda Devi. Three platforms made the site. Righ Singh was romping about after wood and water and made endless chapattis in disgust at our efforts. A rather dreaded day had passed safely and with a certain thrill and satisfaction. We all messed together and sat round the fire. What a pity we could not communicate more fully.

Talk turned to what we would do once out. As soon as we leave Joshimath we become 'mere tourists' but who could miss out the Taj Mahal? [with Machu Picchu one of the few sites that surpasses expectations]. The Ghana Bird Sanctuary was high on my list and we all looked forward to an orgy of Indian food and train journeys. [Noise and crowds were the main shock after our solitary weeks.] A satellite went overhead which we felt an intrusion of civilisation so-called. My hands cracked-open with the roughness of the day's work. Bujgara means birch trees and is indeed surrounded by them. We had a very cold night (only 150 metres lower than Base Camp) and it was a frosty tent that was rolled up. When opened that night in Deodi it was still frozen!

The porters' idea of tea was to fill the kettle with water, milk-powder, tea and vast amounts of sugar and slap it on the fire. When it boiled over it was ready. It was delicious and Righ Singh turned out chapattis on the glowing embers quicker than we could eat them. The sun touched the top of N.D. and it ran down the slopes like something melting.

The day started with a bang and we were soon gripped on the slabs leading to the Tilman Slabs area — really the crux of the route. It was like descending oversteep roof tiles but at least the ropes had been left as it was too dangerous to remove them, even for nerveless locals. Boulders and birch were nothing after that, even the uphill sections.

All too soon it felt we were at the spur with the cairns which gives one of the best views to Nanda Devi. She had put on an extra veil of white overnight. We were sorry to drop beyond for the long flanker down to Ramani but if we lost our goddess we walked into a glory of autumn colours that made up for it: the yellows, reds and purples set off by the deep greens of the pine trees and overtopped by white spires and blue sky. We used Peter's weariness as an excuse to stop the porters at Deodi (the Vestibule), a place of woody bliss. Any hint of breeze brought a ballet of falling leaves.

200

I washed the tent in the river to remove the mud from under it and the frost from inside. Peter, unwisely, commented that the last time we had seen rain had been there. It promptly rained!

The porters vanished into caves and we retired to fall asleep to the odd sound of leaves and water pitter-pattering above us.

Today was a delightful day from start to finish. I was up first and joined the porters for tea. The smoke from the fire went back into the cave and appeared further up the hillside. I'd love to go off on an extended tour with these lads: they are such cheery extroverts. The rain was snow higher up so we shudder at the thought of the others coming out under the new conditions. The porters had been wise in coming early. That depth of snow would not melt off now till spring. Winter had come.

We crossed the river and the trees were magnificent against the snow whiting. Even the path seemed easy, (we had some immunity by now I suppose) so we could relish the spectacular setting which had been hidden while walking in.

Righ Singh pointed out figures away ahead — the tail of a big Japanese gang who had been in the Southern Sanctuary — so we have Dibrugheta ('small stone-god meadow') to ourselves. We reject the standard site and beyond the meadow chose a ledge among the pines where we are now. It is possibly the most exquisite place I've ever pitched a tent.

There was no sugar for the tea as the 4-day-ration had all gone by last night: 7 lb of it! But we had delicious rice flavoured with spices which came from wee paper pokes twisted into Righ Singh's waist-band. The rice was thrown into the pressure cooker and was deemed ready when it began crawling out the safety valve. (We hid behind the trees till it was opened!) There was litter from the USA, Czechoslovakia, Japan, India and the UK which was rather a sad commentary.

We ate to bursting as tomorrow night we are invited to stay at Lata for a party (goat and rakshi) and go down to Joshimath thereafter. So I write this and eat too many jam chapattis, for I may not be able to tomorrow night. It is a job to hold the biro with three fingers hurting. The rain comes on again.

18 October: Hardwar

When I scribbled what I thought would be the last of our news I should have known better. The unexpected is the normal out here. Nothing should be taken for granted. Every 'tale' seems to have a sting in it. I woke at 3 am. It was not raining thank goodness. The porters were still noisy by the fire, laughing, talking and clearing throats. How they can do what they do with so little sleep is amazing. When the alarm went off at 5 nature made me exit — to find the world muffled up in snow. The porters were still round the fire, faces lit, and the forest a mix of monster shadows and new white. Beyond rose the jagged hills and a rush of stars. It was so beautiful I woke Frank and told him to have a look. We pretended not to think about Charles and Stephen still in the Sanctuary.

We crossed the tree-trunk bridge and tackled the 1,000-metre toil beyond. It was more enjoyed than in descent despite the deep, soft snow making it hard work. The Curtain is an incredible fan of rock and it had to be passed by going round over it. Down the gorge was unthinkable. The peaks caught fire as the sun rose and we had another day of crystal clarity and vivid colours. 'Anyone got any film left?' became a regular plea!

The long slope led to an ever-widening view. Nanda Devi as ever filled the gorge upstream. A maze of jagged peaks ranged in all directions. We walked through an arch and on to Dharansi, the highest point of the day. Normally this was a day's march but we had to go on, being low in food and the porters lacking all shelter. Some were walking in plimsolls with only a stick for support. Carrying 65 lb! We wended in and out and up and down. It was not difficult, just constantly dangerous as the shady corners were deep in snow and the sunny places were slippery with mud. We opened one load to find our ice axes. Even one or two of the porters were subdued. For hours every step had to be sure — a great strain on the nerves, with thousands of feet yawning below. Helping the youngest, very frightened porter, took my mind off it a bit. When we were finally onto safe ground my legs felt as they do coming ashore after days at sea: wobbly!

Peter and I passed Lata Kharak (Lata's pasture) and raced on to Bhalta where we downed a litre of water each, paddled, and had a laze in the sun. We did not want it to end, even then. The terraced fields were red, for the harvest had finished and in Lata village, every stone rooftop and terrace had hay drying on it. We sat on a balcony for welcome tea and were given a room in Sher Singh's brother's house. We gave away everything we possibly could as presents and paid our porters. It was small return for all they had given us. We think we are well-off, but we do not laugh as much as do these humble peasants in the far Himalayas.

It was quite a party. I had my 2-litre water bottle beside me and I managed to surreptitiously pour 90% of my drink into it, therby earning a quite unwarranted reputation as a boozer. Peter was emptying his into a big jar in the corner but later discovered it leaked so all the spirit had run under his sleeping bag, which will smell for weeks. There were songs and stories and we forgot awhile the bus to Joshimath and the world of Delhi waiting.

There were no *poochies* (creepy crawlies). We slept well. After early morning tea and chapattis we distributed what we could: the pressure cooker, karrimats, socks, lighters — even the chapatti dish itself. The porters then took our loads down the half hour to the motor road. An hour later a bus came but did not stop. At 2 pm Sher Singh, useful to the last, returned with a lorry. It took an hour to Joshimath, a magnificent run in the bright colours of autumn. We arrived at dusk along with a thunderstorm and were battered by hard-hitting hailstones. The hotel welcomed us and after a final packing we went off to eat: a superb Indian meal with scrumptious rice and an endless series of tasty dishes with it. We paid for it by trading off our ropes and any unwanted camping items we had stored there.

My alarm went off at 4.30 and we went for the bus at 5. It went then too, after a flaming rag had been held under the fuel tank to warm-up the diesel. After eleven hours of mighty drops a mere foot away one's mind becomes as numb as one's bum. Occasional tea or *tiffin* stops were welcome. It was straight onto the train at Rishi Kesh and we are now installed in a seedy hotel overlooking the Ganges. As the river looked and smelt cleaner than we did we had a swim in it and washed away our dirt if not our sins. We are now fit to return to the Greaves in Delhi, by the 'Musoorie Express' (spacious sleepers booked after hard bargaining). Tomorrow it will be whisky and soda on the terrace under the magnolia blossom with servants spoiling us and all this fading into dreams, becoming, for us part and parcel of the legends and history. Just last year a strange and moving legend was added to the mountain which has filled our waking and sleeping all these weeks.

Many years ago an American climber, Willie Unsoeld, later to be one of the climbers to make the first traverse of Everest, saw Nanda Devi and was so captivated by its beauty he vowed to return and, if he ever had a daughter, she would be named after the peak. Well he had a daughter, a vivacious blonde, who grew into a competent climber in her own right. Thus both Willie and Nanda Devi Unsoeld journeyed up the Rishi Ganga as part of an American expedition to try the mountain by a new and difficult route — the prow that faces down the gorge. Nanda Devi fascinated the porters by her name, her beauty and her personality. They simply adored her. The trip went well and eventually the climbers were gaining height on the prow not far below the summit. Willie and Nanda Devi were in a tent on the prow when she complained of feeling ill. It was no ordinary tummy trouble and a few hours later she died in her father's arms — on the mountain after which she had been named. She is still there and the locals believe she was 'called home', being some human incarnation of the goddess-mountain.

Our Nanda Devi days were less dramatic but equally unforgettable: the greatest walking adventure of a lifetime, doubly treasured because access was available for such a short time. For once, we were in the right place at the right time. Nanda Devi is, rightly Goddess of Joy.

BIBLIOGRAPHY
BONINGTON, C., *Changabang,* Heinemann.
MURRAY, W.H., *The Scottish Himalayan Expedition,* Dent.
SHIPTON, ERIC., *Nanda Devi,* Hodder & Stoughton.
    Upon that Mountain, Hodder & Stoughton
TILMAN, H.W., *The Ascent of Nanda Devi,* C.U.P.
WEIR, T., *The Ultimate Mountains,* Cassell.

MAPS
    These are difficult to obtain. A Japanese *kamkarte* at 1:200,000 was the most used of our finds: Uttar Pradesh, Garwal Himalaya, Sheet 2 had Joshimath in the centre of it. Older Indian Survey maps or US Army ones could be photocopied from geographical libraries and other sketches and maps found by researching through the volumes of the Himalayan Journal, Alpine Journal or American Alpine Journal.

10

England

A SOMERSET-AVON WALK

The springs of enchantment lie within ourselves; they arise
from our sense of wonder, that most precious of gifts . . .

(Eric Shipton)

When I walked a six-month route from John o'Groats to
Land's End, a tale told in *Hamish's Groats End Walk* part of
the fun was working out a satisfying route linking these ends
of mainland Britain. My route followed bits of the West
Highland Way, most of the Pennine Way, parts of the Offa's
Dyke path and the South-West Coastal route, all well-used
'official' pedestrian motorways. But, in between, there were
'missing links'. Finding routes through these blanks on the
map provided interest both in planning and execution.

Scotland's Highlands hardly need any official Ways.
Practically every major glen is a right-of-way. The Borders
were a pleasant mixture of landscape and history and greatly
enjoyed. From the south end of the Pennine Way to North
Wales we managed to use canal towpaths for much of the
time. (Like coastal walking this is a neglected area of
activity.) The Somerset-Avon 'missing link' between the
Severn Bridge and the South-West Coastal Path's start at
Minehead was one of the highlights of the walk: a succession
of gentler hills, where a rich historical heritage and
fascinating diversions all added to the general attrac-
tiveness, and it was this link I wanted to return to — partly
to see things I'd missed but also to try and work out a more
interesting walkers' route between Minehead and Chepstow. In the event I frequently had to do parts of it twice
over to satisfy myself on detail, or to return to the car. Some
day I hope to produce a proper guide to it; here I hope just
to give something of its flavour. Strangely, it is in rural

205

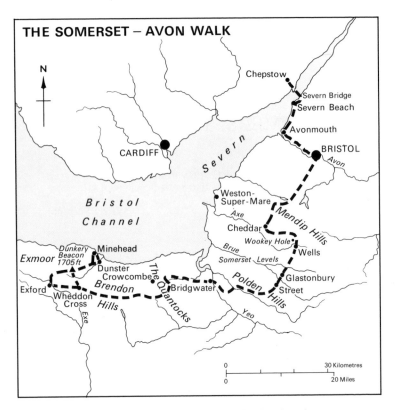

THE SOMERSET – AVON WALK

England, that guides are needed. In Sutherland you can say 'follow the stream for seven miles' and that is sufficient. Scotland's wilds are the better for not having guides but here, with a patchwork of fields, forests, hills and combes, with multi-use for agricultural and recreational purposes I sometimes found it was necessary to give field-by-field descriptions. This however is just an impression rather than a description of the walk. Whether my line or variants are followed, it is still good adventuring.

The walk between Minehead and the Severn Bridge is about 195 kilometres and there are plenty of fascinating things to see en route: Wells Cathedral, the Quantocks, Cheddar Caves, Bristol's *S.S. Great Britain,* and Glastonbury Tor to name but a few. The names themselves should give you itchy feet! Do read up beforehand so as not to miss the good things.

Here is how the walk can be broken down into sections:

DAY ONE : Arrive Minehead. Walk to Dunster or beyond.

DAY TWO : Grabbist Hill and Dunkery Beacon or Wheddon Cross or Exford.

DAY THREE : Along the Brendon Hills to Crowcombe.

DAY FOUR : Over the Quantock Hills to Bridgwater.

DAY FIVE : Somerset Levels and Ponden Hills to Street or Glastonbury.

DAY SIX : Glastonbury, Wells and Wookey Hole.

DAY SEVEN : The Mendip Hills to Cheddar.

DAY EIGHT : Over the Mendips to Bristol.

DAY NINE : By the Avon Gorge to Severn shores.

DAY TEN : Over Severn Bridge to Chepstow.

Minehead can be reached from Taunton by the West Somerset Railway which operates historic steam trains — a good way to start our wanderings. Minehead is a pleasant seaside resort but it is pleasanter still to leave its bustle either for the quiet hills or, by the coast, to Dunster.

Dunster, on a bank holiday, was crowded too but its charms were not to be hidden. There is a castle on the hill (inhabited since 1070), an active dovecote, a tithe barn, packbridge, the historic Yarn Market, a church of rare beauty and a working mill which was first mentioned in the Domesday Book. It is a friendly place and a stay there is a treat. The church is not to be missed nor should the others on the route; they are full of architectural interest, associations and blood-thirsty history, so, though I can't say it every time, do visit them.

Grabbist Hill will test the morning limbs after the delectations of Dunster. It is a woody hill with a maze of footpaths. The view from the top rewards the effort: the sweep of the Severn with Minehead down, down below. I had the bonus of an arch of rainbow framing the scene. The walk along the crest gives sea views on one side and a vivid green patchwork landscape on the other, then the trees take over as you drop down to Wootton Courtenay. We became mixed up in a colourful and noisy meeting of horses and hounds. It was a real 'Tally Ho' sort of place — a day relished by the Scot more used to his desert hills of the north. Grabbist Hill's view so impressed one Victorian lady that she composed the hymn 'All Things Bright and

Beautiful' in which the 'purple-headed mountain' is Dunkery and the 'river running by' is the Avill. After refreshments in Wooton Courtenay I set off to climb Dunkery Beacon, and my route led up through fields and gorse slopes (nature's barbed wire entanglements) to cross the Luccombe–Wheddon Cross road onto the heathery heights. Towering cumulus clouds, a fresh breeze and a clear view made the summit of Exmoor a refreshing spot. There were dozens of people at the big cairn, grabbing brief sunshine in a season of rain. The Beacon is 519 metres high and once was part of a chain of signal stations that were used up to Napoleonic times.

I can never decide whether to hold the height and wander along the uplands of Exmoor to descend to Exford, or to descend more directly to Wheddon Cross, — but usually the weather decides for me. Both places are small villages and on the route between them you can savour some real rural rides as the landscape rolls along. Camping at Blagdon above Wheddon Cross on the Groats End Walk I was made quite homesick to hear the roaring of a red deer stag when I woke to a dewy autumn morning. A child in a neighbouring tent was less romantic. 'Mummy, is that cow being sick?' he asked.

Wheddon Cross has a Scottish touch too in The Rest and Be Thankful pub. I like the distinction of names on the public loo: 'Ladies' and 'Men'. The hamlet is deeply set in the gap between Exmoor's stark heights and the gentler Brendon Hills, which are entirely cultivated or forested, the highest point, Lype Hill, being quite a bit lower than Dunkery.

Lype Common is reached by a marked route through endless fields and gates (I lost count twice trying to check the exact number) on what is the most intensely-cultivated bit of the walk. A motor road runs right along the crest of the Brendon Hills and, perforce, has to be followed. It is not a busy one and there are some tumuli worth seeing (watch out for bulls!), while the dying craft of hedge-laying is much in evidence. Round House on the map intrigued but it was not round at all. Do turn off south for quarter of a mile at the next junction. There you find the abandoned route of a mineral line which ran for five miles along to Brendon Hill, whence it went down the "Incline" and another line to Watchet, the port from which the iron ore was shipped to

South Wales. The Incline was a mile-long, 1-in-4 ramp, down which the waggons were lowered. The top is right by the roadside not long after passing the Naked Boy's Stone.

Raleigh's Cross Inn is passed, (or visited!) towards the eastern end of the ridge. Elworthy barrow is a good spot for a pause for shortly after the road plunges down with knee-juddering steepness – 1-in-6 in places — and there is an extensive view of the Quantock Hills. Their most northerly summit is Beacon Hill and it is in line of sight to Dunkery Beacon. My overnight stop was Crowcombe Heathfield youth hostel, a country house, well-converted and pleasantly run. Reaching the hostel by the best route took quite a bit of working out as this 'gap' between Brendon and Quantock Hills is a maze of lanes, all attractive for walking.

The Quantocks present quite a steep face to the walker the next morning, but reaching the crest gives that sudden 'other side of the mountain' feeling with a big view down Aisholt Common and out to the Somerset Levels. Wills Neck at 384 metres is the highest point and walking to it from any direction is pleasant. My visit was on a crisp Good Friday morning and as I reached the summit the first skylark of the year rose singing into a blue window in the clouds. The Quantocks give sweeps of dark heather brown, rising above the rich greens of the flanking forests. A steep track from West Bagborough gives a quick way up onto the crest. It is worth walking along the heights for a couple of miles, to Black Hill, to savour the scenery which is 'best of English' in character. Some day I want to walk the Quantocks end to end, rather than just making selected crossings or circlings.

The walk out to Black Hill goes by Triscombe Stone (a wishing stone) along the edge of the forest. On a misty day with the beech trees creaking and a buzzard mewing in the murk it can be quite atmospheric. This is the Hare Path, its record of use going back centuries. A motor road, from Crowcombe to Nether Stowey, actually crosses the ridge, and on the map it is liberally marked with arrow symbols. The Coleridges lived at Nether Stowey (Aisholt, across what Coleridge called "a deep romantic chasm", was too remote for his wife's taste) and Newbolt lived there in the thirties — so I'm not alone in my admiration of the Quantocks.

I descended by Ram's Combe to where it merged with Quantock Combe at Seven Wells Bridge, swopped banks and, after passing the chalets of the Scripture Union Great Wood Camp, rounded to Quantock School. On a hot day this section of forest walking is much welcomed. Hinkley Point Nuclear Power Station is a contrasting sight on leaving the trees, then it is back to rural walking to Bridgwater. I went by Pepper Hill Farm to Hawkridge Reservoir, and on by Bush, Pightley and Goathurst. I swear I'm not making up these names. They do exist. Nearby are other gems: Dancing Hill, Oggshole, Wind Down, Rook's Castle, Currypool . . . The map indicated rights of way across the Barford-Enmore parks but these were fenced and ploughed up years ago and efforts at finding routes ended when I found myself up to my knees in sludge: green, cow-enriched sludge. Both Enmore and Goathurst are picturesque Somerset villages where you look at the church and lunch in the pub. One farm near Enmore had a notice which offered, 'Goat's milk, Yoghurt, Farm Manure, Cheese'. The map offered the dotted line of a right-of-way *across* Hawkridge Reservoir.

Bridgwater is a busy market town which is not yet fully geared to tourism. It tends to be congested with traffic. Even the statue of Admiral Blake (local boy made good) seems to be taking a step backwards, cringing from the traffic swinging round the Town Hall. In the quiet of evening, while walking by the River Parrett, I heard the sounds of Grieg's Piano Concerto wafting from an open window so I lay on the grass and relished its beauty. I've only heard it played live once, and that was in Lima, after walking the Cordillera Blanca. Bridgwater to Street does not look far on the map but it is an extraordinary bit of country to walk through in the middle of a succession of hill ranges. The names are all of heaths and moors, drains and sedges. I left Bridgwater by Chedzoy and you can't find a richer Somerset name, unless it's Weston Zoyland, the next village while, between the two, is the Sedgemoor battle site, which was the ending of the ill-starred Monmouth's Rebellion in 1685 and which brought such grim retribution to the west. Weston's church held 500 prisoners after the battle, a score of whom were hanged from the tower; Chedzoy's is marked where the rebel peasants whetted their pikes and scythes before the battle.

I'd actually gone through Chedzoy to walk alongside the King's Sedgemoor Drain, a wide channel and one of the longest man-controlled waters on the Somerset Levels. You can walk a dozen miles along it and not find a single contour line. The 100-metre Polden Hills have an altogether exaggerated feeling of size. They form a crest which runs out into the horizontal world between the Parrett and Brue rivers — a contrasting second part to the day's walk.

The walk along the King's Sedgemoor Drain left a vivid impression for it was a fresh morning of big skies, with skylarks in full chorus in their minstrels' gallery, while the waters were busy with many different species of ducks, some non-mute swans, herons, redshanks and even cormorants on holiday from the sea. There could be no bigger contrast to the M5 which is crossed on leaving Bridgwater. Ornithologists could walk all morning up the drain and then cut north to Street. I compromised by using it for a few miles and then walking up and along the Polden Hills. Walton Hill, with its white stump of a windmill, is a small hill with a big view. I was caught by a hail storm while puffing up to it and when I came out from cowering under my brolly I saw the improbable shape of Glastonbury Tor looming through black thunder clouds and arched over by a double raindow: a tingling experience.

I then came down to earth with a bump as Street youth hostel (a chalet-like place on the ridge above the town) was fully-booked and in Street itself I was unable to find bed and breakfast. My weary steps took me out by Walton (which I was glad to see had a fish and chip shop), but I couldn't find accommodation at Walton either and after two hours of searching I found a bed at the Piper's Inn, miles back on the route! Had I known, it would have been easier to go into Glastonbury, an altogether more interesting place. There I could have stayed in the George and Pilgrims Hotel, founded in the days of Edward III, or at a camp site just below the 165-metre tor, with its fourteenth-century tower. Those interested in ancient sites may well need an extra day here for Glastonbury, Wells and Wookey Hole in one day is a tall order. In Glastonbury it is hard to separate myth, tradition and history. King Arthur and Queen Guinevere were supposedly buried here — a belief recorded in Norman times. (Their presumed remains were re-interred in the Abbey by Edward I.) Joseph of Arimathea traditionally founded a church here on the Isle of Avalon; St Patrick was a visitor before sailing to Ireland and St Dunstan introduced the Benedictine rule which only ended with Henry VIII. Saxon, Norman, Plantagenet, Tudor, all left their mark, creative or destructive. The very dereliction of the site cries its commentary on mankind. It was on Wyrral Hill that Joseph's staff was supposed to have sprouted to become 'The Glastonbury Thorn'. Cut down by the Puritans it produced offsets which survive still and bloom at Christmas.

A route by Queen's Sedge Moor and Pill Moor avoided the busy A39 between Glastonbury and Wells. It was early evening when I arrived. I needed a day for Wells alone as, top of its obvious attractions, it has a good book shop. As we came into the city, a major tourist place with ample accommodation, I saw a cinema queue waiting for tickets to see the film *E.T.* Once I'd found somewhere to stay, I came back, the queue had gone and I was able to walk straight in. An irregular life means films have to be seen as and when possible. *Greyfriars Bobby* in Marrakech or *Monsieur Hulot's Holiday* in Nairobi were probably the oddest combinations whereas *The Day of the Jackal* was made even more effective by being seen in France. An Arab film I saw in Tangier was all Saladin and Richard the Lion Heart, the latter, naturally, cast as the Baddy!

Wells Cathedral I found quite overwhelming. It sits beyond a sweep of green lawn, the moated Bishop's Palace to one side, so you can actually see it well. The west front with its stumpy towers is massive in its bulk but astonishing in the rich carvings of the dozens of figures, royal or ecclesiastical, which decorate it. Restoration work over the last decade has brought them marvellously back to life. It is the interior that is unique however. The soft land of Wells was inadequate to support the tower so inverted arches had to be added to strengthen the building. These have the structural shock of twentieth century work but were made in the fourteenth century. Art and engineering have never been better joined. I stood for a long time just watching people entering and enjoying their expressions of shock and wonder. Some think this a bit of an architectural freak. I love it. But then the whole place is loaded with marvels and delights. The misericords in the choir (old as the building's beginnings) have delightful carvings — one showing a mermaid and a lion, another of a fox preaching to four geese, one of them asleep! Four times an hour everyone watches a 500-year-old clock spring into action as figures of mounted knights dance round on the transept wall and, outside, two knights in armour beat on a bell. Just a couple of miles from the market square is the show piece: Wookey Hole.

It is part of Madame Tussaud's and on display is a collection of spare waxwork heads, rows of them on shelves in weird juxtapositioning. Wookey Hole is primarily an extraordinary natural feature and this and the Mendips geological display makes the entrance fee bearable. The River Axe bursts, full-grown, from the mouth of a great cave system, one of three that are shown to the visitor. Some of the earliest bones of prehistoric man were found here as were a female skeleton and the bones of goats, milking vessels, a bronze brooch, a comb made from an antler, a sacred knife, Roman coins, and a polished ball of crystalline stalactite. The museums here and in Wells display a wide range of animal bones: hyena, mammoth, rhinoceros, bison, elk, reindeer, bears, wolf — testimony of our erratic climate. When we moan at the rain it is as well to remember our mercies as well — like *not* having hyenas in the back garden.

The hill road on up from Wookey Hole warned: 'This road is not suitable for charabancs'. I left it to go up the gorge to Ebbor Rocks. There is no water in the gorge (it has gone underground to reappear at Wookey Hole) and Somerset's red soil gives way to a variety of limestone features. The trees are left to gain the spacious Mendip plateau and it was actually odd to see dry stone walls again. A pretty little place called Priddy was an excuse for a break at one of its two pubs. In August it has a sheep market which has been a regular event for 600 years since it was moved out of Wells during the Black Death. There are several routes to Cheddar, including the official West Mendip Way, which can be followed down to Draycott. I more or less did this. The plateau is so level that it is easy to forget one is actually up on a hill until unexpectedly, one field dips and there is the glittering River Severn and the Somerset Levels, and the odd circle of Cheddar Reservoir. Fortunately there is a quiet road as well as the busy low A371 so one can walk to Cheddar safely. A walk like this gives one a very different view on charabancs! It is possible to cut down fields to the A371 as it enters Cheddar and there are several camp sites, many B & B spots, hotels, and a youth hostel. The last was my goal. Cheddar is a pleasant little town but tacked on to it is one of England's major tourist traps — the Cheddar Gorge and its caves. Lines of shops, tea rooms, and souvenir stalls crowd up to it. Not having to find parking space was one pedestrian advantage. This concentration of tourism is not surprising for the caves are showpieces and Gough's Cave and Cox's Caves were worth queueing for. Minerals in the rock have given the towers and structures some gentle tints 'like Edinburgh rock'.

Having looked at the lower gorge the evening before, I set off to walk along the top of the gorge *en route* to Bristol. I was away too early to use the steps of Jacob's Ladder out of the gorge itself but the viewing tower at the top, which looks like a displaced lighthouse, is certainly in the right spot. It is more or less the last look back over those dominating Somerset Levels. It is all there, from Glastonbury Tor to Hinkley Point (mystery to mystery), with the Quantocks now just eyelashed on the horizon. There is a dip down to the road in the top of the gorge and then on by the intriguingly-named Velvet Bottom. Lead mining went on here from Roman times to about a hundred years ago. Traces of the works can still be seen and the arid tips still reject Nature's attempts to green the poisoned waste. A radio mast marks the route and in just under a mile Beacon Batch (325 metres) is reached: the top of the Mendips, sited on a small remnant of moorland. This is Black Down and it rather recalls Black Hill on the Quantocks, except for the overall cultivation, which is the legacy of limestone. Burrington Combe down the hill on the north has caves too. Goatchurch Cavern was my first descent into the underworld, 'another fascinating part of the great outdoors [*sic*] adventure' as I once saw it advertised! It was while sheltering in a storm in the combe that Augustus Toplady created his hymn 'Rock of Ages'.

A steep walk took me down to Blagdon, with a view of Blagdon and Chew Valley Lakes, long-enough established to disguise their reservoir nature. Blagdon straggled down in sun-catching disorder like a town in Spain. I had a coffee and sandwiches (Cheddar cheese of course) in the Mendip Hotel (which enjoys a superb panoramic view) and then went on by the lake and a teasing of fields, lanes and minor roads to reach Winford for a late lunchtime snack in The

Prince of Waterloo. A cruel ascent took me up to Dundry, a hamlet isolated on its hill, from the encroaching tide of Bristol city. A flight of 156 steps led me down to a road which swept round and down into suburbia and to my first glimpse of the Clifton Suspension Bridge.

You can make of Bristol what you will. It is one of my favourite cities and still retains a hint of its distinguished nautical past. Where you stay and what you do presents only the problem of choice. I made for the Baltic Wharf Caravan Park along Cumberland Road, being the only camp site available. My first visit to Bristol was to its Wine Festival which I sailed to in the beautiful brigantine *Eye of the Wind*, which had just been redesigned after its Operation Drake adventures. The ill-fated barque *Marques* was refitting in the floating harbour near the Watershed Exhibition Centre, and today, Brunel's famous ship, the S.S. *Great Britain*, now rests in the dock where she was originally built. It was in 1970 that millions watched on TV as she was salvaged from the Falkland Islands where she was wrecked in 1886. As the first-ever, ocean-going, propeller-driven iron ship (1843) she represents a vital link in nautical history.

The National Lifeboat Museum and the Bristol Industrial Museum are also south of the floating harbour. The city has really made an effective attempt at revitalising the docks area. When we do things 'on the nail' we are referring to the one-time sealing of a bargain in the local market by putting money on the nail and in Bristol the 'nails' stand along Corn Street to this day. 'The Centre' is the plain name of the centre of the city. The statue in the middle of it is of Burke who looks as if he is bowling right arm round the wicket. The tourist office is nearby and is worth contacting before starting this walk for its 30-page accommodation guide, and leaflets on the Avon Walkway and the city generally. I returned to camp by St Mary Redcliffe (also south of the harbour), a parish church the size and magnificence of a cathedral, which Queen Elizabeth the First thought the best in England. It brought my tally of churches seen on the walk up to a score. Bristol and Clifton have that number within their bounds. This is another place where one could easily spend a full day. Do allow for such extras when working out routes of multi-day walks. Walking should be a means to many ends rather than a narrow end in itself.

The continuation from Bristol is made easy by the Avon Walkway which follows the Avon Gorge to the coast. (You can walk along the river all the way from Bath.) It took me from Clifton Suspension Bridge to Avonmouth's A5 motorway bridge, as big a contrast as you could find. The tide was out when I set off so I had a clear view over to the lock gates of the 'floating harbour' which dates back to 1809. Two miles of river had locks constructed at either end and the river was diverted to a new channel. Bristol's tradition of engineering novelty continues: Concorde is manufactured locally. The Suspension Bridge, like the Forth Railway Bridge, is an unforgettable sight, blending original engineering and design into grand harmony. I walked across it and back and looked down eighty metres to the mud below. Just before the concrete sweep of the M5 bridge there was a hamlet, Pill, sited round a secret creek. A breeze had halyards beating a tattoo on the masts of all the yachts. It is the sort of place that would have made the perfect setting for a Gothic novel. The pilot cutters used to be based here. It was the bends of the river that stopped the over-large modern freighters so now it is all container ships to Avonmouth. The navigation lights off Pill are called Adam and Eve.

The mile aloft on the M5 footwalk was a brutal return to the battering of cars and urban industrialism. If the pollution is not too severe you may make out the Severn Bridge. Avonmouth is quite the most complex concentration of industrial activity I've ever seen. There are huge docks (the tidal range is 15 metres), fuel depots, smelting and chemical works etc. It is so horrendous that it becomes fascinating in itself. On the Groats End Walk I walked through it in early morning darkness and it was like something out of science fiction: noise, bustle, lights, and the arc of bridge beyond. I could still smell fumes ten miles beyond. You can amuse yourself by listing the various types of work you notice in passing. I listed about thirty.

It is worth leaving the road to walk along Chittening Warth into the hamlet of Severn Beach. The contrast was emphasised by the renewed birdlife: gulls and eiders calling on the tide, starling flocks, pigeons, larks, a wren, various warblers, thrushes and blackbirds, waders and magpies (the punks of the bird world), and an owl which was so busy beating along the bushes, it passed only a metre away from my motionless form. Severn Beach has several camp sites, many pubs but a scarcity of B & B facilities. Most walkers should manage to go on over the Severn Bridge to Chepstow but a night here is practicable, or you can catch a train back to Bristol for the night. There is a rifle range between village and bridge which may or may not mean the shore path is closed. Firing always starts at 9.30 so campers can walk through before then. At the pull up for Aust and the Severn Bridge you cross the first contour line since the Avon Bridge: the bridges are the tallest objects for miles. The bridge trembled and swayed as we crossed its mile-long span. It actually bridges the Wye as well as the Severn and was opened by the Queen in 1966 but it is already giving cause for concern. Cars crawled along, nose-to-tail, which made me feel quite smug striding along free and easy. It was almost an anti-climax to descend onto Welsh soil and the Chepstow ending of our 'missing link' walk. I had just become fit and it was over. Maybe it should always be done as part of a Groats End Walk. What about it? Some day? *Your* great walking adventure?

BIBLIOGRAPHY
There is a vast literature on this area so I have only mentioned a few general works I've enjoyed and a few booklets on more particular aspects.
ALLEN, N.V., *The Exmoor Handbook*, Exmoor Press.
BURTON, S.H., *Exmoor*, Hodder and Stoughton.
CLINKER, C.R., *The West Somerset Railway*, Exmoor Press.
COYSH, MASON, WAITE., *The Mendips*, Hale.
FRASER, MAXWELL, *Companion into Somerset*, Methuen.
HMSO, *National Parks Guide: Exmoor*.
LAWRENCE, B., *Discovering the Quantocks*, Shire Publications.
MEE, ARTHUR, *Somerset*, Hodder.
PEEL, J.H.B., *Portrait of Exmoor*, Hale.
ROSSITER, S. (edit), *Blue Guide; England*, Benn.
SELLICK, R.J., *The Old Mineral Line*, Exmoor Press.
WAITE, V., *Portrait of the Quantocks*. Hale.

MAPS
The OS 1:50,000 sheets 181, 182, 172 cover the walk but the 1:25,000 is often more useful: SS 84/94, SS 83/93, ST 03/13, ST 23/33, ST 43/53, ST 44/54, ST 45/55, ST 56, ST 57.
From Bristol to Chepstow the 1:50,000 is adequate.

Scotland
ST. KILDA: WORKING FOR
YOUR WALKS

Man has suffered in his separation from the soil and from
other living creatures. . .and as yet he must still, for security,
look long at some portion of the earth as it was before he
tampered with it

(Gavin Maxwell)

St Kilda has had a surprising number of books written
about it over the years: *Island on the Edge of the World, Last
Voyage to St Kilda, The Life and Death of St. Kilda, Out of
the World, St. Kilda Revisited,* are just some of the titles
which give a hint of the natural wonder and human tragedy
of the place. Very few places so geographically inhospitable
have ever been lived in for long, yet men discovered and
settled on St Kilda long before historical times. The islands
were evacuated and abandoned just over fifty years ago, a
drama that touched a chord worldwide: so much sad history
encapsulated in one remote corner. The wonder is that St
Kilda was ever inhabited for not only is it remote but it is
encompassed by storms and the island group has been
compared to 'shark's teeth scattered in an Atlantic waste'.
Hammond Innes, whose stories specialise so much in wild
locations, and who knew the island used St Kilda as the
setting for his novel, *Atlantic Fury.*

I can vouch for its veracity. The isolation of St Kilda can
be savagely emphasised even by summer storms. On my
first visit there was a huge swell and the wind was whipping
creamy spume from the waves. I retired to my bunk with a
request to be called when the stacks of St Kilda were near
enough for photographs. After what felt like a century there
was a yell to come up on deck. I did so and peered over the

side at the cheerful, sun-dancing sea, then lifted my eyes to the horizon — only there was no horizon. Just fifty yards off was a wall of rock, vertical, green-grown and bird-whitened with the sea sucking at its base. My eyes went up, and up, and up, till my neck was aching. A thousand feet above, the cliffs vanished in a maelstrom of cloud. Welcome to St. Kilda!

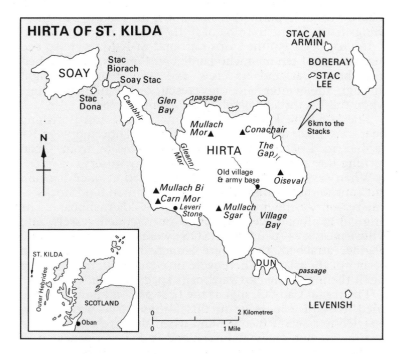

This was Boreray, at 384 metres, the largest of the three major 'stacks' (rocky islets) that lie a few miles east of the main island of Hirta, our destination. It was a stunning encounter, its 'arranging' typical of Kate and Cubby Mackinnon of the *Kylebhan*. Cubby took us through the narrow strait between Boreray and Stac Lee, which is a 172-metre cenotaph, stuccoed with thousands of gannets. About a quarter of the world's gannets once lived here and collecting young gannets *(gugas)* was a regular feature of St Kilda life. A man would leap perilously from a rowing boat onto the sheer cliff and then haul others ashore. They climbed with ropes long before the recognised beginning of rock climbing in England but I have never seen this acknowledged. To this day the people of North Lewis have a right to cull young gannets. Tourists are apt to be a bit squeamish when offered gannet for supper but on St Kilda the gannets meant food, oil (cooking and lighting) and feathers (for bartering); the beaks were used as pegs, the skins as shoes and oil containers. Nothing was wasted. There was no hypermarket just down the road to buy these things from. Come to think of it, there were no roads either!

In October 1759 the storms around St Kilda were so bad that a party of ten men who landed on Boreray one October, lost their boat and its crew and were marooned right through the winter and only rescued the following June when the Factor's boat called on its annual visit.

The last time I headed there myself, our sturdy fishing boat was glad to shelter one night in Tobermory and a second in Lochmaddy, the one-day voyage from Oban turning into a stomach-heaving three-day misery.

When several people were shipwrecked at once it could put considerable strain on the island's limited food stocks — one reason for the invention of the St Kilda mailboats. The original mailboats were hollowed-out wooden vessels, into which messages (usually an SOS) were sealed then, with a bladder attached, these were launched off the south-east corner of the island. There were no beaches on the stacks to catch them and the eastward drift sped them onwards.

The tragic Lady Grange is the first person known to have tried to send a message in this fashion. She was a Whig married to a secret Jacobite and when she threatened to talk was unceremoniously abducted and ended a prisoner on St Kilda from 1734 to 1742. She spoke only English, the locals only Gaelic, and it must have been a horrific exile. Her mailboat failed but a message smuggled out in a roll of tweed worked, though before she could be rescued she was taken to Sutherland where she died in 1745. In 1746 five boatloads of soldiers searched the island for Bonnie Prince Charlie, a fugitive after the disaster of Culloden. It was one place he actually did not go to!

Early in 1876 an Austrian ship was wrecked and nine sailors were rescued. When starvation faced the island an SOS was sent off by mailboat and the message reached the Austrian Embassy in London in six days allowing a quick relief to be mounted. It is a work-party tradition to launch some mailboats; most of ours were retrieved.

St Kilda, through most of its recorded history, was the property of the MacLeods. Originally both the MacLeods of Harris and the MacDonalds of North Uist claimed the islands and it was decided to settle the issue by a fifty mile rowing race from the Outer Hebrides, the first to lay hand on Hirta to become acknowledged as owner. The open boats battled across the open sea and entered Village Bay together. There was little in it as they neared the shore but when the MacDonalds looked set to land first, Coll MacLeod grabbed a weapon and struck off one of his hands which he quickly threw over the other boat so it landed on the shore of Hirta. The MacLeods sold St Kilda in 1931 to the Marquess of Bute who bequeathed it to the National Trust for Scotland in 1956. They have leased it to the Nature Conservancy Council who manage it as, surely, one of the world's most spectacular reserves, a landscape of superlatives.

When we rounded into Village Bay and the sea stopped heaving us about we could hear the put-put of engines and voices and laughter. A white straggle of huts ran up from the shore. Up on the hill a geodic dome and various aerials were evident. A truck came down a road from them. St Kilda was anything but deserted; the army was there and have been on St Kilda since the evacuation. Thanks to the army we had such comforts as electric light, hot and cold water on tap, flush toilets, even a pub, all of which were unknown to the old inhabitants.

The Commanding Officer came out in an inflatable to welcome us: a piratical Welshman whose hobby was driving husky dog teams. People, gear, food, were shuttled ashore and we, the National Trust for Scotland's 'Boat People', returned to our normal colours. We were the last work party that year. The N.T.S. owns the island while the Army lease part of it as a tracking station (for rockets fired from the Outer Hebrides). Every summer N.T.S. work parties have been restoring parts of the old village and these popular expeditions provide one easy way of reaching the inaccessible islands, as well as supplying enjoyable company and interesting work. Accommodation is in restored houses whereas other visitors have to either camp or live on board whatever yacht or boat brings them. Both are options with an element of risk for the winds can be ferocious. The army alone stays through the winter. All their buildings (except the generating house) are linked together by covered passages. In winter ropes are rigged across to the generating house so people can have some protection from the risk of being blown away in gales which have topped the anemometer's maximum reading of 130 mph. Gales have been known to blow for seventeen consecutive days. The first winter when the soldiers were under canvas must have been an interesting experience.

Our restoration work was fascinating in itself but there was still ample time to explore Hirta. We were to enjoy a spell of unusual calm and some really hot weather; indeed at the end of the first day I actually experienced a mild dose of heatstroke. Most of our time was spent restoring the end of a black house *(tigh dubh)* which had collapsed. My companion in these labours was Luigi, an Italian working in Bonn, who will be remembered for his suntan and his eating capacity. Most days we would work till tea time and then wander down to swim on the sandy beach that only appears in summer (winter gales fling boulders up on to it.) Several yachts or boats were usually anchored off shore. It was a scene such as one might have expected on the Riviera, not notorious St Kilda. One day a huge Army Landing Craft came ashore and months of supplies were unloaded: tractors buzzing in and out like ants to their nest. There was always a slight feeling of unreality to our existence.

Frequently we ate outside, one night being joined by round-the-world yachtsman Declan Mackell who said St Kilda was the only place he'd felt it safe enough (from weather and people) to spend all day ashore. Mealtimes were sometimes interrupted by the appearance of the St Kilda mice, a large field mouse sub-species which had evolved on the island. There used to be a St Kilda house mouse as well but its life was so tied up with humans that it became extinct after the evacuation. One story we heard told of visiting scientists becoming very excited on capturing a mouse with feet of an unusual colour. Luckily, before recording this startling discovery in some learned paper, they found out that several mice had had their feet painted by soldiers so they could tell them apart in mouse-racing contests! Even if apocryphal the story deserves to be true. St Kilda also has its own wren. One pair nested above the lintel of 'our' black house. As man is not seen as a predator these creatures and others were never difficult to observe.

Our work party was comfortably accommodated along the long 'street' and well fed by Jess Johnston from Peebles who has been to St Kilda many times. I tended to wander along to the 'dining' cottage for a cup of tea before anyone else was up. On the morning we had chosen to do the circular walk round the island, Jess and I watched two snipe fighting just behind the cottage as we sat drinking our tea. It was a pale, fresh, flower-like start to the day but, by breakfast time it had turned wilting hot again.

The party walked along the street, past "our" black house, had a sip at the well near it, and came to the army road. This we decided not to take and instead sweated up the hillside beyond onto Mullach Sgar to obtain the best view down to the village with its sweep of houses (mostly in ruins of course), the ugly army base and the dome of Oiseval beyond. Everywhere was dotted with *cleits* which were like miniature dry-stone houses and were the deep-freezes of the old St Kildans. Here they stored the various birds and eggs used as food, peat, hay and precious objects like their horsehair ropes — which could rot easily. The *cleits* were dry as they let air through the stonework, and served their purpose excellently. There are over a thousand of them, some even out on the stacks. The island of Dun, which forms one arm of Village Bay, dominated our view to the south. If the *cleits* were a perpetual detail perhaps Dun was the predominating geological feature.

The view out from Village Bay or its hinterland is largely blocked off by the ragged crest of Dun (Gaelic for fort). When we sailed in on arrival we had noticed that daylight showed through it near its seaward end where a tunnel had been pounded out by the waves. It cannot have been many million years ago when Dun became detached from Hirta at the other end for only a narrow channel separates them. The St Kildans rigged a chain down the Dun cliffs and could boulder leap across to this but any landing now has to be made by boat. The army took gangs of us out by inflatable later on.

Landing was adventurous for the less nippy as we had to transfer from tide-tossed dinghy to steep rocks and haul up on fixed ropes. St Kilda was once part of a big volcanic *caldera* and the jagged teeth that still show are the decayed remnants of the crater rim. Dun is long but thin and steep (steep on St Kilda often means sheer cliffs), rising to 178 metres at one stage. The great attraction of a visit is the multitude of puffins which nest there. Just the thought of puffins can raise a smile; Dun has 80,000 nesting pairs.

We spent a long time wandering about Dun, over the yellow lichened rocks, as our courage allowed, sharing the hours with these most comical of birds. How do puffins manage to fill a beak with nine fish, all facing the same way, without losing what they're holding when adding to it? Their frantic flight and fussy antics, their fancy-dress rig, all allied to a serious expression, make them a hilarious study. Anthropomorphism is obviously part of bird-watching fun but we had one more serious task: collecting all the dead puffins we could from the accessible shoreline rocks. We filled several sacks of these sad remains and took the smelly collection to Wally Wright (the NCC warden) who wanted to search the birds for any rings. He has been ringing birds for a decade but a percentage (about 2500 a year) are taken by the pillaging black-backed gulls. On a previous visit to Dun with a delightful, rather older gang of American wildlife enthusiasts we had had a grandstand view of a gull dealing with one poor puffin.

The puffin was grabbed on the surface of the sea and the gull kept thrusting it under water until it stopped struggling. It then proceeded to turn the drowned puffin outside-in as it ripped it apart. A line of feathers floated off on the tide after the stuffed gull laboriously flapped away. Wally had the revolting task of turning the stinking remains outside-out to see if there were any leg rings. As he sat between his two awful heaps a soldier came past and asked what he was doing. As dead pan as a puffin Wally said he was helping the cook. That night the camp were going to have a Chinese speciality . . .

Our gang had several hours on Dun because the weather was so settled. I think we all ended up photographically punch-drunk on puffins and that was only seeing a fraction of the numbers for the outer half of the island is reserved for the birds only. I would like to have gone further on. Nobody is sure whether the map's indication of a 'castle' is real or not. Was there water? Who would live there? Was the name *Dun* taken from a castle or from the island's shape? There are still plenty of puzzles.

Out beyond Dun we could see the hump of Levenish, at 62 metres a small stack by St Kilda standards, wave-swept and spray-torn for much of the year. This very exposure attracts visitors keen to see what life can survive on the borders of possibility.

After our fill of Dun-viewing we set off along the cliffs facing west to try and find the Lover's Stone. There were *cleits* perched on the cliffs too, in places none of us much cared to try and reach. St Kildans, in addition to being strong climbers, also had a remarkable head for heights and a hearty fearlessness. The cliffs were a mix of sheer rock, scree, and exceedingly steep grass. The Soay sheep seemed happy to wander where we failed to tread. These beasts, nimble as goats, dark and oily-coated, are the original old sheep of the islands. Since the evacuation they have freely roamed on Hirta but remain wary of man. *Cleits* provide them with shelter and we soon learned to enter a *cleit* with caution. If it was occupied the sheep would charge out and startle us.

We found the Lover's Stone eventually: a prow of rock jutting up and out over the crags that tumbled to the sea. Only Graeme went right to the point of it so was much photographed by everyone else. He just stood there however whereas the young males of St Kilda had to prove their prowess on airy rock before their intended would consent to marriage. It may seem crazy but a husband who could not climb would have been useless as a provider. The St Kildans had massive, wide, agile feet from generations of going barefoot. The young man would stand with his toes of one foot to the edge of the drop, place the heel of his other foot against those toes, then crouch to place both hands, clenched as fists, against his feet, ending crouched and thrust out over the void in an uncomfortable position. You can try it on the doorstep. They did it on a cliff-top prow of rock.

We had crossed the spine of the island by the Lovers' Stone and while on one side lay the cliffs, on the other was the great hollow of green Gleann Mor (the big glen) with Mullach Mor behind. Embedded in the grass we noticed the wreckage of an aeroplane, which we later learned was a Sunderland which crashed during the war with a crew of ten, seven of them from New Zealand. Two other aircraft came to grief on the then uninhabited island: a Beaufighter which just hit the summit of the island, Conachair, and then fell over the edge into the sea, leaving very little wreckage apart from the tail section, and a Wellington, which crashed 200 metres up on the nearly inaccessible island of Soay. The plane was only investigated in 1978 as till then it was thought to be a German wreck.

Mullach Bi (Pillar Top) only fractionally lower than Mullach Mor (Big Top) was a good place for a break. It was also a good place to photograph the fulmars, those solemn, stiff-winged fliers. We could lie right on the edge of the thrift-nodding cliffs and catch them eye to eye as they rode the updraughts along the rim. They only lay one egg and that after several years spent almost entirely at sea yet, in the last eighty years, they have spread out from St Kilda to colonise the entire British coastline. Nobody has explained this population explosion.

Below Mullach Bi was a site to which our leader suggested we come back one dark night. Here were scores of shearwater burrows: a bird even more unusual than the fulmars. Strangely only Luigi and I wanted to join Graeme for the night on the sea cliffs. We scrambled down in the last light and made ourselves as comfortable as possible for the hours of waiting. A fishing boat's lights drifted on the sea, the only sign of man in the quiet warm night. We dozed. When the darkness was near maximum we sat up, leaning on a rocky outcrop, waiting in the silence. Luigi did not know what was to come and grew a bit restless. Then there was a whirring of wings.

Goodness knows how the shearwaters do it but they crash in, out of the black sky, to land accurately at their nesting burrow entrances. I had not noticed the hole behind me so when the first bird of the night flew in it landed me a thud in the *solar plexus!* Another swooshed past my left ear. Within twenty minutes the night was a bedlam of calling birds, the ripping whir of flight, the bumps and scrabblings of landings. It is impossible to describe. The Leach's and storm petrels were also taking part. Later, the excitement slowly subsided, the silence crept back and the grey tints of day fogged the negative of night. We looked round at a waste of crags and fallen rock; nothing in sight except a few squeaky pipits, and the murmuring fulmars on the ledges above.

I'd first experienced this eerie sensational night exercise

on the island of Rhum where the Nature Conservancy Council did some ringing and study of birds. Their burrows were numbered as well and the same birds came back year after year to the same holes. For years no one knew where they migrated to but ringed birds have been found off the coast of Brazil. How do the young birds know where to go? They are abandoned by the parents and left in the burrows, so fat that they cannot escape for some days. They then have to tumble down over a thousand feet of boulders into the sea, learn to fly and then set off for Brazil to find mum and dad.

You don't rush round Hirta. There is too much to see and the going can be quite demanding. There were plenty of ups and downs and ins and outs before we reached the north-west corner, The Cambir: a clenched fist of rock shaking at Soay across a stack-filled channel. It is sheer or overhung in many places. The map showed a score of overhangs on this western walk besides stacks, *geos* (creeks) and natural tunnels.

The island of Soay has no easy landing place yet every year the St Kildans would land there because of the sheep. The beasts would be pursued individually on foot: a fairly high-risk sport one would think. In the eighteenth century a local bandit was marooned on Soay and his crude shelter is still there. His bleached bones were found with his dirk stuck in the ground beside them. All the accounts of landings make it sound a hazardous operation. The whitened framework of the crashed Wellington could be picked up through our binoculars.

In the Sound, and dwarfed by Soay and The Cambir, there are three more stacks: Stac Biorach (73 metres) a difficult climb, Stac Soay (60 metres) its 300-metre wall tunnelled through by the sea, and Stac Dona (26 metres). Early last century a visitor reported that climbing Stac Biorach was almost a test-piece for the local lads; two men climbed it while he watched, for a quid of tobacco! St Kilda was the true birthplace of British mountaineering but the players being young peasants did not band into an Alpine Club! It was only when you saw the size of birds circling the stacks that the scale came to us. These stacks, off Brighton, would be sensational.

We lunched on this remotest, walled-off corner of Hirta, then chose our own lines along to reach the burn of Gleann

Mor. There was a small lochan where a score of bonxies (great skuas) were bathing and whenever anyone passed one or two would rise casually and then, out of the blue, swoop down on the intruder from behind. At the rush of wings most people's nerve would go and they'd duck or dive to the ground. The birds don't often hit but when they do it hurts! They are robber-birds and pursue innocent gulls, harrying them until they disgorge their food in panic which the bonxies will then dive for, sometimes even catching it in mid air. They are bigger than the biggest gulls and brown in colour and are only found in the northern or western isles.

Some of us spent quite a bit of time studying the 'horned structures' of this glen. These are the indigenous dwellings of a people who settled the glen maybe 4000 years ago and the buildings are unique. Only now are they being studied by archaeologists, in the usual last-minute effort, for they have degenerated faster since the evacuation than those thousands of years before. They had always served as instant *cleits* so their corbelled roofs were kept in order by the residents but after the island was deserted they began to disintegrate. There are a score of them, the unusual feature being two curved arms of stone reaching out from a group of cells. Nothing is really known about them; one has come to be called the 'Amazon's House'.

Coming along from The Cambir we could look across Glen Bay to the point on the other side, Gob na h-Airde, through which a huge passage has been carved out by the sea. A sloping ledge led down across the face of the cliff into this; it looked a possible line of access even for our gang so we went to look. We ran a bonxie-gauntlet along to the point and then had several fluffy bundles of fulmar chicks spitting foul oil at us as well. The tiny mites could puke a good metre and were able to reload and fire with some speed.

The ledge was wide and only at the corner under the archway was it tricky so a rope had been rigged for hanging onto. The cave/tunnel was cathedral-like in scale and feeling. Framed in the arched walls was distant Boreray. The waves surged in and foamed over the rocks. In a storm it must be a fearsome place.

When I came out ahead of the others to take some photos I heard a whoosh and then saw three killer whales in the sea just below the ramp. They were huge piebald creatures, slowly surging along in a rolling frolic. One was much smaller so it was probably a family group of mum, dad and baby. I rushed back to tell the others and we stood watching their big dorsal fins sweeping out to sea even when they were half a mile away. It was the most dramatic wildlife sighting of our stay in Hirta.

We covered all exposed flesh as we began the sun-smiting toil up to the top of the island (460 metres). The afternoon sun was remarkably hot. The view was not as grand as it could be as everything trembled in the heat haze. It was then we decided we'd overnight at The Gap to see the clarity of a sunrise; quite a presumption on St Kilda, but the high pressure was firmly anchored above Conachair. The Gap is the parabolic col between Conachair and Oiseval. Conachair is Gaelic (coming together of the hills) and Oiseval is Norse (East Fell) which points to the mingling of past influences.

Just a few metres down from the summit of Conachair the ground falls away sheer in what, at 425 metres, is the highest sea cliff in Britain. Only on Hoy in Orkney is there anything comparable. It was a dizzy view downwards with gulls on the sea appearing as tiny white dots and the seals looking more like microbes. It is quite impossible to convey the sheer numbers of birds nesting on these cliffs and stacks. It is an avian bedlam. We carefully picked our way down to The Gap.

The bivouac there attracted most of the work party a night or two later. The elusive little petrels inhabit some of the *cleits* at the Gap and their burbling was a companionable noise. We could see the birds when we shone our torch beams through the dry-stone walling. But the object of that night out was to see the sunrise, and we weren't disappointed. It came with glowing lemon, marigold and poppy tints to unveil a silver disc of sun beside the dark silhouette of the stacks. It is one of the abiding memories of St Kilda.

The Gap lies behind and above the village and in our thirsty, sun-weary state on the day of the walk we just could not face Oiseval's ascent so we cut down 'home' for tea and the scones Jess had been baking. We had a swim at the jetty afterwards. A fishery protection boat came into Village Bay. Some days we had a dozen different yachts or boats in to 'Costa Kilda'. The islands had a Royal visit when *Britannia* unexpectedly turned up in August 1971: a fine day of sun and no midges which the whole family enjoyed ashore, exploring everything and making this strenuous circuit walk and visiting Dun. People like Joe Brown and Hamish McInnes prospected for possible climbs (with TV in mind) but *mal de mer*, fulmars, impossible landings and the sheer impracticable situation sent them packing. The highest cliff in Britain remains unclimbed. In 1979 the Gillies sisters, original St Kildans, who had left as children, made a visit. One novelty for them was being able to bath on the island. 1980 saw the fiftieth anniversary of the evacuation and eight original residents made a nostalgic return. A service was held in the restored church.

While it would be possible to write at book length about this fascinating place, I hope that in this chapter I've portrayed something of its special character and its unique circular day walk. We were all very restless on our last day for we did not want to leave. Following tradition we launched our mailboats under Oiseval, finished off a pointing job, packed, visited favourite places for a last time, over-ate, and almost laughed to see the stars stutter out in rain. The boat was late and we left in a rising sea that had the cheerful tub wallowing mightily — which is where we came in. Though St Kilda went down over the horizon it is still one of the strongest of memories, a marvellous adventure.

BIBLIOGRAPHIES
ATKINSON R., *Island Going*, Collins.
DARLING, F.F. & BOYD, J.M., *Natural History in the Highlands and Islands*, Collins New Naturalist/Fontana paperback.
MACLEAN, C., *Island on the Edge of the World*, Canongate.
QUINE, D.A., *St Kilda Revisited*
STEEL, T., *The Life and Death of St Kilda*, Fontana.
SMALL, A. (ed), *A St Kilda Handbook*, NTS paperback.
WILLIAMSON, K. & BOYD, J.M., *St Kilda Summer*, Collins.

MAPS
St Kilda is on Sheet 18 of the OS 1:50,000 but larger scales are advisable. The shop on Hirta sells these and they are also sometimes available from the NTS office, as are some of the books listed.

NTS
Enquiries on publications or work parties to:
    The St Kilda Secretary
    National Trust for Scotland
    5 Charlotte Square
    Edinburgh EH2 4DE

    Telephone: 031-226-5922

THE WALK FROM OUKAIMEDEN TO ASNI

Below is the detailed route as mentioned in chapter three.

(Use the 1:100,000 map sheet of Oukaïmeden-Toubkal in conjunction with this description. The map alone is inadequate.)

Walk up the road to the Tizi n'Oukaïmeden. At the bend in the road on the *tizi* (pass) a path drops westwards. Take this. It wends down first on the right and then on the left of the obvious spur you look down from the tizi. Thuya (juniper) trees. At the first obvious junction (above Gliz) take the right fork towards Agadir, the prominent village on the red spur ahead. Cross the mine road and shortly after turn sharp left at a junction which is not too obvious. This is a poorer path but follow its zig-zags all the way down to the houses, crossing various other possibilities. There are so many houses and paths it is difficult to describe a route but a prominent rock block perched on a pedestal of soil is obvious and this earth pillar can be aimed for and the sunken lane below it is taken to bypass the lowest habitation, just above the river. There is a fine view up the valley.

Just follow the track as it traverses northwards, with an attractive view over terraces to the three villages of Tidili. The path wends round a side valley and through these hamlets. At the third, instead of going into it, cut down to the river and follow the bank down to cross at a bend to the left bank. The path climbs to a spur and from a later spur descends in many tight zig-zags back to the river side. Keep by the river which is crossed to reach the village of Tinoughâr. Once through it the path is easy to follow: it climbs high up in initial zig-zags to traverse above the gorge, which here joins the main river coming down from Tachddirt.

An isolated hill stands in the main valley (purple and tawny in colour) while behind it the vivid red slopes are cut by an obvious road. As this isolated hill is passed the track starts its determined descent to the river: a succession of hairpins, with ilex trees now mixed with the juniper. The path amalgamates with a road which can be seen wending down to ford the river and join the main valley road to Imsker. The riverbank is a delightful picnic spot and it is worth lying up until 5 pm and finishing the walk in the cooler hours into dusk.

The road reaches Imsker through fruit trees and an oakwood. Skirt the village and just as you leave it the village well can be seen to the right. Take the path by it and not the road continuation which can be seen scarring the slopes ahead. The path zig-zags down into the tree-filled valley you look down on and crosses the river (sometimes a bridge) to the village opposite. Skirt this beside the river and at the first fork bear right. The route runs through fields and trees and eventually skirts by the riverside to cross once more at a cave-bitten cliff. (If the river is not easily forded there is a path on the right bank which rises up the hillside a bit and down again to rejoin the basic way.) After crossing the river walk down the valley bottom and re-cross the river by the obvious bridge. The valley road fords the river to use the right bank down to Asni (it joins the original '*piste*' from Asni up to Oukaïmeden, now only a jeep road), but as it is without shade, of grimly hard surface and devious in its line the original path is best followed.

The road has rather obliterated the start of it but if you walk on the left edge you will see the break down. There is a great variety of shrubs and flowers with lots of lavender growing wild. The power line to Oukaïmeden can be seen on the hillside above. Wend on through ever-richer farmlands. The spur opposite ends as the valley from Imlil joins ours. This doubles the width of the flat, fruit-tree filled valley. The path runs into a *seguia* which entails a bit of hopping back and forth. Just after this there is a branch path going uphill to the big village of Tansghart. It is not visible at the junction but as you twist up you pass under the Oukaïmeden powerline. Walk into the village and turn left at the white mosque to leave by a wide lorry track which eventually joins the proper road. The views back are rewarding! The road slowly contours down to Asni. The T-junction is marked by a concrete block (an old French-style signpost) and you turn left here down to the last fording of the river. There is usually a bridge. The delights of Hotel du Toubkal await.